Singletree From Tennessee

The Life Story of
Alma Dukes Biggs
As written by her own hand

Compiled and edited by
Lisabeth Foster

Copyright 2003
by Alma D. Biggs

ISBN 0-89315-404-0

All rights reserved. Written permission must be secured from the publisher to use or reproduce any part of this book, except for brief quotations, critical reviews, or articles.

Printed By Lambert Book House,
Florence, Alabama 35630 USA

A Singletree From Tennessee
by
Alma Duke Biggs

Acknowledgments

To Lisabeth Foster

Without you this would not have happened.
Thanks is such a small word,
With a tremendous meaning.
You have been my right arm.

To Ralph Foster

The steering Committee of our team. Thanks.

To Jack Wilhelm

Thanks for your time and interest, and for your help.

To Marge Green, Author of "A Life With Wings"

My friend said, "I do not claim originality for every thought in this book. I have garnered many gems of wisdom from countless sages, and with God's help I am trying to pass it on to my children, grandchildren, and others.

To Margie and Basil Overton

Thanks for your patience and words of wisdom. My friends indeed are Basil and Margie Overton.

Contents

Foreword

Acknowledgments

Preface

Introduction

Now, The Story	1
Loads To Pull	18
Keep On Keeping On	33
Hard Times	55
Book Satchels And Lunch Pails	65
Southern Holiday Cooking	86
Annapolis Avenue Church	102
Whispers In The Wind	109
Sunshine	174
Knoxville Days	213
Our Honeymoon And After	235
Making Ends Meet	276
Our World Turns Upside Down	299
Solo Flights	313
Volunteering	356
Changing Times	378
Achievements And Tributes	382
Genealogy	407

Foreword

Someone has said, "If you live long enough, sooner or later everything will happen to you."

I have been blessed with a long life. Having been born in 1908, I have lived in portions of eleven decades. Many momentous events have happened during these years, especially in the United States, and I have enjoyed being a part of a heritage that made life better for me. I hope I can contribute to a legacy that will make life better for others, especially for my children and grandchildren.

They have encouraged me to "put on paper" some of the details of my life. Ironically, the metaphor "singletree"—used throughout the book to refer to me—probably has little meaning to most of them, since it is a term from the distant past which is slowly disappearing from use. A singletree is a bar to which chains of a harnessed horse are attached to pull the load.

At times, I have been referred to as a person who serves such a purpose in my family: to give direction and "keep everyone between the ditches." I take it as a compliment, but feel at times that such a distinction is more of a responsibility than I can fill and more of an honor than I deserve.

Preface

For my children, grandchildren, and great-grandchildren, and perhaps "kith and kin" and neighbors who are interested in hearing it like it was in 1908.

This is my story, but it is your book:
YOU ASKED FOR IT!

A Singletree From Tennessee

Singletree - a bar to which chains of a harnessed horse are attached to pull the load.

The speed with which my near century has passed is almost unbelievable. The year 2002 seems a good time to tap into the knowledge of those who have lived until this time. At this writing, I am 94 years old. How dramatically the way of life has changed during my lifetime! Through my stories I want you to see, feel, fear, and join hands with me as I recall what we called "the good ole days."

I am thankful for my reasonably good health. I can still readily bring to memory happenings of my early life. My hearing is greatly impaired, so I depend upon and trust my "Aides."

There is an old proverb that says, "When an old person dies, it's as if a library burns." A great bank of wisdom and experience is lost forever. Please help me preserve some of these fact and figures. They are yours for the asking.

For the information of all who desire to know the relative proportion of fact and fiction regarding this reading: The story is true to the best of my recollection and knowledge. All names are real. The characters were actual residents of East and West Tennessee and North Alabama. Their personalities and abilities as described are as nearly accurate as possible. Some descriptions may vary because sometimes our minds "play tricks" on us.

Many people have given me friendly aid and encouragement along this long and tedious journey. Although I cannot remember all the people who have helped me, you know who you are. I thank each and every one of you from the bottom of my heart.

THANK YOU
ADB

INTRODUCTION TO

A Singletree From Tennessee

Now as I try to lay the cornerstone for the family that continues keeping on and on through good times, trials and tribulations, I want my children, their children and their children to embrace this story as a part of their life. I want them to know that they too can be synonymous with the "load pullers of yore," and, as the tug chains of life are fastened to new singletrees, a few of these experiences will flash in memory's eye as your hands are laid to the plow and you look to the sky.

Now, The Story
A Singletree from Tennessee

Joseph Fleming Dukes and Maud Milstead were married February 25, 1906. The ceremony was performed at Pocahontas, Tennessee by Jim Reed, Justice of the Peace. The happy couple bought a small house with a few acres and called it home.

Joe was considered the "catch of the day." He was a handsome, blond, young man who might have been described as "a tippler" toting a gun and riding a prize horse. Good looking Maud, though not a beauty, was charming and easy with friends. She had beautiful black hair and soft brown eyes and a smile for everyone.

Both families seemed to approve this romantic match. Maud was quick tempered, and most of the time things went her way. Joe was very laid back with a happy-go-lucky attitude that everything would turn out alright.

At a very young age, Joe lost the sight in one eye during a freak accident, but being a child he was able to live and manage his disability very well. In fact, not many knew this was his cross to bear. His blind eye did not mar his appearance. In spite of this, the girls thought he was very good looking.

Joe Fleming and Maud Milstead Dukes

This Certifies that

Joe Fleming Dukes
of Pocahontas Tennessee and
Maud Milstead
of Pocahontas Tennessee

were by me united in

Matrimony

according to the ordinance of GOD and the Laws of The State Tennessee at Pocahontas Tennessee on the 25th day of February in the year of our Lord 19 06

Jim Reed J.P.

Witnesses

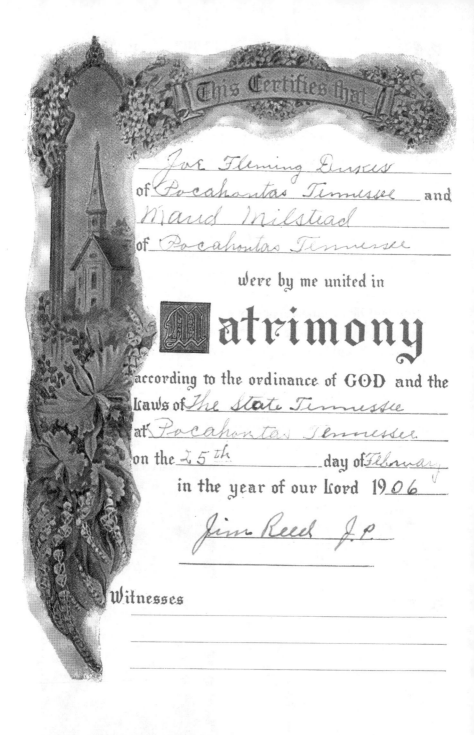

Alma Born – 1908

The Doctor's office, a small frame building, was located in the center of the town of Pocahontas, Tennessee. Dr. Joe Alexander, the only doctor for this entire area, lived here and took care of ALL the sick and afflicted, as well as the delivery of the offspring from generation to generation.

Dr. Joe Alexander's Office

In many a lonely dull life, a home call by the DOCTOR was, in itself, better than the medicine he prescribed—simply because his visit assured the patient that he was alive in a world that cared.

On October 26, 1908, Dr. Joe was excitedly called to the home of Maud and Joe. With the aid of the midwives, women of the neighborhood, another little girl was born and placed in the arms of the proud mother and beaming father. Dr. Joe was their friend and neighbor in a time of need again.

This information came to me by word of mouth: "My great aunt on my paternal side married a young Italian artist and adopted Italy as her home. She did not come to Tennessee often but the last visit was made when her nephew (Joe and wife, Maud) were expectin'. She asked to name her first Great Niece. The name of the little blue-eyed girl immediately became ALMA LEE DUKES. (My family never visited Italy.)

Alma Lee Dukes

Alma had a sister, Vada, who was born January 26, 1907, a year before Alma was born. Alma never knew her. Vada died in a tragic accident on November 14, 1907. This tragedy is related in the story about Alma's parents.

Robert Arlton Dukes, "Geronimo"

June 11, 1914 changed my way of life. I was six years old and thought I knew it all. This was the day my first little brother was born. All at once, it seemed I became a baby sitter. It was my job to rock the baby until he went to sleep, and then watch his every move until it was naptime again. It was not that I didn't like doing this; I just wanted to be outside playing with Allene, Marlin, and all the others in my class at school. But it seemed I had a really important job.

Robert Arlton Dukes was my little brother's name. He was named for Papa's father, but Grand Pa called him Geronimo: for whom or why I do not know, but it stuck. I think he was Grand Pa's favorite.

Arlton and I grew up to be real pals – that is, until Dr. Joe and the stork left another bundle at our door. Then the *new* arrival had to be rocked.

Lewis Milstead Dukes, "Shorty"

Lewis was born September 23, 1916. He was named for the Milstead family. He grew up fast and became very tall (6 feet 2 inches). The nickname "Shorty" became his trademark. I was 8 years old, and I readily became his baby sitter, or baby carrier. People said, "That child will be one-sided from toting that baby on her hip."

My brothers and I were blessed with our home ties—Mama and Papa struggled to give us the necessary tools for a good life, and especially often reminded us of The Golden Rule.

Pocahontas, Tennessee

Pocahontas, Tennessee? How did a small village in Tennessee, which influenced my family and me for so many generations, know about another Pocahontas? Or did they? American history tells us that an Indian "Princess" lived from 1595-1617. She saved the life of Captain John Smith, a Virginia settler, who was to be killed by her tribe. Pocahontas married John Rolfe, a Virginia settler, in 1614, and they went to England. Many of the greatest Virginia families claim to have descended from her.

Are we descendants of this Princess, too? At least our hometown carries her name. What do you think?

Perhaps the painting of the Indian Maiden will help us to have a mental picture of our Pocahontas.

Indian Maiden

She is tall, like a young tree in spring,
Slim as the willows that seek the shadows of streams.
Her voice releases one note of music, then many that echo through valley and forest.
She is gentle and loving,
Fleet as the deer that runs from the hunter,
But she can be sad and silent,
Still, more still than the stream frozen in winter.
She is quick with her laughter
And like a sunbeam
She flits between forests of trees
And frolics as one with the breeze.

"Anon"

Pocahontas In 1908
As I Remember

Pocahontas, Tennessee was a carbon copy of many other small towns built along the Southern Railway tracks in Hardeman County, Tennessee. The town was neat, charming, and as lazy as the muddy Hatchee River that winds its way on the outskirts of town like a rusty brown snake. The slow moving river provided the setting for many happy hours of picnicking, swimming, and just playing for all who would take time to notice the constant struggle of this stream to make contact with the mighty Mississippi River. Families were born and raised here in the same, unexcitable way generation after generation. In fact, after all is said and done, they were nourished on the same legends and ordeals. They managed to survive their ups and downs. The Golden Rule was a common bond that spread over the neighborhood, (The Golden Rule, Matthew 7:12 and Luke 6:31) the rule of doing unto others as we would have them do unto us.

The Pocahontas people were not high or noble or mighty; they were just ordinary folks like the Atkinsons, Swinfords, Reeds, Rolands, Wardlows, Tiplers, Van Dorns, Fortunes, Carrs, Campbells, Alexanders, Willie B. Jones and Milo and Modena, Sheas, Brewers, Warrens, Milsteads, and many more good people—like the Dukes.

Picnic in Pocahontas

Catfish caught right off the Hatchie River at Pocahontas

Fish Fry

The Hotel In Pocahontas

Dollie Shea, Madam At Pocahontas In 1908

A road running North and South divided the population in Pocahontas. In summer the dust was usually ankle deep, and in winter the red sticky clay was almost knee deep. The merchants put planks between the wooden walks and the cross-overs of the road for the protection of the long skirts of the women shoppers.

A yellow frame, two-storied hotel graced the East Side of the road. The Post Office, church buildings, and grocery stores made up the West Side. Because the "painted ladies", or ladies of the street, were permanent residents of the hotel, not much else was on that side. The hotel originally accommodated two classes of guests. The two-story yellow building was built to serve passengers and workmen on the newly constructed railroad; it was also maintained as a brothel that served the same travelers.

Hard Castle Bottom was a swamp area that ran west out of town. It was just a little less than a sink hole in wet times. After automobiles were made a part of our existence, everyone feared crossing Hard Castle Bottom.

Uncle Josh and Aunt Sally Dowdy lived right at the crest of the hill. They would sit on their front porch and await the next SOS call. Finally, the loud drones of a motor struggling to be freed from the mud would come loud and clear, one of the many casualties that got mired up in the swampy mud. Uncle Josh would say, "Aye doggie, Sally, it must be a Buick." (Ford was the favored car in those days.)

The town well was located right in the center of the community. This was the meeting place to hear the news, both good and bad. All church buildings had large bells that were used not only for their services but also as fire alarms and to signal disasters and other important happenings.

The one-room schoolhouse was located on the hill known as Baptist Hill, and it was within walking distance of all the students. Pocahontas had three places of worship for its citizens. The Methodist building was probably the oldest of the three. Many of the senior population belonged to this group. People from distant countries who had adopted this area as their home met with those who attended the Community Church.

Young Years

There was not much exciting going on in the life of a young girl six years old in the years 1914 and 1915. I guess I just required the normal amount of attention and was spoiled rotten! Everybody said, "She is a pretty little girl," and some even ventured to say, "and shows signs of being smart, too."

1914 was a big year for our family. On June 11, 1914, Dr. Joe delivered a bouncing baby boy at our house. He was named for his paternal grandfather, Robert Arlton Dukes. He was a real joy, and Grand Pa Milstead nicknamed him Geronimo. I started to school that year, and my life seemed to take a big leap into the unknown. There is so much that needs to be recorded here that it is hard to know where to begin. So just listen.

After two years our family increased, and attentions had to be shared again. I was no longer the only object of affection. So now I introduce you to two little tow-headed boys who really became my charges.

Robert Arlton Dukes *Lewis Milstead Dukes*

Robert Arlton Dukes was the third child born to Joseph and Maud Dukes. He was born in Pocahontas on June 11, 1914. He and Helen Jean Jones eloped on June 11, 1937. Helen Jean was born in Brownsboro, Alabama, on November 12, 1918. Robert died July 28, 1987.

Two daughters were born to this union: the first, Pamela J. was born April 17, 1948. She married Gary Chowning (born October

14, 1947) on June 11, 1970. Their children are Brandon Dukes, (born May 6, 1975) and Natalie Dianne (born March 19,1979).

The second daughter, Teresa Fields was born April 13, 1951. She married David Denny (born January 2, 1949) on June 16, 1973 . Their children are Joshua (born May 25, 1977) and Davis (born December 25, 1980). Joshua married Maria Watson on April 7, 2001.

Lewis Milstead Dukes, the fourth child of Joseph and Maud and Alma's youngest brother, was born September 23, 1916. He married Della Pearl Harrell (born November 1, 1918) on December 1, 1945. There were no children. Lewis died May 31, 1986, at 70 years of age.

Alma's Baby Sitting

Alma ran down the brick walk with its patches of daffodils like spots of gold on the grass along the side. She opened the screen door and called, "Mama, Mama, I'm home."

No sound was heard from any part of the house, but a thin smiling woman appeared in the doorway.

"Alma, is that you?"

"I'm here, Mama."

"Come here and help me with the baby. He's cried all day."

Alma went to the crib and patted Lewis.

"He's alright now, Mama. He's stopped crying. I went to the kitchen and got some 'lasses from the wooden keg and gave Lewis a lick. He likes 'lasses. He's smacking his lips."

"Did you give that baby molasses? What a mess you must have made, and washday not for three more days, and clothes drying when they will in this weather," she sighed.

"Well, he's happy now," Alma giggled.

Mama felt guilty as she put a few more stitches on the quilt. She tried to finish it up while Alma watched the baby.

Hot Soup

Papa opened the back door and entered the kitchen – "Maud, we're home," he called. He didn't hear a thing. He called again, "Maud, where are you?"

She answered in an aggravated tone, "I am in this side room, cleaning up this sticky mess. Alma left the cork out of the molasses keg, and it spilled, and she tracked it all over the place. Tend to the baby for me." Mama felt guilty spending the whole day away from the baby, not being able to finish the quilt and do her other household chores for cleaning up the mess.

Papa tiptoed over, cautiously peeped at Lewis and, with a sigh of relief, said, "He's asleep," and under his breath, "Thank Goodness." He surely didn't want to get tied down rocking while supper was being made in the kitchen. He really wanted to read the "Commercial Appeal." Things were happening, and all the men ought to be able to talk about what was going on. Maud just wouldn't understand that.

"What happened at the store today?" she called from the kitchen.

"Nothing, everything quiet," Papa answered. In order to make conversation, he said, "I think the fall rains have set in."

"That's not smart thinking, Joe. It's coming down in sheets outside right now.

"Is it?" he said, giving her a sidelong glance with his pale blue eyes, but he did not reply further. After many years of married life, he had learned that it was more conducive to peace to leave his wife with the last word.

Even with Papa's newspaper knowledge and traveling salesman's reports, we were totally unaware of the pressures that existed in far away places like Corinth, Mississippi, a few miles away and Memphis, Tennessee, which was 60 miles, an unthinkable journey.

"Joe, you all come on, I made a pot of soup for supper. It's a good night for hot soup."

Papa thought back to all the leftovers that must have gone into that pot. Of course, it was an easy meal for Mama since her time had been taken up with other things. He got up out of the chair and slowly entered the kitchen saying, "Alright, I like good, hot, fresh soup."

There was not much conversation as we ate our cornbread and hearty bowls of soup. We were all anxious to get back to the warm heater in the room that served as a sitting room, bedroom, Saturday night bathroom, as well as other incidentals necessary to a family's comfort in an otherwise cold house.

We were all tucked in bed early. Arlton worried about our horse, Old Prince, because of the cold, but he was told to go to sleep. I told him, "He'll be alright in the morning."

The glow of the kerosene lamp that held the night shadows at bay was blown out, and it gave up with a flicker that seemed to say, "I want to keep burning, bigger and bigger, and perhaps someday I'll be an eternal flame."

The Church Of Christ At Pocahontas

The Church of Christ at Pocahontas had its beginning over a century ago. Brother T. B. Larimore, founder of Mars Hill Bible Academy near Florence, Alabama, held the first gospel meeting in 1872. He made the following statement, "The material at Pocahontas is excellent, consisting of men and women of firmness who are settled in life."

T. B. Larimore

The people all readily agreed to meet together every Lord's Day to worship God. Soon after this protracted meeting, a church building was erected. A tornado destroyed this structure in 1880. In 1907, another meeting place was built.

Grandpa and Papa both were very active in the work of the church. Papa was taught at this place. When I was approximately nine years old, about 1917, Brother J. A. Foster from Texas held a meeting of two weeks duration. He impressed me so (along with the teaching instilled in me since my infancy) of the importance of becoming a Christian that I boldly walked down the aisle one night as the congregation sang, "Just as I Am," and I made the good Confession. The next morning, I was baptized in the muddy Hatchie River. They say this river is the only natural stream in this part of Tennessee.

As I walked into the water, I could feel the mud oozing up through my toes, and I was led out about waist deep. This could have been a frightening thing for one of my age, but I was prepared for all this and was so thankful that I had the courage to make this step in my early life: "Before the evil days come."

One principle adhered to by the Church of Christ in the way of a theological tool is the statement, "Where the Scriptures speak, we speak; and where the Scriptures are silent, we are silent."

I Remember

Luke 22:19 says, "And He took bread, and gave thanks, and brake it, and gave unto them saying, 'This is my body which is given for you: this do in remembrance of me.'" I Corinthians 11:24 says, "and when He had given thanks, He brake it and said, 'Take, eat: this is my body, which is broken for you: this do in remembrance of me.'" Jesus, our Lord, built an eternal memorial out of the fruit of the vine and unleavened bread. The Lord's Supper is to help us remember Him and his sacrifice. It is by no means expensive; yet, it is the most appropriate memorial that exists.

Someone has said that our memory is just like a church spire, and I quote:

1. It generally overlooks the neighborhood.
2. It records the comings and goings of people and time.
3. Things abide with it—important things, curious things, odd things, and trivial things.
4. It is a register of life.

My memory book has many unopened pages, and I am trying to use my mental key to remember and reveal some of my life's untold stories. Some are fascinating and some uninteresting and silly. You pick and choose. My cup of memories runneth over, one drip at a time, and seems to pause for each one of you to take your first sip.

Sunday School

I cannot remember when we did NOT go to worship. Since the congregation at Pocahontas was small and struggled to keep alive, we did not have a regular preacher. Our Sunday service consisted of what is called Sunday school. I was enrolled into this small class at a very tender age – probably four or five years old. My teacher was Miss Lessie Tipler. She was proclaimed by all to be the beauty of the beautiful, both inside and out. She would hand out small biblical pictorial cards with a Bible scene and the "Golden Text," a quote from scripture. This was our study material for the next week.

As the children of this class grew older, they advanced to a class with workbooks designed for more progressive study. Song books, study material, etc. was all ordered through the "Gospel Advocate" in Nashville, Tennessee. From the earliest remembered days until this day, Sunday school has been a part of my regular Bible study. Thank you, Miss Lessie, wherever you are, for taking each step with me toward a Christian foundation. You taught me how to behave without seeming to preach. You said, "Good or bad is decided in wills of self, not God, but as you will."

I continued faithful with this small congregation until we moved from Tennessee. Practically all the Milsteads are members of the Church of Christ. Papa's family is all of the Methodist faith.

There was an old itinerant preacher called a "circuit rider" who showed up with his Bible under his arm and ready to preach the word. He rode a big black horse and carried a large knapsack. Preacher salaries were unheard of in those days, but a filled knapsack was a blessing. He would be paid with everything from chickens, eggs, potatoes, meal, smokehouse meat, and all good things homegrown and home-cured. He was most thankful for any small gift—even a kind word. We all appreciated his visits and the basic Bible lessons he left with us. He was a true pioneer of the Good News, and we all looked forward to his next visit which would come in about two months. His name was Brother Wheeler.

Loads To Pull

The Country Store

Early in the year of 1909, the Country Store became a reality. Papa begged, borrowed, and saved a small sum of money and was able to open a one-room Country Store.

He was a people person, and soon the store was the gathering place for the early morning gang. They shared the latest news, good and bad, and took advantage of the warmth from the big, red-hot, pot-bellied stove. Some were skipping early morning chores at home and some were making up yarns and aiming at the corroded brass spittoon nearest them. It was soon noised abroad that if help was needed, just see Joe. He became a partner with the sharecropping dirt farmer from season to season. He carried the grocery bill for the lumberman from payday until payday. He furnished anyone, black or white, with what the store contained of the necessities of life until better times came their way.

Joe's store was magic, one big room crammed full of life's happiest desires. The long counters were filled with glass jars containing mouthwatering peppermint sticks, chocolate kisses, and big two-for-a-penny cookies. Big barrels lined the floor and contained the items that became staples for all kitchens: salt, flour, cheese in big hoops, baking powder, and self-rising flour. There was coal oil (kerosene) for the lamps in cans whose cover spouts were plugged with Irish Potatoes.

The Country Store soon outgrew the premises, and after a necessary addition became THE GENERAL STORE. The assembled fragrance that hung in the air was as permanent a fixture as the kerosene lanterns suspended from the ceiling. This odor of oil, cheese, leather, bacon, lard, and wisps of curls of tobacco smoke became a part of the visit to the General Store. The kegs of big, fat cucumber dill pickles submerged in brine were retrieved by a sharpened stick and enjoyed bite-by-bite all day.

A visit from the traveling salesman was always a bright spot in the day. He would appear with a cigar cocked in the corner of his mouth, telling bawdy stories and with no thought beyond cards, wine, woman, and selling his wares. This was a big diversion for everyone from everyday worries.

The store was graced by the appearance of female customers only when a real emergency arose. About the only thing that would bring the ladies in was the need of yard goods, thread, and snuff. The latter only if they were completely out and just had to have a "dip." This was a real emergency. Otherwise, the men folks did the snuff buying, too, to keep a family secret that even their own womenfolk used it.

The entire atmosphere of the store was friendly and warm, especially in the wintertime. Empty nail kegs were scattered around and up close to the pot-bellied stove for the sole purpose of encouraging tale telling among the men folks. Twelve o'clock was the time of day for opening cans of sardines, putting on pepper sauce, which was on the house, and eating cheese and crackers around the red hot stove. Each rugged nail-keg-philosopher had a tale of his particular liking stored away for this time of day, being sure that he would top the other fellows, such as the time Papa came home, telling us about the murder of Old Man Nethery. He told about some of the boys in the neighborhood being out 'possum-hunting' and finding the old man in a well. A perfect crime never solved!

People in trouble could always find a friend or credit behind Joe's counter. One day he pointed to a man on the far side of the road and said to me, "Alma, see that man?" The man did not even look toward the store. "He owes me an account," Papa said, "so he takes the far side of the road." Another day I was at the store when a man came by with a wagonload of groceries. Papa said, "Where did you get all those groceries?" The man answered, "At Mr. Shea's store. I brought in a load of wood and sold it to him for the groceries, Mr. Joe. I didn't think you sold for cash." That was the general opinion of how Papa dealt with the rank and file, so sometimes the cash went to the other merchants.

"Alma, always remember," Papa said, "It's not so much how much you owe, but how you treat the man you do owe." He always manifested sympathy to those who just couldn't pay due to circumstances, but he had no patience with the "dead beats."

Every Saturday night, Mama would start worrying about Papa coming home from the store with all the money that had been collected from the migrants in town. She would stand it as long as she could, then she would bundle up and go to the store in order to come back home with him, in that way assuring him of adequate protection. But for security, he depended more upon his trusted weapon than his wife.

There is no time quite as busy in the Country Store as when election time comes around. The discussions of how our affairs were handled at Bolivar, the county seat, and why the party votes were split went on and on. Then there were far away rumblings regarding a war. Everybody thought we ought to elect a man for the White House who would keep us out of war.

Papa always said, "The little man can be the big man if everybody pulls together."

One day the men were gathered around the big stove, sitting in straight chairs, warming their shins and hinder parts as the warmth penetrated the whole room. A man looked up from the task of lacing and tying his high top shoes. He was wearing a gray shirt of some linen and wool-like material carefully buttoned to the collar. He had a long slim face creased by the wind and weather and deep set eyes with glints of light in them. His eyebrows were very bushy. He was the regular letter carrier. This was my Grand Pa Milstead, ready to carry the United States mail.

Stephen Albert Milstead was a loyal employee of the U. S. Government. He made the following statement about the importance of his job. "Neither rain, nor snow, nor heat, nor gloom of night will stay these carriers from the completion of their rounds." He stated that the government in Washington had just issued this slogan to them.

Grand Pa was in the store that morning to pick up some items for mail customers who were unable to make the cold trip into town. Papa said, "Mr. Milstead, did you see the prices posted up at the Warren Store? I'll beat them, I'll sell you corn at 30 cents per bushel, not shucked and shelled. My eggs are 5 cents per dozen, hen eggs not turkey eggs. He might be kin to you, but I can beat him when it comes to giving a bargain."

The following was taken from a Warren Ledger dated 1906 and 1909. This store was similar to our store, also located near our store.

Saloms	.20 cents	Mederson	1.40	Paster Rent	4.00
Crax	.10	6 yrds Calaco	.42	House Rent	4.00
Roson ears	.10	Kniff	.75	Merchant's	
Tirkey eggs	.10	Union suits	1.00	License	16.50
Orngs	.10	Wagon tung &		Coat Suet	9.00
Stake	.20	Single trees	3.20	Hat	3.00
Shugar	.25	Horse shoing	1.00	Shoes	1.50
Broken eggs	.05	1 Curry come	.05	Hoes	.15
				Load of wood	.65

Sails May 1910 — $199.77
       June   360.39
       July   327.72

The General Store was a symbol of some of the most care-free years our country has known. It was the center of social life in hundreds of tiny communities across America.

Papa Decides to Remodel Our House

Thanksgiving and Christmas of 1908 passed at the Dukes' house without much ado. Even so, they did bundle me up both times, and they hitched Ole' Prince to the buggy, and over the hill we went to Grandpa and Grandma's house. We spent the traditional days with them and the other members of the family. As usual, the big table was just groaning with all kinds of holiday dishes. Each family had contributed their specialty. Mama brought the big white coconut cake and a gallon jug of real boiled custard.

At the end of the day, we came home and settled in for the night. Papa pulled his chair closer to the heater and said, "Maud, I think we are about to outgrow this little house. Things are lookin' pretty good, the farmers have made fair crops, at least the sharecroppers—both white and black—are breaking even. They are endin' up just where they started last Spring, havin' nothin' but owing nothin'." Papa and Mama had become accustomed to this way of life. No matter how fruitful, their labors had been for someone else.

"The economy in general is not too bad," Papa continued, "This might be the right time for us to remodel our house. What do you think? I could take time to oversee the carpenter work and I think I could recruit enough labor hanging around the store to do the work."

"I am so glad you mentioned this," Mama said, "I've been dreaming of more space, but was afraid to bring up the subject."

All this talk set the plan in action for a bedroom here and a bigger kitchen there, some storage space, and a big front porch. Mama said, "I always wanted a porch that faced the east so my flowers would get full benefit of the morning sun." They spent several hours with pencil and paper, and they finally decided to actually start on the project.

Living in a house under remodeling is not easy. Everything was piled into one or two rooms. Cooking was done on a two-burner laundry heater. Day to day living was a make do effort. Mama was determined to "hold her tongue" and make the most of what seemed an endless task. Everything was stacked on top of everything else, with just enough room to push through from front to back. The workmen were tearing out walls, windows, and doors. It seemed we were not really living but just existing.

Ruth And Edgar's Visit

Then an exciting message came from the big city of Sheffield. Aunt Milo's (Grandma's sister) daughter had just gotten married. The daughter's name was Ruth Freeman, and she had married an older man whose name was Edgar Ingul. Well, Ruth was bringing Edgar to their ancestral home, Pocahontas, for a honeymoon trip.

"They can't stay here in this mess," Mama said right off. "They'll just have to make a short visit to Papa's and Mama's house."

As it turned out, Ruth wanted Edgar to visit us, and they did come knocking on our door. With a make do kitchen, Mama could not cook a full meal, but she did fix a pot of stewed Irish potatoes on the stove that morning. Ruth was known for her critical ways about everything. After taking a bite of the potatoes, she said, "This tastes just like a mad wasp smells." That broke the camel's back, and the welcome mat left the front door.

Some time later, after they had gathered their belongings and gone back up the hill, Mama said, "You know Joe, a mad wasp might really have fallen into the pot from all the hammering and sawing." From then on, if something was served that we didn't like, "It surely tasted like a mad wasp smelled." I think that was the last visit from Edgar and Ruth.

With all the hammering, nailing, fussing, and screaming going on in and around the house, Mama was hearing the call of Spring, for her attention to the yard and garden. With each coming of Spring, we are reminded anew of what a wonderful time of year it is.

It was very early Spring, and I was a toddler, just old enough to be a "hair in their biscuits." Every time the door was opened, I insisted on being outside helping with everything in the yard. This year Mama declared the blossoms on the dogwoods, redbuds, and all the fruit trees outdid themselves. "I'm convinced, she said, they are the most gorgeous trees God put on our earth." As young as I was, the new leaves and flowers did not bring me the deep appreciation that Mama had for them. She puttered 'round the yard, checking beds for crocus and other early blooming bulbs and shrubs. She finally said, "With all that is going on, I will just wait for another Spring. I will soon have a nearly new house, a yard surrounded by a paling fence, and perhaps lots of bulbs, shrubs, grass, and all the beauty that goes with a well manicured yard, instead of working myself to death today."

I want you to have a mental picture of our remodeled house, yard, barn, garden, and little farm. Our house was now a pretty, neat frame house located in the center of a four acre plot, and it was on a lane that led one way to town and the other way to the school house, and on to Grand Pa's house. Papa had ordered four big oak rockers for the front porch, one on one side for Papa and one on the other side for Mama. Our barn was at the back of the lot and seemed larger than the house. I guess the horses needed more room.

Our front yard was in its glory that Spring. The jonquils appeared like spots of gold in the green. Stars of Bethlehem and other small wild flowers, sweet williams, hyacinth, honeysuckle, and all the flowering shrubs struggled for their place in the sun. Tulips nodded toward the small pansies and seemed to be inviting them for a dance. Then the dry weather came in.

The back yard was kept barren and swept clean as our kitchen floor. This was where all the play activity took place. It seemed to be the gathering place for games such as hopscotch, marbles, pitching dollars and horseshoes, jumping rope, and any other activity that came to mind.

Our entire surroundings were "so homey" and well kept in comparison to the other middle class homes that were bordered with honeysuckle and ragweed lots. Those houses always had a British-like Bobby's hut along side them. I never understood why these places of refuge and relief were not at least partially hidden with scrubby Tennessee pines and cedars, or better still why they were not strategically located behind the "big" house. Oh well, anyway our "slip didn't show." Mama had seen to that.

The Outhouse

Our outhouse, or "johnny" as it was called, was about three and one-half feet by four feet. The front door was almost as wide as the building in order to accommodate the big people of the family. The only semblance of furnishing was the bench that reached across the whole back wall. Our bench had three sizes: A big circular hole, a middle-sized circle, and a small circle. Two or three old Sears Roebuck catalogues were provided for the users' convenience.

Early one morning, I had the natural urge to pay this little sanctuary a visit. I ran through the door without noticing the place was already occupied. All at once, I screamed, "Mama! Mama!"

DUKES' SANCTUM

She called back from the house, "What is it?"

"Come here quick! I'm in the closet, and there is a big snake in here!"

She came running, picking up a hoe as she passed the side fence. She ordered me, "Stay right still".

Sure enough, she soon saw what I saw, a big brown snake right inside the door where I had stepped over it. We were both scared to death of snakes, but necessity caused Mama to take a stand. She began to poke and prod the thing until it stuck its head up where she could hit it with the hoe.

When Papa came home, right away he said, "You were lucky to stay out of the strike of this one, for it is a copperhead, a very poisonous snake found in this part of Tennessee." After this, I was always very careful to inspect the surroundings of this little hut before entering, that is if time permitted.

A big story grew out of the snake incident. Papa would never be outdone at spinning a yarn. He said, "That was nothing. Let me tell you kids about a snake. See this scar?" pointing to his prematurely bald head. "One day I was walking home from town, which was about three miles to the Dukes farm, I came upon a big snake down at Hardcastle bottom. It seemed there wasn't enough room for me and that snake to pass each other, so I decided to tackle him. I cut a forked stick and caught the varmint by the head. Then right quick I picked him up by the tail and cracked him like a whip. His head flew off. I'd heard my brothers telling about the Jones boys doing this. I guess this gave me the courage to tackle a thing like this. Anyway, when his head flew off and the fangs caught right up here in my bald head."

We doubted this story because we had heard Grandma Dukes tell about the time a tree limb fell, and hit Papa on the head, and made a scar. We had long ago learned to appreciate his big yarns. We all agreed that it made a good story, and, as young'uns would come along, they would be told the same stories with the same big eyes and adoration of their hero Grandpa.

Old Prince
The Faithful Load Puller

"Where's Arlton?" Mama asked excitably. "Sister, have you seen Arlton? Where is he?"

"He got the back door open by himself and went running up the path to the barn. I think Papa's up there," I answered.

"Is he bareheaded? He'll be sick. I'll declare, that child will come down with pneumonia, being out in this damp. Your Papa will be real upset."

"Oh, don't worry, Mama, I'll go get him." I picked up a stick outside the back door and skipped gaily up the much traveled path toward the rambling barn, calling, "Papa, Papa! Is Arlton up there?"

Papa's voice was heard answering, "Yes, he's with me. We'll be to the house in a minute. Old Prince has got a nail in his foot. You run on back."

As I ran back toward the back door, I wished for springtime, but Christmas comes first, and then I had heard my Grand Ma say, "Spring can't be far away."

As I reached the back door, although it was almost dark I could see my Papa coming near the house with the lantern, making just his feet and legs discernable, but "RR" was tugging right along side his pants leg, chattering like a magpie. He was trying to get Papa's attention and, with wide eyes, he asked, "Papa will Prince be alright? Do horses go to heaven? Can he run any more? Do horses lay down to sleep? Prince will have to, now, won't he?"

Papa patiently answered, "Yes, Prince will be alright. He will be out in the lot in the morning before you get up, you'll see. He is a big fine horse, and horses are real strong. Just you don't worry about him anymore."

Papa had a real love for horses, and it seems his first son was trying to walk in his steps. There was always a beautiful rubber-tired buggy and one or two prize-winning horses at our disposal.

Mama loved hitching the buggy to one of the horses and trotting off up the hill to Grand Pa's. The harness hung on a nail inside the barn wall. In no time at all, she could have the horse hitched up, and with the singletree properly attached, they would be ready to go. The horse was ready to pull his load.

The Weasel Story

As the rain pattered softly on the roof and everything in the house was quiet, even Lewis—we thought he was sickly, but the truth was he was just plain spoiled—we all went to bed and to sleep.

At about 9:30, the middle of the night to us, Mama heard a disturbance out toward the chicken house.

"Joe! Joe!" Maud whispered, nudging him.

"Uh? What's wrong?"

"I heard something bothering the chickens, get up and see."

"Oh, Maud, that's nothing, just the Rhode Island Red is cold and trying to squeeze in between two old hens." With this remark, he turned over and went back to snoring.

The squawking got louder and louder, and soon Maud could stand it no longer. She jumped out of bed and ran toward the back door. Out into the rain she ran, not even stopping to grab a shawl, and she tumbled down the back steps.

"Maud! Maud! Where are you going?" Joe called, "Are you crazy going out on a night like this?"

She called back over her shoulder, "I'm going to see what's bothering them chickens. Couldn't get you to move." She got up and started running again, and she ran smack over a big chicken coop left in the path. Arlton had been using the coop as a cage for his pet rabbits.

Hearing all the commotion, Joe jumped up and hollered, "Maud, Maud! Are you hurt?"

Without answering she called excitedly, "Come here quick, I'm in the chicken house with a weasel. I've got him hemmed in the corner, hurry! Joe, you are so slow!"

"Hold him till I get my pistol." Joe replied. Like a white streak in his long underwear, he ran back to get his gun.

"Oh, we'll get him," he said. Shakily pointing the gun in the general direction of two glistening eyes made discernable by the sudden peep of the moon from sodden clouds.

"Get back Maud," he said, anxious to show off his marksmanship before his wife. "I'll shoot in the corner." The trigger was pulled with much shaking of the hand and the legs of the long underwear; then not a sound was heard.

The weasel, sensing an opportunity for escape, scurried between Joe's legs and was out the door in a flash.

Visibly embarrassed, Joe said, "Well, I'll be, but he won't come back. We sure scared him. I know he won't come back."

The chickens settled down. He turned to go back into the house when he noticed Maud holding her hand. "What are you holding your hand like that for?"

She said, "It hurts, hurts awful."

"What did you do to it? Did that weasel bite you?"

"No, Joe, I fell over that chicken coop and burst the wen on my hand. See. It is all puffed up. I told you over and over to move that thing. Now see what you made me do."

Joe looking at her hand said, "Sure is puffed up. What do you do for a burst wen?"

"I don't know. It's the first time I have ever burst one. I'm afraid I am going to have to have my hand cut off." Then thinking she could never quilt any more, she said, "Guess the good Lord was right when He said, 'All things work together for good for those who love the Lord.' I just finished the quilt!"

Looking at her hand again, Joe said, "No, Maud it will be alright. Old Prince stuck a nail in his foot. I put turpentine on it. Come on in, I'll put turpentine on your hand, you'll both be alright."

She was, and the wen was gone, and the weasel was gone, too.

The Memphis Fair, 1917

Since business looked good, Papa wanted to treat his family with a real trip. He asked, "Would you like to go to Memphis to the big fair?"

"Yes!" I yelled. I was nine, and Arlton, three. Lewis, only one, didn't quite know what was going on, but he joined in the yelling, "Yes! Yes!"

This had all been talked over between Grandpa and Papa, and they had really planned to present the announcement in the form of a question. Papa was the organizer of the affair as he had been to Memphis before, and he knew about things such as hotels, restaurants, and special sights.

As the time grew near, we all became more and more excited.

I asked, "Mama, can we go to the zoo?"

"What's a zoo?" Arlton shyly questioned.

"Oh, you are too little to know, but it's where all kinds of animals are kept," I quipped.

He said, "Oh, yeah! Snakes and weasels and things, I think."

When the day arrived, we were all packed up and ready to take off. The air was charged with excitement. We caught train No. 35 and arrived in Memphis after dark. Papa and Grandpa had a friend in Memphis, Mr. Walter Jones, who met us and pointed out some of the landmarks. Mr. Jones said, "Let's go up in this office building and look around." Once inside, he led us to an elevator, the first one we had ever seen. Motioning with his arm, he herded us inside. The elevator went up six floors so quickly that everyone lost their breath. We all giggled and decided that if this one got us all back down, elevators would be real nice for the barn loft back home.

And guess what? I told my friends at home later. "We took our first elevator ride, and it TOOK OUR BREATH." The old saying, "You can take the boy out of the country, but you can't take the country out of the boy" fit us that day! I am sure we did not try this again, for Grandma said, swaying slightly, "This makes me dizzy."

We were all amazed at the bright lights of the big city and the bustle of the busy streets. I held Mama's hand, and Papa was in charge of Lewis and Arlton. Grandpa was in charge of his family, which now consisted of Marie, Myron, and Merritt.

We ambled along from the station up toward the main street. I decided Papa was trying to show his ability at settling the family in a big city. He kept looking up. I was sure he was reading the bright colored signs. Just then Grand Pa spelled out loud, "C A F E," and then, he said, "Calf," softly. "Joe, what does that mean?" he asked.

Papa explained, "It is a place that would be just fine for our supper."

We went in and found a table big enough for all of us – all ten of us. The waitress handed the grownups a menu, but they didn't know what the foods described really were. Finally Papa said, "Just bring us all bacon and scrambled eggs." He leaned over and whispered to Mama, "Guess we are getting our breakfast tonight." She mumbled, "I guess so."

The next morning, everyone was up early, at his or her usual time and maybe earlier. Grandma said she just didn't sleep at all, for the people just didn't ever go to bed. The clomp, clomp, clomp of the horses on the brick streets was totally unfamiliar, but she did love to hear the horses go by.

The day was full of new and exciting things. To please the children, the zoo came first. I didn't like the looks of any part of it or the smell either. "You all just go on in, and I'll just wait here at the gate," I said.

I had seen the elephant house; the big elephant head made of plaster of Paris was enough for me. I just didn't want to see the real elephant head, trunk, or anything. But they said, "No, you will have to come with us." So I went part of the way inside, but they couldn't budge me to go further, even though the head was just make believe.

All the others liked the zoo. I liked the merry-go-round and the ride on the little train. Once I got a taste of the merry-go-round, that was all I wanted to do. Marie got really mad because she had to stay with me while I rode and rode the merry-go-round.

As the grown folks looked at the agricultural and livestock exhibits, Myron suddenly called out to Grand Pa, "Papa look at this hog; it weighs 700 pounds. Sure would make a lot of sausage!" Still looking at the 700-pound pig, Myron said, "Papa, it's as big as a rhinoceros." Papa, not believing his eyes, read the sign and said, "It really is a pig!"

"Whooooo," Myron exclaimed, "I never did see a pig like that."

Mama and Grandma just loved the woman's building with loads and loads of cakes, pies, jams, and jellies. They were sure they could equal or outdo some of the things they saw. Anyway, they would surely try when they got back home.

While in his meandering around the fair grounds, Papa discovered a monstrosity in the form of a patented storm house. It closely resembled a big oil tank like those you see on a railroad car. Anyway, he being storm minded just couldn't resist this of all storm houses.

The day had been long, and everybody was all tired out and money'd out, too, so the clan went to the station to catch the train back home. With happy memories of the fair, not so happy memories of the zoo, and a brand new storm house, loaded and ready to accompany them, home we went. The storm house was neatly buried at our back door for future use. It was guaranteed against Mother Nature's fits of temper, and, rightly so, not a member of our family was ever blown away by a storm.

Winston, standing. Nieces: Pam & Teresa Dukes, center. Becky, first, David, last, seated.

A Later Trip To The Memphis Zoo

Keep On Keeping On

Survival By Making Do

While Papa was busy with the long hours at the store, being chief clerk and bottle washer, Mama was keeping the home fires burning and the chores of every day living moving as smoothly as possible. Fall season was coming on, and I required extra special attention. It seemed to Mama that her work never ended.

People moved more slowly then. They ambled across the road in front of the public well, shuffling in and out of the stores. They took their time about everything. There was no hurry, nowhere to go, nothing much to buy, and no money to buy it with.

During the late summer months, Mama was in charge of preparing the food supply for the hard winter months to come. In early Fall, there would be dried fruits, peas, beans, and other such staple foods preserved. All our vegetables, chickens, pigs, and dairy products were almost at our back door. We always had a big garden and even cold weather greens, collards, onions, etc. on into the winter.

Grandma had taught her daughters the different ways to preserve food. She taught by demonstrating how to wring a chicken's neck, or to place the neck on a chopping block and whack it off with a hatchet. The headless chicken would run around the backyard for a while and then finally flop over dead. A black pot was on the stove steaming with hot water. The chicken would be plopped into the boiling water. Then the feathers could be easily plucked. The chicken was now ready to be cut into "special pieces," like the pulley bone, and fried the Tennessee way.

Our folks would say, "Neighbor are 'specting company," and out to the back yard to catch a chicken and wring its head off they would go.

Recipe: One cup flour, 2 teaspoons salt, pepper. Chicken washed and cut into pieces. Put a half-inch of lard into pan, heat until hot. Drop pieces in, and turn until walnut brown on each side. Cover pan and cook at low heat 20 to 25 minutes. Make gravy out of drippings left in the pan. Umm-good!

Hog Killing Time

No day was more important than hog killing day. When ice began to show up on the mud puddles, the right day was near. Hog killing brought the real supply of meat from the kitchen to the dining table in different delicious dishes.

Hogs were usually slaughtered about a month after the first frost, because the cool weather kept the meat from spoiling. This was a time of hard physical labor, and it involved all members of the family, plus other neighbors and friends invited to help on this day.

A huge neighborhood barrel was used by everyone. On the day before the hogs were killed, Papa would hitch a horse to a slide and bring the large barrel near the big spring at the back of his small farm. There it would later be filled with hot water. Two sizeable black wash pots filled with water were set on bricks, and a roaring fire was set under each one. Soon, both kettles were boiling and waiting for their charge. When the water was the right temperature to remove the hair from the carcasses, it would be poured into the big barrel, and then the actual slaughtering began.

The experienced slaughter men were ready and waiting for the signal to use their hammers. Joe would fire one shot from the pistol he wore on his hip, and the blow from the hammer would hit the spot right between the hog's eyes. The throat would usually be cut so that the blood could drain from the body. The dead hog would then be submerged in water two or three times, while the men held the animal by its feet. When this was done, the men would lay the hog on a platform made of logs and scrape the hair off with butcher knives. Then the hog was hung up by its hind legs and its stomach split open so the entrails could be removed. Clean water from the spring would be splashed to cleanse the insides thoroughly. They were left hanging a few hours to cool before taking them down. After cooling down, large butcher knives were used to cut the hogs into hams, shoulders, middlings, and more. When each piece was trimmed, the lean scraps were put into one tub and the fat into another. Some of the fat and part of the lean was ground into sausage. The rest of the fat was rendered into lard, poured into a lard stand, and stored in the smokehouse joined to the back porch. The lard was used for all kinds of frying, and the cracklings were used to make bread. Other organs, liver, brains, and pieces were also used; nothing was wasted. Even the ears and jowls were to make souse meat, and the feet would be pickled. Finally, all of the meat was stored in the storehouse. Preserving the meat often determined how well the family lived for the next months. Further preservation was carried on in the smokehouse, where other

parts of the animal were smoked and salted down. Small fires of oak and hickory wood were burned, and this smoking process went on until all the meat was cured. Usually, a special effort was made to lock the smokehouse to keep out those who would steal the precious meat.

Home Chores

The day after Hog Killing, cooking was a must. Some of the women were up the day after, making sausage like their mothers had made in both East and West Tennessee and in North Alabama.

Recipes

Fresh Pork Sausage

After the men had cut and prepared the hams, shoulders, side meat, and other cuts, the women and children usually had the job of grinding the sausage. Grand Pa Milstead normally put up his sausage with the rest of the meat. He called it corn-shuck-smoked-sausage. He would take the corn out of the shucks and fill them with fresh sausage. When stuffed he would hang the sausage from the rafter to be smoked with the other meat. Grand Ma would fry the sausage and fill quart jars with fried sausage covered with grease and sealed. The sealed jars would be turned upside down so that the grease would harden to seal the top of the jars. Later they were placed upright again, ready for opening on a cold winter's morning.

- Measure three times as much lean pork as fat pork
- Salt to taste
- Add sage as liked
- Add black pepper and red hot pepper

Cut meat into small pieces before grinding. Sprinkle seasoning over meat. Mix well and grind. *A hand turned grinder was used, and it was important to have the blades razor sharp.* Now it's tasting time or sample time—fry and taste. Um, good!

Crackling Bread
This bread was always enjoyed at hog killing time.

- 2 cups cornmeal.
- 1 T salt
- 1 cup cracklins: thick skins of roasted pork broken into small pieces.

Use enough hot water to make into dough, thick enough to make into small loaves. Bake in a moderate oven, 400 to 450 degrees, for approximately 45 minutes.

Souse Meat

- Pig's head or feet soaked in brine to pickle. *Comes only with hog killing time.*

Scald, scrape, and clean pig's feet. Leave in salt water for about four hours. Cook until the meat falls off the bones. Strain liquid off. Combine meat and juice. Season to taste with salt, pepper, allspice, cloves, and a small amount of vinegar. Chill over night, turn out on a platter, and serve with lemon slices.

Pig's Feet

Put four, clean pig's feet put in a pot and cover with salt water. Then add the following ingredients.

- 3 cups vinegar
- 1 onion
- pepper to taste
- 6 cloves

Boil until the meat slips off the bone, about two hours.

Our Grand Maws said, "When we get up early and see the East turn to orange, you kinda forget morning aches and chills. You just plain know that God is in His place and the Good Book says, 'I can look upon the hills from which cometh strength.'"

Our Grand Mothers were masters at using what they had. They *could* make a silk purse out of a sow's ear. They had to live off what the land had to offer. Hard work meant a big appetite, and our Grand Mothers and Mothers had to sorta mix ways of cooking, and they did powerfully well. The family enjoyed the vittles that hog killing brought to their tables. They were ever thankful for the little things of life, especially good food and friends.

Country Ham and Gravy

Fry country ham, and leave drippings in pan.

Red Eye Gravy
Add a small amount of water to drippings, and bring to a boil. Gravy will be brown.

White Gravy
Add the following to pan drippings
- 1 TB flour
- cup milk
- cup water

Stir until thickens.

Sausage Gravy
Add crumbled sausage to white gravy.

I remember seeing this definition of gravy at a school in Chalybeate, Mississippi. Gravy: "The substance of things hoped for and the evidence of things not seen." (Faith, Hebrews 11:1)

More Hillbilly Cooking
*Homemade Corn Hominy was made by
my Grandmother, Minnie Milstead*

Nothing edible was ever thrown away that could possibly be salvaged. Even the wood ashes from the fireplaces were a necessary ingredient in the preparation of Corn Hominy. Every home had a spot for the "ash hopper." This operation was usually located at the far end of the back porch. The hopper, usually a wooden keg, was filled with wood ashes. Water was poured over the ashes, and this drained liquid became strong lye. My grandmother, Minnie Milstead, made Homemade Corn Hominy by soaking dried corn in the yellow lye water until the skin peeled off the corn kernels. Then the skinless corn was made ready for a long time boiling. The next time you see a can of hominy in the grocery store, you may wonder who taught grandma to concoct such a dish. Try it. You might like it!

More Home Work

Time seemed to fly on eagle wings, and, as the new year neared, plans were made for the hustle and bustle of this season.

A few more outdoor jobs had to be attended to before the calendar called for a New Year. The soap barrel, which was almost empty, must be checked. The barrel was rolled out to the ashes to start a new batch of lye soap. Spring with all of its "Spring Cleaning" would call for a lot of soap and elbow grease.

Lye Soap

Annual bacon and lard drippings from the kitchen were saved and mixed with water. As the wood fireplaces accumulated ashes, they were removed to a large barrel that was usually kept outside on the back porch. When a warm winter day appeared, water was poured through the ashes. These ashes were from oak or other firewood. As the water dripped through the ashes, a highly acidic fluid was produced. This acidic water was gently mixed with the drippings and boiled until a thick jelly was produced.

This homemade lye soap was not only the most commonly used soap, but it was the only soap available to all people out in the country. It would surely cut the grease.

Since we did have "The Store," we were able to have some "store bought soap" for our Saturday Night Baths, when one big tub of water was heated and everyone had a tub bath. The bath water was then poured on the flowerbeds.

Lye soap was our disinfectant, especially when fresh. When used before the lye had dissipated, it was so strong it would eat the skin off our fingers.

Every Monday was WASH DAY – almost rain or shine. The big black iron pot was uprighted, filled with either rain or well water, and brought to a boil by pine and other scraps of lumber saved for the purpose. Three big wash tubs were used in the laundry process. One tub always had the scrub board, waiting for the stubborn stains and smudges that held on through the boiling lye-soapy water. The next tub was a semi-rinse to take as much soap out as possible. Then came the tub of water with a dash of bluing for a last rinse. The blue would keep the white things white. We would wring each piece by hand and allow it to drip. Then each would find its special location on the clothesline. Mama was so-o-o particular as to how her clothes looked on the line. Each item in its place, namely sheets, pillow cases, table linens, etc., then the wearing clothes. Overalls, dark shirts, socks, and other colored things were at the end of the line. Now, pray for a sunny day. All the shirts, many blouses, and other things were starched stiff.

Tuesday was Ironing Day. Ironing was done by hand using "flat irons" that were heated on the stove. Everything had to be sprinkled for easier ironing, for the sun had made them bone dry. Maybe the GOOD OLD DAYS were not so good after all.

Our Water Supply

Our back porch, which we entered by the kitchen door, was used as a catch-all. At the far end of the porch was the location of our well, known as a shallow well. I am almost hesitant to talk about the water we used. I am sure much surface water (and other contaminants) must have found their way into the well after big rains. The well was covered by a well shed, but surface water must have headed that way. Water was drawn about a gallon at a time by the use of a bucket and a rope. A wash stand was located by the kitchen entrance and provided a place for a bucket, wash pan, and soap dish. The towels were hung on the porch post, and the common dipper had its place on the other side of the towels. In summer, the trees provided plenty of shade, but that part of Tennessee had to make provision for hard winters, sometimes below zero. Then these items were brought into the kitchen.

It was an order that the children must wash their hands before each meal, whether the water was cold or hot.

Wash tubs and big barrels were kept at the corner of the house in order to catch each and every drop of water that might fall. This water was used mostly for washing clothes, watering vegetables, and watering flowers. Water would not be saved too long, for it provided an ideal breeding spot for mosquitoes. The tubs would be full of wiggletails if left long in hot weather. This sounds gruesome, but we had to make do, and we did. Our family escaped many diseases and health problems. How? I think because the slogan at our house was: "Eat your breakfast, and you will feel better!"

Uncle Dick's Garden

An old black man named Dick Winston must have been on the Dukes' annual payroll. He took care of everything, and as I remember, he was the only one allowed in "our" garden with a hoe. He was permanently cross-legged, I suppose, as a result of something like polio. This was a disease that crippled many people, and it especially seemed to attack the black people. Finally, science found a remedy. Dr. Salk made his wonderful discovery, and polio was almost wiped out. Anyway, Uncle Dick was our trusted and tried "Jack of All Trades."

With Mama's "green thumb," she was always sticking flowers in between the onions and cabbages. Then the "fur would fly" when her meticulous helper had been too much help and pulled the flowers out of the cabbage row. She, with her peppery disposition, would quickly reprimand Uncle Dick. He would say, "Miss Maude, I didn't see no flowers, and anyway Mr. Joe likes a clean garden." That ended that—for a little while.

Uncle Dick told us about his childhood and how he coped with his affliction. His parents tried every thing to separate his twisted legs—even had him sleep with padded logs between his legs. All home remedies were used, but they were to no avail.

Our kitchen shelf was loaded with home remedies. Mama would only call Dr. Joe for a real emergency—like having another baby. She took care of everything, even to doctoring. She used home remedies.

Home Remedies

She would say, "These really work, and look at the money I save, Joe." With the coming of cool weather, Mama would tie a ball of Asphidia around our necks, and this was a fixture until the next warm days. It smelled to high heaven, but she said, "It works." She said, "I do this because my mother did it and her mother did it," and on and on. The ball of Asphidia was used as a preventative.

The shelf was full of different colored bottles with remedies for "what ails" anyone of the family. I would say that you need to check with your own doctor today before trying these remedies, but we were convinced they worked.

Pain	*Paregoric*
Pneumonia	*Soak a flannel cloth in hot tallow (animal fat) and turpentine and place over the "lung area." Keep as hot as the patient can bear. This works!!*
Croup	*A tablespoon of brown sugar soaked in turpentine or kerosene (coal oil).*
Cuts & Scratches	*Wrap in coal oil and sugar.*
Burns	*Beat egg whites and cover burned area.*
Cold Feet	*Warm a brick in the oven and wrap well. Lay at the foot of the bed.*
Toothache	*Press a whole clove against the exposed nerve.*

Sometimes a traveling Medicine Man would appear with miracle drugs such as Groves Chill Tonic, Watkins Liniment, and Lydia E. Pinkeham Tonic for the ailing ladies. The proverbial medicine shelf contained camphor, quinine, castor oil (awful), calomel and Epsom salts, Vick's salve, mercurochrome, and much more. Many of the tried and true remedies came from the fence corner Herb Garden (Wild). Like these:

Poke Sallet, Not Poke Salad

Poke sallet grew in all fence corners, and when young and tender was picked and mixed with young mustard greens for table use. The root of poke was declared to be poisonous, so par boiling was necessary before eating. Also some cooks enjoyed boiled poke seasoned with pork drippings and scrambled eggs. We liked it both ways. Boiled poke root water added to bath water was a recommended cure for the "itch" that children picked up at school. We tried this remedy, and the word allergy was heard along with swelling and fever. We will never know whether the poke worked, the allergy alerted us, or the itch had run its course. But this was the first and last poke water bath.

We continue to the cook the poke in the Spring because it acts as a blood thinner and is a wake up—get up call for each day. It works, too. It is a tonic full of iron, rich in Vitamin C, phosphorus, and other minerals. The following is typical of sallet recipes. It shows the special style of vocabulary and penmanship often imparted to young brides by women of the South.

Sallet and Corn Pone
by Elizabeth Hubbard Morris, Walker County, Alabama
great grandmother of Louella McCollum

Sallet

Go to sallet patch, pik yer own plum full sallet leaves. (Leave turnips in ground to grow fatter). Go to tub by well, put sallet in tub with big handful salt, cover with fresh drawed water. Let float til leaves air perked up and bugs n worms have fell to bottom of tub. Meanwhile go put big pot on back of stove with hunk salt belly. Add a measure of salt and sugar, some salt pork grease, and big pod pepper from garden on string. Let simmer til yeve washed sallet 3 times in clean cold water. Then add sallet to pot, stir with fork till all is wilted down. Cover and li cook till tender, jist stirrin nuff to keep pot from bilin oer. Note - in spring cook poke with sallet, makes it betterr anything.

Corn Pone

Put 2 cups plain coarse corn meal in bowl. Add nuff cold water to make stiff dough. Put out cones in hand an lay on greased griddle. Stroke with fingers to make purty. Bake in hot oven til brown.

Hickory Tea

Mama's cousin, Cordelia Crocker, lived about a mile down the road toward the store. Cordelia had two girls, Gwynne and Mable, and missed the joy and heartache of dealing with a male offspring. Therefore, she encouraged the attention of Arlton in her direction.

Cordelia's house was always topsy-turvy. A tub of unironed clothes constantly had a place in the dining room, and they were only ironed as needed. We had dinner at twelve o'clock, but Cordelia cooked late in the afternoon. She made hot biscuits at every meal, and Mama only cooked biscuits early in the morning. Arlton had decided he was welcome any hour of the day at Cordelia's house, which she encouraged, trying to entice him in every way.

Arlton seemed invariably to feel the pangs of hunger when he entered Cordelia's house, and he expected a hot biscuit. She was amused and happy to grant his every wish. This very easily became a habit, even though Mama had warned both Cordelia and Arlton against these unannounced and uninvited visits, and had strictly forbidden him to go without her or without her permission. This charge went unheeded. The habit continued for some time. Mama decided she would teach Arlton that she was his Mama, not Cordelia.

One day Arlton stepped out of the house with a biscuit and stood face to face with Mama who held a switch in her hand. He didn't wait to be told to go home, but started in a trot with Mama close behind. Up the road apiece was a place where water stood most of the time. Arlton stopped, looked back, and said, "I can't get across, I can't get across!" As Mama drew near, she wrapped the switch around his legs and said, "You got across coming up, now you can get across coming back." Arlton knew she meant what she said as she began to switch him again. He jumped the puddle, and the Hickory tea was applied every step of the way home. He ran into the house and crouched under the round dining table, having to be coaxed out for supper. After that he said, "I like to go to Cordelia's house, but I want Mama to go with me." It only took one application to cure him. The above incident made a special impression in my memory because this was the type of discipline that molded my ideals of right and wrong.

Inventions

Come with me as I turn the sentimental pages and recall the appearance of new inventions as they emerged from the minds and hands of the artisans. Do you remember a yoke of wall-eyed oxen tugging and straining as they pulled the heavy load on a covered wagon. I do! Oxen are different and hard to handle.

I especially remember the percolator, the refrigerator, and the red checked tablecloth; the first auto, the first airplane, the one-room schoolhouse, and the pot-bellied stove; the deep-rutted country lanes; hog killing time; fresh chicken from the backyard to the black iron skillet, fried golden brown; and crisp corn pone, polk sallet, turnips and greens; the big iron wash pot; and milking time early every morning. I remember the old wooden churn bringing butter from the sweet milk and rich cream; clabber milk churned by the fireplace; and the rich golden nuggets of sweet butter. Then came the radio, the telephone, the television, and eventually push-button everything, and finally to the present day computers and the Internet.

Our icebox was a well-insulated, box-type cabinet that would hold a chunk of ice weighing 100 pounds. Ice was brought to us on train Number 35 from Corinth, Mississippi. A black man, who drove a one-horse shay would meet the train and deliver to each home the ice, covered in tow sacks. This kept us cool for another week.

I am listing some of the noteworthy inventions that have made our lives different, easier, and certainly more sophisticated than those who lived before us.

It seems only yesterday that horse and buggies were the acceptable and appreciated mode of travel. However, suddenly the picture changed when the automobile made its debut. History tells us that the first automobile was built in 1901 when the 425 gasoline powered Oldsmobile was put on the market. Then on October 1, 1908, Henry Ford introduced his Model T for sale for $850.00. This bit of information came from the Ford Motor Company via the Internet: "The incredible success of the Model T: The little company kept improving its machines and making its way through the alphabet until it reached the Model T in 1908. After 20 years of experimentation, Henry finally saw the fruits of his labor with the introduction of this model. It was the vehicle he had wanted to build since his first Model A in 1903. A considerable improvement over all previous models, the Model T was an immediate success."

Grand Pa purchased one of the first Model T's in our part of the country. The car almost looked like a buggy. The wheels were very tall, the back ones taller than the front to help run in the deep muddy lanes. The spokes were wooden and highly varnished. A spare tire was mounted on the back. An extra tire, pump, patches, and a candle to defrost the windshields were included for emergencies. The horn sounded loud and clear and had the word, Claxton, embossed on the bright brass.

The first models were all equipped with the clincher type tires. To change a tire was a major operation. Grand Pa hated the thought of a flat tire and decided he would make a change in Mr. Ford's creation. He had seen a substance advertised called "ESENKY". This was a sponge rubber type material to be packed into the tire, which proved to be as uncomfortable as a log wagon with steel rims. I never heard the word, ESENKY, before or after this trial run. I think he went back to the tried and true clincher type tire. Your guess is as good as mine as to what happened to the ESENKY Manufacturers.

Each Sunday morning, the seven-passenger rig would be driven right up to the church building, and the whole congregation would plead for a ride. The interior was upholstered with red leather. Lights were mounted on each side of the body. The carbon lighted lamps cast a glow over the brass lamps.

"She was a beauty," and with Grand Pa at the wheel, curious heads would turn and say, "Who's that?"

As we whizzed along the country lane, the live stock would race away and even jump fences. We were all so proud to be a part of this: THE BIG PICTURE.

GRAND PA'S PRIDE AND JOY

By
Alma D. Biggs

The first model T was something to see,
A bright red streak—What could it be?

Huffing and puffing down Hardcastles' Lane,
Our little town will never be the same.

The spokes hummed while turning round and round,
The engine purred with a joyful sound.

The window covering of Isinglass made,
Would surely keep out both sun and shade.

The tires were all "Esenky" filled,
No chance of a flat up or down hill.

A ride was fun for each girl and boy,
The bumping and jumping just added to the joy.

"The pride and joy" of the 'good ole days' came
Rushing by with one big wave.

Thanks again for the Model T,
It made everyone happy as they could be.

Out Of The Past

Have you ever seen a telephone mounted on a wall? In approximately 1913, a wooden highly polished box with bells appeared on our walls. All the families living on Pocahontas Lane shared the party line. As a consequence, everybody knew what was going to happen and what had happened.

One day Mama was talking to Aunt Myrtle and she said, "Maud we better hang up. There is a bad thunderstorm right over us." The lightning was streaking everywhere, but Mama had one more bit of gossip to share. Then Myrtle heard the sudden ear-splitting boom, lightning had hit the telephone wire. The telephone box was in pieces, lying on the floor. Mama cried, "Big balls of fire are all over the place!" Mama's hair was singed off around her face. She seemed to be glued to the receiver, which was still in her hand. Everyone in the community was soon aware of the balls of fire. They all agreed that Mama and Aunt Myrtle were very lucky. Mama always told us not to use the telephone when it was stormy because of the danger of possible electrical shock. We sure listened to her after her incident.

Soon after we moved to Sheffield, as a treat, Mama would take us to the big department store in Florence. We, of course, were "just looking," for there was little money, especially for new clothes. Times were still so hard that things were used to the limit. Nothing was thrown away until it was worn out clear through, but we did like to "look." Something at Rogers' Department Store that fascinated me were the little cups that traveled on wires above our heads from the sales person to the office where change would be made. Then the little cups would come sailing back down to the sales person. (A far cry from the computers of today.)

Remember the first Goodyear Blimp? Remember the story about Orville Wright and his brother's flying machine? On December 17, 1903, Orville Wright was the first man to fly. He remained aloft, flying 120 feet in twelve seconds. The same day Wilbur made a flight of four miles that lasted fifty-nine seconds. The brothers' lift off was from Kitty Hawk, North Carolina. We have come a long way during my lifetime. What next?

Let's Not Forget Electricity

I have mentioned several items, and from our memory book many more could be noted that could never have been of value to us without the discovery of electricity and its power. Therefore, harnessing electricity is the key that makes our world turn.

History tells us that a man by the name of Henry invented electrical devices as early as 1832. Fifty years later, the control of this power was put in general use, and now we use the power for just about everything. In 1925, power plants at Muscle Shoals were built to harness the waterpower of our own Tennessee River. Wilson Dam, then being at our back door, made electricity ours at the push of a button. The Rural Electrical Act was set up in 1935 to generate what was called "cheap electric power" for use in all our area. This brought on notable advancement in the use of untold appliances. Progress was being made right here at home.

Today, without electricity, we are like a crippled bird. The push-button era is here, and we say, "THANK YOU" for all the blessings that have come along with it.

The Crippled Airplane

As I remember, this incident happened in Pocahontas in 1922. Lewis was six and Arlton eight years old. We heard a loud crashing sound coming from the sky, and it seemed to be from somewhere in Hard Castle Bottom. This wet marshy land was located about two miles from our back property line.

Sure enough, the strange roaring sound excited the whole neighborhood, and we all rushed to see what was happening. We found a small aircraft that had been forced into an emergency landing. It was almost inside our pasture.

When we reached the scene, we found the pilot outside the plane, only a little shaken from his ordeal. He was from Corinth, Mississippi, and was headed for Memphis, Tennessee. He was lucky to be able to land in the middle of soft mud.

We all gathered to see our first airplane. I had Lewis by the hand and was calling Arlton to take bigger steps so he could keep up. Just as we neared the plane, the pilot started the motor and it generated a whirlwind. I looked over at Lewis and saw his bare head. His hat was going round and round as the wind had picked it up so high that we couldn't catch it. All we could do was say "Good-by hat."

As it turned out, a replacement part had to be ordered to fix the plane. So we had an airplane parked right in our back door for several days. The nameplate showed it was made by a company called Curtiss. This was our first encounter with a flying machine that would not fly. The experience caused Lewis to lose his hat. The plane was finally repaired, and as he left the roar of his motor was like the thunder of the sky. We hoped he had a happy landing.

Late Spring 1917
Storm Houses

On hot Spring days, I would hear Papa say, "Better be ready, for it looks like it will be stormy tonight."

Sure enough, about dark, we would see a constant lightning flicker in the West, and hear a low rumbling of thunder.

Usually we would all go to bed and, about the time we were fast asleep we would feel the presence of Mama in the room. Then she would say, "Children, get up quick. Grab a quilt to wrap up in, for a tornado is coming. Your Daddy is outside watching the clouds, but he says it looks bad and is headed right this way. Alma, run and get the tinker bell."

All the time, Mama was running around, picking up a treasure here and there that she just couldn't leave behind to be blown away.

"Arlton, did you leave that ax in the storm house?" asked Papa.

"No, Papa, I had it out in the back yard, cutting kindling like you told me."

"For goodness sake, we are sure in a terrible shape if the house blows in on top of us. Just would have to stay until someone dug us out. Hurry up, come on Maud," Papa urged, "we'll never make it." Every time weather threatened, with all this last minute preparation, the storm was usually over before we got settled in the place of safety.

Uncle Byrd, his wife, and their daughter lived across the field from my family in a northwesterly direction. Many times in the spring months of May and June, that was the stormy time, they would look across the field at about dusk, and Papa would say, "See Byrd coming. He must think it's going to be pretty bad tonight."

Margie, my cousin, and I would be all wrapped up in our blankets. When we would climb down the storm house ladder and settle in. We would giggle and pretend to be Indian Princesses. Then the storm would hit. Papa and Uncle Byrd would grab the chain that held the door and hold with all their might. Papa would say, "You all be still, it will be over in a minute." The storm would pass over, but the mark of such frightening experiences left on us young children will never be forgotten.

I told my mother, "Mama, if I ever get married, I'm not going to scare my children to death about the storms."

Mama answered, "We'll see."

Later I had these thoughts about the storms. It was mid-Spring, and the children had turned bronzy brown from being out in the sun. Horses sweated through their coats, flicked their tails, and kicked up their hind hooves, trying to get the horse flies off their bellies. Early in the evening the storms would come rolling in. Great flashes of lightening would streak across the sky. Fright would come with each thunderbolt, until finally the calm came and the sense of fear disappeared. The clouds that came with the hot weather were still floating around and finally stretched across the sky. Then, like a miracle, the rainbow colors appeared with the whole spectrum— red, orange, yellow, green, blue, indigo, and violet—a perfect rainbow in the heavens. The above description is a picture of our known world in West Tennessee after the passing of a storm cloud. God gave us the rainstorms, and I love the rhythm of the rain. Every shower brought profit to some, pain to others. I write this for you at the end of another beautiful Spring day with tulips, red buds, dogwoods, and iris blooming all over the place.

Changes in seasons seem to have grown more noticeable as I have grown older. As a child in our yard playing, I could only be aware of leaves changing and flowers blooming, but today, oh, yes! I see the result of God's handiwork. As the great psalmist, David said in Psalms 8:3-4, "When I consider thy heavens, the work of thy fingers, the moon and the stars which thou has ordained, what is man that thou art mindful of him and the son of man that thou visited him?"

1917
Blackberry Pickin'

After the storm, while my Uncle's family was still at our house, Margie said, "Aunt M, let Alma come over to our house tomorrow and go blackberry pickin'."

"Alright, right after dinner." Mama said.

I put on my bonnet and got a big bucket and sauntered over across the field. Margie was out in the yard under a big oak tree.

She said, "Let's swing awhile."

So being company, she said she would swing me first. I sat down on the board in the rope swing and said, "Push me high, now, run under me, I'm not afraid to swing real high."

Margie Dukes

The door opened and Aunt Lillie appeared saying, "Margie, watch out for snakes."

Margie answered in her droll way,"A-l-r-i-g-h-t, M-a-m-a, I'll find one if I can."

We took off down the road skipping and jumping. I reached up and discovered that I had left my bonnet lying under the tree by the swing. Margie said, "That's alright, you won't really need it."

"You know," she said, "I really don't like to pick blackberries or eat 'em either, but I do like to get way off down in the field so Mama can't always be calling me to do this and to do that."

I said, "I like berries, 'specially jam Mama makes, but you know what I sure don't like? Chiggers, and there always seems to be more chiggers in a blackberry patch than anywhere."

"Chiggers don't like me," Margie said, "Guess I'm too thick skinned like my Grandma Dukes."

Time passed quickly, and Margie looked up and said, "Sun's going down, we had better go home." So we hurried back down the lane to the yard. I was afraid my Mama would be worried, so I ran to pick up my bonnet. When I looked I saw with fright that the crown was full of a big snake, a spreading adder snake.

"Margie! Margie!" I hollered, "Run and get a hoe or something quick! Snake!" I spilled all my berries and practically fell over my bucket.

Margie called, "Mama! Mama! Alma's bonnet is full of snakes."

The girls ran toward the house. By this time, Aunt Lillie had reached the spot. The snake had disappeared. Aunt Lillie said in a scolding voice, "Margie, I told you to watch out for snakes."

"I guess I did, for I really found one," Margie replied.

"Alma, this is another big snake tale for Uncle Joe," laughed Margie.

Aunt Lillie Dukes, wife of Byrd Dukes

Hard Times

1914-1918
Post War Recession At Home

We know that this worldwide conflict did not touch our American soil, but we did not escape untouched. Our whole world was in an upheaval as it had never been before. In telling "my story," I feel I must try and help you understand that the dark nights of life always send us back to the glow that makes the pathway bright.

This conflict was known as World War I, as if there might be a World War II somewhere in the future—and there was. Even though this war was not fought on Tennessee or Alabama soil, I feel that your generation and on and on should know, at least in part, some of the consequences of "War." World War I so affected our lives, and especially my own life, that I think it only fair that I touch on some of the tragedies of this unbelievable atrocity.

As history unfolds in front of you and yours, you will ask the question, "Why?" In my research to answer this very same question, I have found that the historians have taken both their time and abilities to try to tell us why. Here is their answer.

Austria and Serbia were perpetually at war. Austria issued an ultimatum to Serbia, which Serbia did not honor. Archduke Francis Ferdinand (1863-1914) became heir to the Austrian throne in 1889, and the violence that erupted as a result of his murder by Serbia on June 14, 1914, brought on World War I. His wife was murdered in 1915.

The real political struggles—racial conflicts and jealousies; power lusts for conquest and trade; hostile divisions nested in Austrian Serbian hatred—go back far in European history.

In 1914, war was declared immediately by Austria, Hungary, Germany, and others. France, Great Britain, Italy, Japan, Serbia, and the United States of America formed an alliance in 1917. Twenty-nine nations were involved in this conflict. It was truly a world war.

America sacrificed approximately 126,000 of our finest young men. It is estimated that the war cost Germany and her allies around 186 billion dollars. Kaiser Wilhelm abdicated to Holland.

Armistice Day was November 11, 1918. Maybe this bit of history will help us to understand the post-war recession. A few days called "Boom Days" came at first, but this gave only false hope.

1914-1918
Economy at Home

No one from our immediate family was drafted into this war. Some of our neighbors' boys were "over there." At my young age, I was not too much concerned with stories coming from so far away. As always, when a nation is at war, there is plenty of industry and everything seemed to be prospering.

Our Christmas of 1917 was almost forgotten. This had been the last time the whole Milstead family celebrated any event because changes were made, looking toward better times. Also, Grand Ma died, and Aunt Madge died of the flu in 1918. We were very concerned with the economic conditions around us. The "flu" of 1918 was epidemic.

The war ended November 11, 1918. Troops were discharged by the thousands and were arriving home daily. The Southern Railroad was the lifeline for our homebound boys, and it proved to be our greatest source of revenue for our weakening economy. The railroad also provided work for many poverty-stricken breadwinners.

After the short-lived boom days, we could feel a constant let down in the flow of business and money. Business had practically disappeared from the country store that was our livelihood. Papa could not stem the tide of what was happening to our country. Our whole life was becoming an atmosphere of unbelievable poverty.

Papa said, "We are too poor to paint and too proud to whitewash. There is always the dark brown taste and green smell of want at the tip of my nose."

I said, "Oh well, if we can't have steak, we will just eat beans."

At this time, the "golden candles of life" were flickering, and economic darkness was falling over the entire world.

>Poverty, or to be poor is a
>State of the mind, not
>Necessarily a condition
>Of the pocket book.
>We were broke,
>We had no money,
>But we were not poor in spirit.

1914-1918
Falling Prices

"Hard Times" spread over the entire country. There was a real financial slump. Prices for farmers' crops fell below the cost of producing them. Cotton usually bought at 40 cents per pound was, of necessity, being sold at 10 cents per pound. Thousands of people were out of work, causing much suffering, especially among our rural folk. Many heads of families had lost their means of livelihood, and homes were faced with poverty. Recession came upon our secure little world. We woke up to realize that everything we counted important was slipping away like sand through a sieve.

Papa dealt in crossties and lumber, mostly for the railroads; yet, all at once, there was no demand for these items. His lot was entirely covered with ties, which actually lay there and rotted. He could look out and, with panic in his heart, see what in reality was happening. I had always thought the bank had lots of money. One day, when I insisted that something be purchased, Mama said, "We just can't buy anything,"

"Just write a check," I insisted.

Then she finally, with hesitancy, tried to explain that there was nothing left. Checks were only to be written when there was money in the bank. I was really totally lost, for we had absolutely nothing. Papa had tried to explain to me that everything would be alright. In my childish way, I believed him and trusted in the future. But finally I did understand and realized what was happening to us. Papa was completely broke and without a "trade." He was bewildered and stunned. I would not have to "tie a knot in a handkerchief to remember" the beginning or the ending of these days. I kept asking myself, "WHAT ARE WE TO DO?"

1918-1919-1920
Grand Ma Dies, Grand Pa Remarries

There was not much of great interest happening around Pocahontas during this time, except war talk. The Armistice had been signed. It was now a "big picking up and putting together" project for the whole world, it seemed.

Grand Pa was the local weather vane from being under the sky day after day. He could "read" the clouds.

One morning before he left for the daily mail route, Grand Pa called Mama on the new contraption named a telephone. He said, "Maud, your mother is not feeling well, please look in on her later in the morning."

Mama didn't wait until later. She went straight to the barn and put the saddle on old Prince and almost galloped over the hill. Grand Ma was really sick. They called Dr. Joe who advised she see a specialist. The specialist lived in Memphis.

The men hurriedly put some planks together and made a litter to carry Grand Ma from their house to the railway depot. They very carefully lifted her onto a cot, and placed her in the baggage department of No. 36. She complained of severe pain in her side and back, and fever indicated infection.

At Memphis, she was diagnosed with acute appendicitis. All available treatment was administered, but to no avail. The appendix had ruptured, and infection had spread throughout her whole system. Grand Ma died in the hospital in Memphis. "Whispering Hope," her favorite song, was used at her funeral.

Her death left Grand Pa with youngsters on hand, the house to take care of, garden work, and then his job. He quickly realized he needed help. Mama and Papa just locked their doors and moved to the house on the hill. Mama was responsible for the running of both families: Grand Pa's three—Marie, Myron and Merrit (who was about my age)—and the three of us. This was a sacrifice on all of us, but it worked out fairly well from necessity.

Then someone decided to help. Grand Pa was introduced to a lady from Selmer, Tennessee. Her name was Emma Stone Brooks, a widow with no children. They were married about three months after Grand Ma died, which came to be a real sore spot. The Joe Dukes family put the key back into the door of their own home. They had gone the second mile, and were glad they had been able to help.

As far as I know, life at the Milsteads was a struggle to be a family. Marie and Myron both resented someone in their mother's role, something they were not ready to accept. Merrit, being the youngest, found a tender spot in Miss Emma's heart and accepted this new development in his life.

For some reason, I never knew why, Grand Pa was granted a transfer to Sheffield, Alabama. Maybe they thought a change would improve conditions. In 1920, they rented a Southern boxcar and moved lock, stock, and barrel to the 600 block of Annapolis Avenue, Sheffield, Alabama. Grand Pa begin to walk the streets with a Bible under his arm. The three children (Marie was now a teenager) were enrolled in Sheffield

Miss Emma Stone Brooks, Grand Pa's second wife.

Merrit Milstead, Grand Pa's youngest child, who accepted Miss Emma's love and care.

schools. The Milsteads called this house their home until they both died.

P.S. Old Charley, the horse, ate all the flowers, dishes were broken, and chickens died on the train trip.

Alma's Grand Pa carrying mail in Sheffield, Alabama.

1919 – 1922
Economy Of The Roaring Twenties

The "roaring twenties" brought a breath of hope. But it was so shortlived that it really made no great difference. Then came the days when everybody was in the same situation: broke but still proud and not greatly worried. The straw that broke the camel's back and threw us into a panic was the notice of foreclosure on our home. Now Papa had to figure out ways and means of escaping total disaster. The bank did force us to give up the only home we had ever known and loved. We salvaged only a handful of personal items through blood, sweat, and tears. Then we began suffering the consequences.

1923-1924-1925

Since Grand Pa had moved the family to Alabama, we seemed to think that things might get better for us if we made a move there also. In 1923, with our hearts breaking, we loaded our few belongings onto train Number 35 which was headed East: This meant Sheffield, Alabama. We rented a small house on 4th Street, which we called "home" for a short time.

My brothers and I were enrolled in Sheffield High School. I was ready for my fourth year at a fourth school. This new world came to me as a different way of life, and it was not easy.

Papa was ashamed of our rented house. We would go out the back door to avoid a neighbor or prospective friend. After many days of job hunting, he became a victim of depression. He made it known that he wanted to turn around and go back home—to the only home he had ever known—Pocahontas, Tennessee. This is what he said, "In the autumn, the leaves looked down from whence they came, and I heard a call saying, 'Come back, and things will be the same.'"

What we all needed was a "JOB," so food and clothing could be returned to our place in life. Starvation was a fact, and malnutrition was a twin with the same life style.

Marie and Hubert Elope
She Was Like My Sister

The year was 1921. It seemed everything was going smoothly at Sheffield High School; that is, for everyone except Marie Milstead. The main reason she protested moving from Tennessee was the fact that she would be separated from her sweetheart. Though in their teens, they were deeply in love. Hubert Brewer made her forget the grief from her mother's death, and most of all the hurt that came with Grand Pa's remarriage.

Today was the day she had marked on her calendar that Hubert would come to Sheffield. He would be waiting when the last bell rang at school. She hurriedly left her classroom, and, sure enough, when the big door opened, she saw him waiting for her. The sun was shining for Marie.

Hubert had ridden the train and had no transportation. However, a streetcar ran between the Tri-cities. They walked to the trolley stop and soon caught a streetcar to, of all places, Spring Park in Tuscumbia, Alabama. The return train home had to be boarded there. They strolled around the park and Big Spring for awhile before much was said. Then finally Hubert gently took her hand and said, "Let's not go back to your house in Sheffield".

Marie turned to face him, then whispered, "Oh, where would we go?"

He answered, "Let's catch the next train going West."

"What do you mean?" she asked, knowing in her heart what he meant.

"We could go to Maud's house at Pocahontas tonight. It would be late, but I could go across the street to Grady's for the rest of the night. Then tomorrow, we can get married somewhere, somehow."

"Get married! Are you crazy? You know Papa would have a running fit! No, this isn't the answer, as unhappy as I am. We will just have to work this out – sometime."

They came to a big log, sat down, and were very quiet for some time. Then Marie told him, "You know how Papa feels." She stood up, put her hand on his shoulder and said, "We will just have to wait."

Later, he remembered her expression, which seemed to say, "All right, let's go."

"Do you love me?" Hubert asked, as if expecting her to say again, "No, I can't."

But she said, "You know that answer."

He said, "Come with me now and get your things."

"You know my Papa; he would never give his approval."

"All right, there is another way. Let's elope."

Marie thought she had heard of someone eloping, though she didn't quite understand what it meant.

Hubert anxiously said, "We will have to hurry to catch the train."

"No, Hubert I just can't do it."

He knew she was hesitant to even try to take such a step.

"I could not hurt Papa, Myron, and Merrit by leaving them here in a strange place, even though he does have Miss Emma. They look to me since Mama is gone."

Hubert said, "I know, but look how unhappy we both are. I don't want to hurt your feelings, but I don't give a continental about your Papa, your brothers, or anybody else. Come with me, now, or I will go home to stay. Whatever that means, you figure it out."

"Oh! No! Hubert, I do love you, and I can never be happy here. Don't tell a soul - let's just go. Let's do; what did you call it? Elope."

And they did.

As the wheels clicked, Marie grew more nervous, thinking Grand Pa might have the train stopped. But this did not happen. He just let the wheels run faster and faster toward Pocahontas.

It must have been in the middle of the night when a knock came on the front door of the Dukes' house. Maud said, "Joe who could that be? And in this rain!"

He cracked the door and stood there shivering, a blast of icy wind came through the narrow opening. There stood Marie and Hubert.

"Well, of all things! Get in this house before we all freeze to death." Lots of explaining took place in a short time. Finally, as I peeped out of the warm covers, I saw Marie coming toward my bed. She was just like an icicle, but she did manage to tell me a little of the excitement.

"That sounds like fun." I said, "When I get married I want to elope, too."

The next morning, the Dukes and Grady (Hubert's friend) were up early, getting ready to go to Corinth for "THE WEDDING."

Somehow, some way, by somebody, they got married. Late that afternoon, they came home as Mr. and Mrs. Hubert Brewer.

The Brewer family worked fast and furiously all day fixing the wedding supper. A gracious plenty was served to the kith and kin, the neighbors and friends.

Mr. Brewer soon had a little two-room cottage built on his farm, and Papa, through his store connections, bought the necessary items for playing at housekeeping. The newlyweds lived in Pocahontas for several years, and then Hubert secured a railroad job. He finally became a conductor, and they moved to Sheffield.

There is no question but that theirs was a happy marriage. Hubert petted her to death, and she was spoiled rotten. They had a little boy and named him Jack Warren Brewer. "Since Marie was contemporary with me in age," Alma said, "I always thought of her as my big sister. I miss her so much."

Marie was born in 1905 and died in 1984. Hubert was born in 1900 and died in 1953. Jack, their son was born May 8, 1927 and died January 14, 1998. His death was announced as follows:

Jack Warren Brewer died January 14,1998 at El Dorado, Arkansas, where he had resided for several years. Jack was the son of Hubert and Marie Brewer. He was a Grandson of S.A Milstead. The family worshiped at Annapolis Avenue Church of Christ from its early days. Jack and Katherine were the parents of three children, Jane, Gary and Chris. Funeral services were held at El Dorado on Saturday, the 17th of January 1998. Katherine still resides in El Dorado, Arkansas.

Book Satchels And Lunch Pails

In the years from 1889 and 1895 (approximately), Brother A.G. Freed established a teacher training school at Essary Springs, Tennessee. Schools in the South were rare. An advertisement ran in the Gospel Advocate for a teacher minister to establish a school and preach at Essary Springs, Tennessee. Brother Freed answered the ad and was hired. This school was the forerunner of Freed-Hardeman College, in Henderson, Tennessee. The Dukes' farm was located near Essery and was convenient for the Dukes' children to attend. Even though this new school was operated by members of the Church of Christ, and the Dukes were Methodist (very much-prejudiced), Joe (my father) was allowed to enroll. It is not known how long he attended. We do know that he became an excellent Bible student and enjoyed the singing schools. He had an exceptional tenor voice.

N. B. Hardeman, President, Freed-Hardeman College

After Brother Freed resigned and moved to Henderson, a young man reestablished the school and it operated in the original setting for many years. This young man was Mr. (Professor) I. N. (Ike)

I. N. Roland

Roland. He had been a student of Brother Freed and was very thorough in his work. He was tall and spindly looking. His family said his appearance and actions did not promote popularity, but this criticism was not justified because he was a man of many excellent personal qualities. He was unusually smart, dignified in manner, but foremost he was a teacher with a thirst for knowledge and a zeal for imparting that knowledge to others.

C.P. Roland, Dean

Professor Roland was born in 1868 and died in 1950 at the age of 82. This is the man who taught me reading, writing, and arithmetic from the first grade to the eighth. He was my teacher, my mentor, and my example.

In 1914, Professor Roland became principal at the Pocahontas school. He brought a young girl to teach the elementary children. Her name was Miss Grace Paysinger. She would become a daughter-in-law of the Rolands. She married C. P. Roland in 1916. In later years, she wrote in a book, Walking Down Memory's Lane, "I have always been glad that I taught Alma Dukes to read."

In October 1914, I was six years old and started to this school, a one-room school house in Pocahontas.

The Rolands lived down the lane toward town from our house, and every morning I would swing on the fence gate waiting for Professor Roland to come by so I could join him for the early morning walk to school. I would always try to have the proverbial apple to hand him as a token of my appreciation. Maybe it was truly the shadow of a bribe, but I hope not. I do remember him complimenting me on my behavior and desire to learn. Oh, well.

"I am the first person standing on the left with my head turned."

Pocahontas School Days

    Papa provided as well as he could for his family. He encouraged us in the importance of holding our heads high, getting as much education as possible, and, all in all, pulling ourselves up with our own boot straps with the help he and Mama were able to provide. And he encouraged us by emphasizing the importance of the help of the "Good Lord."

    Within walking distance of our house, the school house was a one-room building with a partition in the back. We climbed a couple of steps to an improvised stage. This stage was used for the many school entertainments, such as box suppers, fiddlers' contests, and school plays, usually performed in the interest of fund raising. The room smelled of chalk, mold, and linseed oil.

    Spotted unevenly over the hilltop, cedars softened the ugliness of the entire picture and covered the outhouse. One side of the outhouse said, "Boys," and the other side said, "Girls." I always blushed when I held up my hand and asked to be excused.

Almost everyone in our town, for the space of two generations before, had been exposed to the administration of religious justice, strict regulations, and double use of the long terrible stick known as the "pointer;" yet, the impartial schoolmaster, whose cold gray eyes showed just a hint of crinkle at the corners, seldom put it to use.

At first, I was afraid of Professor Roland, our Ichabod-type schoolmaster. But I soon learned my way around many things. Everyday, promptly at ten minutes until eight, I would come out of my front gate as my principal turned the corner. Books took up at eight, so I would automatically fall in step with him, trotting most of the time to keep up.

Miss Grace Paysinger taught the elementary grades. Acting as Professor Roland's assistant, Miss Grace earned a lot of good experience in handling "bad boys." Professor Roland backed her up, and he was not afraid to get rough, if necessary. At the end of the session, Miss Grace went home to sew on her trousseau, for she and Clifford Roland, son to I.N. Roland, planned to tie the knot. And in August of 1916, as a member of the Roland clan, Miss Grace moved to a Tennessee town called Maury City.

During the time when Miss Grace and Professor Roland were still at the school, Lewis, Arlton, and I had adopted a baby goat. The teachers would come to our fence and watch the boys feed the goat with a bottle. This baby goat grew up to be a big billy goat, and Miss Grace would invariably say that it had a good "upbringing."

Thank you, Professor Roland. I still owe a great debt of gratitude to Professor Roland and especially Miss Grace for starting me on a GOOD UPBRINGING!

I really had learned to appreciate and like this thin, wiry, intelligent man that so many people claimed to dislike. They simply did not understand him. He was so smart, and I wanted to learn and learn. I just liked to be near by when he was explaining difficult things to the older groups.

My School Friend, Myrtle Rollison

I had a friend whose name was Myrtle. Her Pa had something no one else had: a team of huge, wall-eyed, cud-chewing oxen.

At our lunchtime, I'd say, "Myrtle, I'm going to run home, but I will be right back. You save me a biscuit out of your tin bucket, one with a hole punched in it, filled with molasses!" There was just nothing that tasted as good. Too, I liked her because she thought I was lucky because my dad had a real store with everything good in it. Sometimes, I'd beg Papa to give me a jawbreaker, and I'd slip it to her. This was a real treat for Myrtle.

Dave Rollison's oxen were used for plowing and hauling heavy logs. One day, while Myrtle's Pa was trying to get his balky team to move, I was standing close by, and he was using some mighty big words. I had never heard swearing, and I didn't know what it meant.

"Myrtle, what is your Papa saying to the oxen?" I asked.

"Oh, Alma don't mind Pa. That is just he-man talk he is using to get em' going. He's not really mad. It's just the only thing they understand 'sides the whip."

Mr. Dave Rollison said he had to use a different language in handling the oxen than in driving horses or mules. He said the horses were geared up from mouth to tail with all kinds of harnesses, including the SINGLETREE. Then when all hitched up, they would wait for the words, "Get up" and "Whoa." To go to the right was "Gee" and to the left was "Haw."

Our pretty horse, Prince, understood all these orders, horse talk. But Mr. Rollison said oxen were different. He said a horsehide whip was always used, and a wooden yoke went under the neck, which was fastened with tied cords. The pop of the whip indicated what the oxen should do. The whip was seldom used as punishment.

Business Ventures

After hearing about how to handle oxen by the stories Mr. Rollison told the boys, Lewis and Arlton decided to enter the business world at their tender ages, using his team as their example of "load pullers".

Arlton said, "Remember how he hitched his oxen with a yoke around their necks and then hitched them to a slide to pull heavy loads? Let's do that! Only what will we hitch? Let's catch some mice and hitch them to a sardine can."

So, they caught six mice in an open trap and hooked them up. The mice balked in a corner and would not pull. They decided to try lizards. After catching the lizards, they held them down by the tail. The lizards wiggled and scratched and made a lot of noise. Mama came rushing out of the house to see what was going on. She let out a scream,

"You all turn those reptiles loose! I hear they will bite you, and they are poison!"

No move was made. Mama picked up a peach tree switch and said, "Now! Now, what will you do? I will switch both of you." The boys went running and the business venture was forgotten. They sure had a lot of fun trying to get those mice and lizards to pull a load.

Playing Church

The boys and I played many improvised games. We especially liked to play church. We would find a nice cool shelter under one of the Tennessee Pines and drag up logs for our pews. We would all three sing songs we had heard at church. You would actually think we were headed in the right direction when we bellowed out, " I am bound for the Promised Land." Then Arlton would pray and thank the Lord for everything, including the little green lizards. I would try to end his endless plea with a gusty, "Amen." He misunderstood and thought I said, "Lay them in." He caught Lewis and tried to baptise him. The struggling, screaming and kicking took the place of religious shouting. I then loudly did say, "AMEN."

More Pocahontas School Days
My Most Embarrassing Moment (I Think)

When I was about nine years old and in the fourth grade, Miss Grace had moved away, and Professor Roland was in charge of the entire school. One day he asked me to go to the blackboard, up two steps and onto the stage. I was told to "phrase" a sentence before the whole group (meaning to diagram it, pointing out the subject, predicate, verbs etc.).

We were not required to wear uniforms to school, but my daily winter outfit might have been called Alma's uniform, for I came attired with about the same dress each day. My uniform called for long-legged white underwear (legs stuffed down into black stockings) and high topped shoes, an under garment made of cotton flannel colored gray, and whatever dress had been made ready by washing and ironing. Under all of this came the black sateen bloomers. These bloomers had elastic in the legs to make them blouse, a drop seat fastened with three big black buttons secured by black buttonholes. However, from many ups and downs, these holes had become stretched and would not hold the buttons. So up the steps to the blackboard I marched. When I took the first step up, the whole seat of my black bloomers dropped down around my ankles.

Mostly instigated by a teenager named Roy Nelms, the laughter caused the others to stomp and cheer. Roy was an egotist and a self-proclaimed ladies' man. He thought the girls were all crazy about him—and some were. He later became a successful auto dealer. He very likely did not realize the lasting hurt he had caused. Children can be so cruel. However, all is forgiven, Roy.

Some boys will be boys – sometimes a handful. Duggan Rawson filled an eraser with chalk powder and threw it at the blackboard. Professor Roland thought that Brett Newland had thrown the eraser, and to punish him Professor Roland hit Brett with a geography book. To retaliate, Duggan took out after the teacher and gave him a black eye. All in all, Professor Roland could handle the big bad boys.

I am injecting our "Gypsies Tale" here, because this visit with the Gypsies happened when I was a preteen attending Pocahontas school with my classmates, including Charles, as you will soon see.

Gypsies

Everyone was aware of the annual visit of Gypsies. The word Gypsies meant fear to all of us, especially the children. We were all aware of how Gypsies lived, moved and, most of all crouched.

Late in the day, Papa came in from his busy store day and announced, "We are going to have company—the Gypsies are coming this way! They have been spotted down near Hardcastle Bottom."

Most of the time, neighborhood news traveled slowly. But this was not true when there was some unusually juicy gossip, or when a caravan of Gypsies was traveling our way. Then it was made known to all by the backyard telegraph. The Gypsy people traveled by covered wagon and by foot, and there were usually fifteen to thirty of them in one company.

Gypsies were a nomadic people always on the move. They had swarthy skin from living under the open sky. They dressed in gaily-colored clothes, with rings on most of their fingers, huge earrings, gaudy bracelets, and heavy chains around their necks. Without exception, they were followed by a pack of dogs that examined every rock and tree, barking as they traveled from campground to campground. Big iron pots hung under their wagons and made a clanging noise.

When the Gypsies were as far as thirty miles away, sometimes word would reach the store by a traveling salesman or someone visiting or traveling through. There were so many interesting stories about Gypsies, and the stories began the minute we heard that they were on their way. We would begin to put everything that was loose under lock and key. If it were late in the day, we would be sure the hens, hogs, livestock, and everything living was safely tucked away in its proper place and a lock put on the door. It was well known that the gypsies would steal anything that was not tied down or locked in. We would hear stories about them that would make our hair raise, and then we would beg to sleep with Mama and Papa. Usually it would end up with me sleeping with Mama and the boys tucked in beside Papa. As it happened, this unusually fine summer afternoon was no exception. Arlton and I were in the yard playing hopscotch—and Lewis was just in our way—when we looked up and saw Papa walking in giant strides, toward the house. At the same time, we hollered, "What's wrong Papa?" We were asking over and over, without giving him a chance to tell, even if he'd had a mind to. We all pounced on the porch at the same time. Mama opened the door, and Papa said just one word, "Gypsies!"

"Land sakes, Joe, where 'bouts are they?" Mama asked excitedly, pushing us into the house at the same time.

"They're 'bout here already and sent word ahead to ask if they could camp in our field straight across from the barn," he answered.

Now, everybody knows it is a fact that if the gypsies camp on your property, they will not steal from you but from everybody else for miles around.

Mama said, "Surely you told them to go on. There is no where around here for them to camp."

"No, I told them they could camp, provided they would move on come morning," Papa declared.

Papa had always secretly enjoyed the visits of the gypsies. They were known to be shrewd traders, and he always felt he came out on the big end of their deals. Why, the last time they came, he got his horse, "Old Prince." The Gypsies just got store-bought things. Papa figured he was a natural born trader. By this time, we were so scared and excited that we huddled together and said in unison, "Papa, are you scared? Papa, are you scared?"

He assured us that he wasn't scared, but I noticed him touching the pocket that contained his gun and telling Mama he believed he would go back to the store to keep an eye on everything tonight. But on second thought, he would get old man Jones to stay at the store and keep watch, and then he would come on back and be with us.

Well, it is a good thing he did, because it seemed as if we had just dropped off to sleep, Mama with me and the boys with Papa, when we heard the rain beating down on the roof and a pounding on the door at the same time. Papa reached for his gun with one hand and pulled his britches on with the other, while mumbling half-asleep, "Who in tarnation would be out on a night like this?" He'd forgotten for a minute the guests in the field. By the time Papa got to the door, we were up and crouching (similar to the Gypsies) right down behind him, ready to help if he needed us, and curious to see what they looked like this time.

"Can we sleep in your barn?" one Gypsy man asked. He was the head of the clan, and he stood in the doorway with his nose not ten inches from Papa's face. He spoke in what was an unknown tongue to us. We thought this must be what the preachers had told us about. It was actually broken Spanish.

"You can, provided you move on as soon as morning comes." Papa answered in what surely sounded like a quivering voice to me.

"Papa, are you scared?" I asked as he closed the door.

Mama said, "You hush, Alma. You know Papa is not afraid of anything."

I don't believe we slept another wink of sleep the rest of the night, knowing there was a storm going on. We would have been in the storm house except for the Gypsies being in the barn. We stayed put because Mama thought the good Lord would surely take care of us this time, with the Gypsies all around. By daylight the next morning, Arlton and I were dressed. We sneaked out of the house before breakfast and ran toward the barn. We darted from tree to tree for fear the gypsies would spot us. It sure was a good thing we came out when we did because they were all headed down toward the creek, down behind our barn. The men were dressed in rough, course clothes, and the women were flashy in all colors imaginable. Their skirts were full and long enough to almost touch the ground. Each skirt had great, big pockets on the sides. We soon learned they were full of trinkets, presumably picked up on stops prior to ours. Anyway, you can be sure the pockets were always put to use. We felt we were safe as long as we kept our distance and stayed behind the trees. We watched as they built a fire and began pulling what appeared to be dried sausage out of a dirty-looking knapsack. They scouted around to find sticks suitable for sticking hunks of dried meat on which they held over the fire. They had all found a stick and were heating and eating this dried meat when they began to look straight toward where we stood hidden behind the tree, and they were mumbling something. I was sure they were plotting to skin us alive. I thought I had gotten us into this, so it was up to me to get us out of it, some way. As bravely as I could, I stepped out and motioned Arlton to come behind me. By this time, one of the gypsies took a step in our direction, holding out some of this dried sausage. (I honestly believe they were trying to be friendly and share their humble larder with us.) But shaking so I could hardly stand, and with my teeth rattling worse than that big rattler Mr. Carr killed down near the creek, I grabbed Arlton's hand, and we started running as fast as we could toward the house screaming, "Mama, Mama! They're trying to poison us!"

By the time Mama ran for Papa, and Papa ran for the house, and we all ran toward the camp, they had packed up and started moving out. Papa looked down in that direction, pulled out the gun, and started firing while shouting, "I'll teach you to try to poison my young'uns."

The next morning, Papa was in the back of the store by the stove. He was thinking about the Gypsies. He knew they were really gone and afraid to come back in this direction. The door opened, and Mrs. Wardlow entered. "Joe," she greeted him, "tell me all about what happened last night. I heard you shot in the direction of the Gypsies' camp. You really didn't shoot to kill a gypsy did you?" Papa quickly explained in part what had happened. He knew she would go to and fro telling the neighbors everything he told her and more, too.

At that moment, Mrs. Nethery, a good friend of Papa, entered the store. Anxious to wait on her, Papa asked, "What do you need, Van?" Her face flushed, and the real reason for her trip wavered in her mind. Looking around to be sure she was the only customer, she said, "A pound of boiling meat. And Joe, drop me a bottle of Garretts in the bottom of the sack, one of the big ones. It seems I just can't keep snuff in the house for Aunt Dorn." With the sack tucked safely under her arm, she hurried away. Papa thought, "That woman, she's not fooling me! They are good neighbors as long as they stay on their side of the road."

History tells us that the ROMA GYPSIES have been in the Americas since 1498 when on his third voyage Columbus brought some of these people to the West Indies. They have been called "the hidden Americans" because they choose to remain in seclusion. Gypsy life is kept separate, and parents do not send their children to public school for fear of intermarriage. "Out West" has been their adopted homeland, but they are a roving nation that lives off the land. They are described as a lazy family that has developed the fortune-telling business, maybe as their second job. They are a lazy, fun-loving people with musical talents. – "ADB"

More Pocahontas School Days
Teacher's Pet

One day at school, I heard someone say, "Alma is teacher's pet."
"She is teacher's pet."
"Let's don't play with her any more."
I noticed, with hurt feelings, that some of the girls ignored me. I could hear them whispering and tittering behind my back. But you know what? I didn't care, I really didn't care. I said to myself, "I'm smarter than they are, get better marks, and have never had to stand in the corner with a dunce cap on. I have never had my hand spanked with that paddle with the hole in it." So I just didn't mind if they wanted to act that way. Maybe I had some self-esteem after all. So I decided since the girls didn't want to play with me, that I would get some real attention where it counted. I called all the important ones, the boys: Myron, my Uncle Charles Marlin (he's the good-looking one), and Murray. I said, "You all come over here. I've got something to tell you." I knew all boys liked to hear about Gypsies, and I had a real story for them.

They hesitated, not 'specially wanting to come when a girl called, but one by one they ambled up and curiously asked, "What is it?" All at once, I was the center of attention, telling about the Gypsies, and how they camped in our field.

I liked Charles. His daddy had a store and pulled teeth in the back room. He had pulled my teeth, so I felt I knew Charles really well. All big-eyed and big-eared, the boys stood and listened to the happenings, and Myron questioned, "Alma, are you sure they tried to poison you?"

"Yes, come down after school, and I'll show you where they camped. The ground is all trampled down, and I think there are some of the logs still burning." Of course, I stressed how I had saved my little brother from being poisoned and maybe being kidnapped. I told them not to ever let a Gypsy see you peeking at them from behind trees. But I told them, "My Daddy knew what to do, and he surely scared them off." All the neighbors already knew about Papa shooting at the clan, but it really sounded brave to me. My Daddy honestly protected his family.

"Alma, you are a hero. No, girls can't be heroes. But Alma, you are something!" Charles exclaimed.

All of the girls sensed something exciting was going on in our little group, and one by one they came up asking, "What's happened! What's happened? Tell us!" No sooner had the teacher's pet disagreement come up, it had been dissolved. The little group forgave and forgot, and we were all friends again.

At the next recess, we were all out together on the flying jenny, which was made of a board nailed to the top of an old cedar post with an iron spike. To make the iron spike real slick, green onions were stuffed around it. Professor Roland came out of the school door and said, "Little girls, go play 'Ring Around The Rosy.' Big girls, go play 'Farmer In The Dell.' You big boys come on, and I'll beat you pitching dollars. You little boys can watch, for it's almost time for books."

I was so happy when we went back into the school building, and Charles said, "Alma you are sump'n!" His name was Charles Shea. He was in my class. He was my first real sweetheart. Maybe the feeling was puppy love, but there is something about childhood and teen sweethearts that never happens again. I think it was a first in my lifetime.

It happened in 1922. I was fourteen and in the ninth grade. It was so exciting! He had said, "Alma is sump'n."

Charles Shea, My First Love

No "bumps" can be compared to "goose bumps" caused by just the sound of his voice. Maybe it was puppy love. Charles was the only one who brought sunshine into my life during those dark days.

Murry Wardlow, My First Date

Murry asked me, "Does your Mama let you date?"
I answered, "I don't know."
"Let's ask," he said.
I got permission and had my first date at about twelve years of age.
He walked me to—you guessed it—church. I wore a white middy blouse suit, starched so stiff it could have stood alone. My hair was shining and my nose, too. Murry came my friend and left my friend.

Boarding School Days

Nothing very exciting seemed to happen at Pocahontas School for the next few years. We went to the same building, had the same teacher, studied almost the same textbooks, learned reading, writing, and arithmetic, and for the most part had the same playmates. I will say as Miss Grace said, "About all I can remember is studying, walking to school, sometimes in snow and sometimes in rain."

Pocahontas School was not state accredited, so when I reached the ninth grade, Papa persuaded Professor Roland to let me keep attending the one-room school and be tutored by a real professor, Professor Roland himself. This was agreed, so I was taught the first year of high school in a class all by myself. Many times I have thanked Professor Roland for a great school experience, until I was thirteen years old.

The sophmore year was a different story. I had to go on to school, but where would I go? About twenty-five miles from Pocahontas, Chalybeate, Mississippi, had what was called an Agricultural High School, where students mostly from rural areas came and lived in dormitories. It was decided that I would enroll at this school. I was fifteen years old, but I was very small for my age. This life was so new to me that I hardly understood what was happening. The girls were, as a rule, overweight and very limited in other than farm ways and means. I guess I almost became a big sisters' pet. The girls thought they were my guardian angels, and I had nothing to fear. Yet, being so far away from my home was my cross to bear.

I wanted to come home! One weekend, on a Friday, Papa loaded the family into the big Oldsmobile and headed for Mississippi. The rainy season was taking its toll; deep ruts and mud were everywhere. When school was out, we loaded up, dirty clothes and all, and headed for home. It rained! It rained, and it kept on raining with sleet pellets hitting the hood of the car. The ruts became deeper and deeper, and the tires slicker and slicker, until finally with a "bang" one tire gave up. What would we do now?

Papa said, "Maud put the blankets around the children, and I will go up the hill where I can see a light and ask for help." Mama didn't like the idea of staying in a mud hole in the dark by ourselves, but she did not have another answer. Papa came back with two of the men of the family, and all together we persuaded Mama that the only thing to do was come up to their house until the morning. The family was more than pleased to have someone come and break the monotony of rain, sleet, and maybe snow. After we were served a gracious plenty, a table full of vittles, the children were bedded down on pallets. Some of the adults slept on pallets also, as the family had one extra bed. We children liked the idea of being in the room where all the talking was done, but we were soon fast asleep.

The next morning, the sun woke everyone, causing an early rising. After we had our repast of country ham, red-eye gravy, scrambled eggs, blackberry jam, hot biscuits, butter, and lots of home ground coffee, we thanked our new friends. With the help of the two men and two mules, the car was pulled out of the ruts to firm ground. This experience introduced us to real hospitality and a new family of friends. But Papa said, "No more Chalybeate for us after this school year." So we began making plans for next year. I was almost sixteen years old and in the eleventh grade (a junior); where would I go?

As the new school year approached, much talk went on as to where I would go to school for my junior year of high school. Finally, it was decided that I would make application at Middleton, Tennessee. Middleton was about fifteen or twenty miles from Pocahontas.

"How would I make this trip every day," I thought, as I listened to my parents' discussion. The Southern Railroad's schedule offered one new thought. Investigation was made, and it seemed it was the most feasible of all the suggested ideas: I became a regular daily passenger, morning and evening.

Southern Railroad System

The trains of the Southern Railroad System operated on steam created by coal heated water. There was a coal chute at Pocahontas where they reloaded fuel. The trains ran on iron rail tracks held together with cross ties. Walking the railroad tracks was one of the ways we passed many afternoons. Black smoke belched from the big smoke stacks, the brakes hissed, the bells rang. When the coal bins were filled, the whistle sent the signals to proceed. All the members of the train crew wore uniforms with brass buttons polished and shining in the morning sun. I rode this train every morning to school in Middleton, Tennessee, and back home again in the afternoon.

These trains were called "locals" and were the earliest railway transportation powered by steam. Number 35 ran from Sheffield, Alabama, to Corinth, Mississippi; to Pocahontas, Mississippi; to Middleton, Tennessee; to Grand Junction, Tennessee; and then on to Memphis, Tennessee. This was the morning train. They usually made a stop at the coal chute at Pocahontas. Number 36, the afternoon train, returned about 4:30 P.M., then on to Sheffield. Number 35 made it possible for us to have out-of-season fresh vegetables and many other needs not available in our small town. Every Saturday a freezer of ice cream would be delivered to the depot then picked up and wheeled to the town well.

Ice cream had to be my favorite food off train Number 35. When I was young, ice cream was a nickel. It wasn't often that I had a nickel. I would go to the well and get my treat. Miss Henrietta Campbell would carefully place the ice cream on top of the cone to make it look like a lot. I found out early in life that you had to push the ice cream down into the cone with your tongue, or it might topple off. Then came the best part: licking the ice cream and letting the soft, sweet concoction slip down my throat, also catching the drips. The idea was to make the cone last as long as possible. Who knew when I would get another nickel?

Miss Henrietta Campbell, the town's jack-of-all-trades, especially in photography, had long ago been assigned the duty of dipping the ice cream at five cents per cone. In hot weather, the cream would melt and run down her arm, but that seemed to make no difference.

Miss Henrietta also took pictures of everything and everybody: weddings, babies, all kinds of community gatherings, and any newsworthy event. She always carried an umbrella, rain or shine.

The Tennesseean

I would catch the local Number 35 train in the morning, attend school at Middleton all day, and then take the Number 36 in the middle of the afternoon for home. It has often been said, "Where there is a will, there is a way," and I must have had the will to have an education.

These local trains were combined into a route and finally made up-to-date. The route was called the Tennesseean. Regular stops were scheduled. The trip would begin at Memphis, Tennessee, and then proceed on to Middleton, Tennessee, to Pocahontas, Mississippi, to Corinth, Mississippi, to Sheffield, Alabama, then to Knoxville, Tennessee, and finally to Washington, D.C.

The Tennesseean was the Cadillac of the line, equipped with a beautifully designed dining car that offered delicious meals and private meeting areas. It also offered the comfort of private toilets that spilled out onto the wild blue yonder.

From an economical standpoint, the railroad was a blessing to so many families. I remember some of the family names of people who used the trains or worked for the railroad: James and Cecil Edwards, the Hydes, Hubert Brewer (conductor), and many more Sheffield residents.

One of my memories is of a black man with a one-horse dray. He and his horse would meet the train and pick up ice for our community. He would deliver the ice to various homes. Our meager supply of a few days would be delivered in a big bundle covered with toe sacks and placed in our icebox, which was well insulated. The box would hold about a 100-pound block of solid ice. We took special care in opening and closing the door of the icebox. It was like a gift from heaven and required our special care.

Sheffield School Days

The last of 1923 or early 1924, we made a drastic move. This would be my last year in high school. Having already attended three other schools at two other places, I did not easily agree to this change. I thought I did not want to leave Pocahontas. Charles was there.

Arlton, Lewis, and I were enrolled in Sheffield schools. I did not find that Sheffield High accepted me. I was an outsider. Belonging to no clique club and having no new friends, it was just too much to try and fit into this type situation. I think my report card reflected the hurdles I had to conquer. Anyway, I graduated from Sheffield High School in 1925 at age seventeen, without Charles.

This was a real challenge for me. Don't do it to your children.

SCHOOL DAYS

YEAR	AGE	GRADE	TEACHERS
1914	6	1	I.N. Roland, Pocahontas, Tn.
1915	7	2	Miss Grace Paysinger, Elementary (married and left
1916	8	3	In 1916)
1917	9	4	I. N. Roland
1918	10	5	I. N. Roland
1919	11	6	I. N. Roland
1920	12	7	I. N. Roland
1921	13	8	I. N. Roland
1922	14	9	I. N. Roland
1923	15	10	Chalybeate Agriculture High Chalybeate, Mississippi
1924	16	11	Middleton, Tennessee High Middleton, Tennessee
1925	17	12	Sheffield, Alabama High Mr. & Mrs. Creel

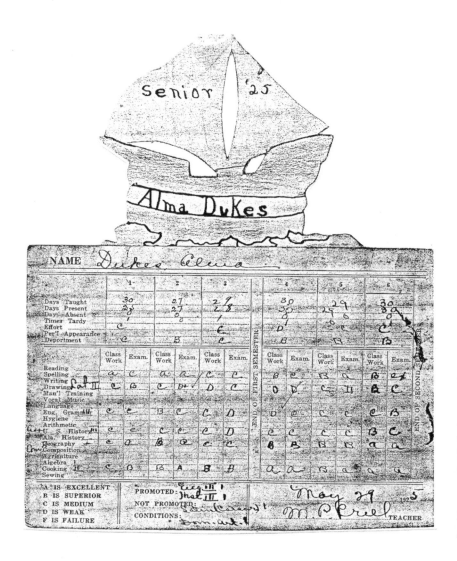

Alma's Graduation, 1925

SHEFFIELD HIGH

Alma and Lewis, 1925

Southern Holiday Cooking
A Christmas At Pocahontas
December 1917

Christmas at the Community Church was always celebrated about a week before Christmas Day. The members of the congregation were all busy making plans so plenty of gifts would be on the tree for everyone. The men were in charge of finding just the right tree, usually a cedar or pine that would reach the ceiling. Committees were carefully making ornaments, putting candles in all the windows, and in general creating an atmosphere of Christmas spirit. Real candles and garlands perched on every limb. The decorations were strings of popcorn and crepe paper chains of all colors, especially red and green.

Decorating the Christmas tree, an annual event at the church building, was designated for everyone in the whole area. It seemed to me that everyone took part in this community Christmas tree. Each family would bring sufficient gifts for the members of their family to have something to open, as well as any other gifts they felt inclined to put under the tree.

The tree was approximately ten feet high, decorated with strings of popcorn and colored paper chains made by the children and just loaded with icicles of tin foil. The lights were real candles, and of course, there was always a standby crew of big boys who carried buckets of water to quench any fire that might threaten to destroy the whole gala scene.

Papa would play Santa Claus. At this time, I was getting very suspicious about all the secrets and whispering. On the night before the affair, the house would be abustle with sneaking pillows, quilts, and other stuffing into the bedroom where no one could enter. "Your Papa is dressing," would be the answer to our knocks.

Papa made a perfect Santa for he was so jovial and had a real good sense of humor, like the time he gave Mama the box of snuff off the tree and Grand Pa—who was a leader in the church—a tin of tobacco. He was always pulling something on someone, right in the midst of town, even at other times during the year.

This whole celebration was the highlight of Christmas to so many people living in and near Pocahontas. There were a large number of children whose families had such a dull, meager existence. This was a very happy time.

Papa made the children laugh, but in some instances adults were seen with tears flowing, because their sons were in the service and absent at the gathering. We did not have anyone serving in World War 1, but there were many families in our area who had sons "over there." Our hearts went out to them at this time, and many prayers were asked for peace on earth.

After the special event, it was usually bitter cold, and there was plenty of snow and ice under our feet as we trudged home. However, we were blessed with a warm feeling of love toward everyone. The message seemed to be that life was leading us somewhere, somehow to a brighter day, echoing from the carols we had sung. We remembered that Christmas is a time for sharing and recalling the love that was given to us. Time was pointing to the fact that the old year was fading away to make room for the new one: 1918.

1917
Christmas At Our House

I am nine years old. Is there really a Santa Claus? The season, may be referred to as Winter, but the chunk of Winter that was especially known as Christmas in Pocahontas was like Christmas everywhere. And in the eyes of a nine-year-old, Christmas is just indescribable. Excitement is everywhere and in everything. It seems to me that at the height of all the Christmas preparations, I would come down with a cold, coughing and generally complaining. Mama was a great believer in all the home remedies, coal oil, turpentine, Vick's salve, and goodness knows what else she would pick up as she would be on her way to heat up an old iron skillet and drop a flannel cloth in the hot utensil. She would mix all these ingredients and would always say, "Put plenty of lard in so it won't blister." I hardly ever did blister, but Arlton was so thin-skinned he would be red and crying in a very few minutes after the hot applications. I believe she called it applying the "hot poultice," which must be made of old flannel. As unprofessional as this may sound, I am sure it saved many a child from a bout with the old fashioned pneumonia, which was almost surely fatal at that time.

Anyway, I would usually have to stay in the house while Papa and some of the neighborhood boys would go in search of a tree for our house. This was a real task for Mama, and I usually knew just what we thought Santa would like in a Tennessee cedar. There would be a wrangle as to how tall, full, and big around it should be. This tree was for our very own.

Our Christmas preparation started soon after Thanksgiving. Looking and wishing from the Sears Roebuck catalogue from Chicago, Illinois, wore the pages thin. When Mama was ready to make an order, she would have a hard time finding enough information to make out the description and numbers of the items she wanted.

All at once I would notice that there would be more stove wood to be carried into the kitchen. We always had a pile of wood right outside the kitchen door. One person could be kept busy firing the wood burning range stove. This stove was so pretty, black with silver trimmings; it had a nice big warming closet to keep victuals warm from dinner to supper time, also a big hot water compartment so good for Saturday night baths.

About a week before Christmas, Mama would say, "Let's all pick-out hickory nuts, tonight." If Papa had pecans at the store, it would be pecans. Everything seemed to be shaping up for the big day of baking. Cakes would always be made in advance. A big lard can was saved back for the purpose of storing the cakes. I would always beg for a piece of cake as soon as they were fresh baked, but Mama would say, "These are for Christmas." I told myself, "If I ever grow up and make a cake, I will eat it then and there." Every cake Mama ever made, I believe, was for a certain time and purpose other than right now. Anyway, the large lard can with a wide, gaping, cavernous look seemed to be eagerly awaiting to gobble up cake by cake before we children knew what was happening.

The tall pie safe, with its pierced metal doors making a heart-shaped design, was the unforgettable source of fragrances from a mixture of apple, mince, and other spicy delicacies.

Mama said, "A fresh pork ham is a must for our table." She was very careful in selecting the proper size. She made it a point to attend the neighbor's hog killing in order to get her prized fresh ham. This juicy, choice piece of meat would be salted down for several days. It must be covered entirely with salt. It then would be removed, washed off, and put into a  kettle large enough for circulation of water around the ham. The meat would be cooked for hours until the meat seemed to pull off the bone. Then skin would be pulled off, and several dashes of ground pepper would be sprinkled here and there, and the ham would be set aside until Christmas. Incidentally, this is just about as delicious a meat as you can imagine. Of course, our kitchen was always stone cold, so the meat, cakes, pies, and everything prepared in advance had no chance of spoiling before the big day arrived.

Right here and now I cannot refrain from setting down some of the favorite recipes that were a must on the side table on Christmas day. The recipes on the yellow pages with all the scribbling of additions, subtractions, and improvisions written are for sure tried and true many times over. The recipes are from Grandma Milstead and Aunt Minnie's aged and much used cookbooks. These are a must at Christmas.

Now, with everything in readiness for Santa, as far as we children could notice, Christmas Eve was very much the same as other pre-holidays, except everything seemed to settle down with quietness. As dusk arrived, Mama would say, "You all get ready for bed, and go to sleep, for everyone will be getting up early in the morning."

At her suggestion, I would strip down to my gray outing petticoat and long-handled underwear and climb into an icy bed in the middle bedroom. It always took until the wee hours for this bed to warm up to where it was real snuggly, and then it was time to get up.

This Christmas was much like all the others, except I thought I was growing up to a point where some things should be explained to me. I thought later maybe Mama would take me aside and talk about spring and things coming to life and maybe explain to me about the birds and bees. But not my Mama; this did not happen, I just kept my ears open and learned a little bit. And I did not find out about Santa Claus *this* night.

When I finally got warm enough for sleep to come, I slept hard and fast, for I had already decided I would be awake about the time the old man with his reindeer came. I didn't know just how he would get to our stockings hanging around the stove, for we didn't have a chimney, and this is what I wanted to see. Well, sure enough, I heard noises, which seemed way in the night. I thought this must be what I was waiting for. I opened my eyes, and there were Mama and Papa fumbling around in the dark with sacks of goodies, apples, oranges, nuts, and hard candy. They were filling the three stockings, we had

hung around the stove before being tucked in. After a while, I decided it would be safe to venture in and inspect what days before had been smuggled into the house, for this very minute. I crept very cautiously into the room and looked about. I felt of my stocking and decided things weren't too exciting, and after all I had really discovered the deep dark secret of "Santa Claus."

Feeling guilty for what I had done, I crept back into bed and fell sound asleep. I was awakened the next morning by Arlton and Lewis who loudly announced, "Get up! Santa has been here!" I took my time getting there, being more or less disappointed and downhearted about the whole idea. Mama said, "Alma, look in your stocking." She handed it to me. I turned it up side down, and the goodies spilled all over the floor. When I looked down, I couldn't believe my eyes, for down in the toe of the black stocking a little box had been hiding. I excitedly open the gift, and right there was the beautiful opal ring, my birthstone that I had dreamed about for days. I put it on and ran to everyone dancing up and down, with all the excitement and happiness a little girl could express. At the same time saying, "Merry Christmas! Merry Christmas! Thank you, Santa Claus."

After we all settled down, we had breakfast, and then we put on our Sunday clothes. We were getting ready to go to Grandpa's house. All the family, the Milstead side that is, would take turns having their Christmas dinner. Of course, the big day was Christmas day at Grandpa and Grandma Milstead's house on the hill. Then each day would be a feast day, as each family would take their turn at hosting. By the end of all this feasting, nothing would taste better than cut-off turnip greens, black-eyed peas, and hog jowl on NEW YEAR'S DAY.

Grandpa's House

Southern Cooking

Recipes

About our recipes: Many of my tried and true recipes came from the kitchens of both of my grandmothers. One was born and reared in the Smoky Mountains of East Tennessee, and the other grandmother called West Tennessee her ancestral home.

Many of the recipes were jotted down with a notation, for example, "Aunt Minnie's chicken and dumplins." Some were written on faded-yellowed scraps of paper, such as "Shuck Beans from East Tennessee." Also, there were luscious Christmas deserts scratched on Christmas cards, one with the note, "Ruby's chocolate cake." The goodness of scratch made victuals never fade, so I hope you will take time out and just experiment with some of these hand-me-down recipes in your push-button kitchen.

I even stumbled upon a large cook book called "The Encyclopedia Cook Book." It was identified by a note inside as once belonging to a chief petty officer, Ray O. Williams, U.S. Navy, USS Saratoga, 1932. How this book came into my collection, I do not know, but I wish I could say to Mr. Williams, "Your cook book is still alive and active. I wonder how many of your people and my people have enjoyed this warm-hearted reminder of the richness and flavor of the American food scene?"

Holiday Recipes
From The Kitchen Of Maude Dukes

Right after Thanksgiving, Mama would start putting the Christmas spirit in her kitchen. Aunt Myrtle would say, "Maude have you baked your fruit cake yet?" Mama would answer, "Lands no!" Then she would frantically start checking the boxes at the store to see if the candied fruits, nuts, and spices had arrived from the wholesale store in Corinth. The recipe for her fruit cake had been used by the Milstead cooks for generations. The oven of the black cook stove was now brought to life, for it was time to cook!

THE FRUIT CAKE

Steamed Fruit Cake

- 2 cupfuls of shortening
- 2⅔ cupfuls of light brown sugar
- 9 eggs
- ½ cupful of molasses
- ½ cupful of strong coffee infusion
- ½ cupful of grape or fruit juice
- 1 tablespoonful of vanilla
- ½ teaspoonful of soda
- 5½ cupfuls of general purpose flour
- 3 teaspoonfuls of any baking powder
- 2 tablespoonfuls of cinnamon
- 1 tablespoonful of cloves
- 1 tablespoonful of nutmeg
- 1 teaspoonful of salt
- 2 pounds of raisins, chopped
- 1½ pounds of currants
- ½ pound of candied cherries
- ¾ pound of citron, cut fine
- ¼ pound of lemon peel, cut fine
- ¼ pound of orange peel, cut fine
- 2 cupfuls of blanched and chopped almonds

Cream the shortening and sugar together. Beat the eggs and add, stirring until well mixed. Add the molasses, coffee, fruit juice, and vanilla. Dissolve the soda in a tablespoonful of hot water or in the coffee, then add to the mixture and stir. Sift the flour, measure the correct amount, reserve 1 cupful for dredging the fruit, and sift the remaining flour with the baking powder, spices, and salt. Add the flour to the above mixture and beat. Add the fruit and almonds, dredged with flour, and stir until thoroly mixed. Pour into 2 large or several small loaf pans lined with wax paper. Whole almonds and candied cherries may be arranged over the tops of the cakes. Place in a steamer and steam 3 hours. Remove to a slow oven (300 degrees) and bake for 1 hour. Cool and store to ripen.

The cake was stored away in a lard stand. Granny white apples and a sprinkle or two of wine were packed around it. The lid was then tightly closed. A peep into the can brought forth the most delicious taste bud tingling smell—but we had to wait.

Blackberry Jam Cake

Mama called this cake Jam Cake with Christmas filling. I believe with all the goodies from each kitchen this would have to be my favorite cake.

BLACKBERRY JAM CAKE

½ c. margarine
1 tsp. cinnamon
1 c. buttermilk
1 c. coconut
2 c. sugar
1 tsp. cloves
2½ c. flour (self-rising)
2 c. black walnuts
2 c. blackberry jam
4 eggs
1 tsp. soda
1 box raisins

Cream margarine & sugar. Add eggs one at a time, beating after each addition. (Thoroughly mix 2 cups flour, spices &soda) Add flour and milk alternately, beating after each addition. When mixtiure is smooth, (dredge nuts, raisins, coconut in ½ cup flour). Add nuts, raisins, coconut and jam to mixture. Grease bottoms and sides of three 9-in. cake pans. Put greased wax paper in bottoms. Bake in 350' oven for 30-35 mins. or until sides of cake loosens from pan. Use fruit filling or caramel icing.

FRUIT FILLING:
2 c. grated coconut
Rind and juice of 2 oranges
1 sm. can crushed pineapple
2 c. sugar
2 T. flour
Juice of coconut

Mix sugar and flour. Add remaining ingredients and cook over med. / low heat in a heavy skillet until very thick. Spread between layers, on top & sides of cake. Sprinkle generously with coconut. (This was my mother's recipe of many years ago

Snowwhite Cake
(Coconut)

This cake is the proverbial white cake for Christmas. It is the most beautiful, luscious, festive cake that can possibly be made in the country kitchen. Mama knew the secret that was revealed once each year. TRY IT!

Snowwhite Cake: Two-thirds cup white butter or any good shortening, two cups white sugar, three cups flour, one-half teaspoon salt, three teaspoons baking powder, one cup warm water, one teaspoon orange extract, eight egg whites beaten.

Sift flour three times with baking powder and place in refrigerator with eggs to chill before beating the latter. All ingredients may be measured and chilled overnight if desired.

Cream butter and sugar well, at least 10 minutes for nice texture. Add warm water gradually, one-fourth cup at a time. Alternate sifted flour and beaten egg whites and finally add flavoring.

Pour batter into two layer cake pans, dividing batter equally. Bake in moderate oven 15 minutes, and increase heat gradually to 375 degrees, cooking until edges begin to draw away from the pan. Remove from oven and turn onto cake racks to cool.

TO MAKE FROSTING, use four cups sugar, two cups hot water or juice from a fresh coconut, four egg whites, beaten stiffly, two large or three small coconuts grated, one teaspoon orange extract.

Place sugar in large saucepan and pour hot water over it. Boil rapidly until syrup will form a soft ball when tried in cold water. Have egg whites beaten stiffly and pour one-half cup of the hot syrup over them, slowly beating constantly. Let remaining syrup cook until it spins a long thread. Pour slowly over egg whites beating constantly. Add flavoring. Beat until thick and smooth.

Spread one layer of cake with icing to depth of one inch. Add a layer of fine grated coconut one inch thick. Do not mix coconut into the icing. Add another thick layer of icing and top with another layer of cake. Cover top and sides of cake with icing as thick as possible.

"This cake is almost candy, it is so full of thick layers of icing and grated coconut.

Old Fashioned Stack Cake

Stack cake filled with sweetened and spiced home dried apples served as the Christmas fruit cake. And when a girl married, everybody came bringing a layer for the cake and the popularity of the bride was determined by the height of the cake. Everybody made it by different methods and varying ingredients. I remember that my mother cooked the flat thin layers on top of the stove.

These amounts should make about 12 to 15 very thin layers:

- 4 cups sifted flour
- 2 cups sugar
- 1 teaspoon salt
- 4 1/2 teaspoons baking powder
- 1/2 cup melted butter
- 4 eggs
- 2 teaspoons vanilla

Combine dry ingredients in large mixing bowl. Make a depression in center and add cooled butter; eggs and flavoring. Mix thoroughly. Turn out on floured board and knead in about 1/2 to 1 cup sifted flour or enough to make a dough that is about as stiff as pastry. Pinch off enough of mixture to roll to a diameter of 8 or 9 inches. Place pie tin or plate over dough and cut around. Bake on slightly greased cookie sheet for 3 to 5 minutes, or until brown in preheated 450-degree oven. Cool and spread cooked dried apple filling between layers. Brush top with melted butter for glossy appearance and store for a day or two for more flavorful eating.

Filling:

- 1 lb. dried apples
- 1/2 cup sugar or to taste
- 1/2 teaspoon ground allspice
- 1/2 teaspoon ground cinnamon

Add enough water to fruit to almost cover. Cook until soft; mash and season with the sugar, allspice and cinnamon; mix and cool. Cover a cake layer with the mixture and continue to stack and cover until all layers and filling have been used. Brush top layer with melted butter.

Exa's Rolls

When our children were young, A local drug store called, Spalding Walgreens, had a food service counter and the big drawing feature was Exa's rolls. I am including this recipe in our collection for safe keeping for generations to come. Exa's rolls were deliciously delicious. They would float like a summer cloud in the sky and roll lovers would drive for miles just to reach up and grab one.

CHICKEN DUMPLINGS
2 cups flour
⅓ cup shortening
2 teaspoons baking powder
1 teaspoon salt
Enough sweet milk to make soft dough

Make up dough and let stand for a while. Roll as thin as possible and cut in squares or strips. Use large container for chicken broth. Drop layers of dumplings in boiling broth and allow to boil over each layer before adding another layer.

Cover and cook 12 minutes, season with milk and butter if desired. Chicken may be boned and cut in strips then added just before serving.

Exa's Roll Recipe

HOT LINE NOTE — I have the recipe for Exa Warren's rolls that you asked for Monday. The same woman who taught Exa how to make the rolls also taught me. The recipe is: one cup potato water, one cup scalded sweet milk, one cup melted shortening, one yeast cake dissolved in warm water, one beaten egg, one half cup sugar, one fourth teaspoon salt, flour. Mix potato water, sweet milk and shortening; let cool until lukewarm. Add egg, sugar, salt and dissolved yeast cake, mix well. Add about two cups of flour, beat well until it is the consistency of pancake mixture. Cover and keep in warm place one hour. Add enough flour to knead into biscuit dough texture. Let rise until double in bulk — about one hour. If ready to use, pinch off desired amount, roll out and dip in melted butter and place close together in baking dish with sides. Let rise again. Punch down unused mixture and place in refrigerator. Mixture will last about two weeks in refrigerator.

— Here is the recipe for old time egg custard. Three eggs beaten up good. Three fourths cup sugar, one tablespoon of corn starch, two cups sweet milk, one teaspoon of vanilla, and sprinkle on nutmeg. Cook at 350 degrees.

Maude's Ambrosia

6 oranges peeled and sectioned
½ cup sugar, or to taste
1 coconut grated
1 small jar maraschino cherries
cut into pieces

Place layer of orange sections in glass bowl; sprinkle with sugar and cherries. Layer with coconut. Repeat layers ending with coconut. Chill. Serves about 6

Chicken And Dressing West Tennessee Way
(The way my grandmother, her mother, and her mother made chicken and dressing and gravy.)

• Use a medium-sized iron skillet, and make regular southern cornbread, using buttermilk and egg or eggs. Bake and set aside to cool. Actually, day old bread of both kinds, crumbled together is better.

• Use equal amounts of cornbread and white bread, left over biscuits (today, leftover hamburger buns might be handy). Mix crumbled bread, add salt, pepper, and sage (whole leaf or ground). Add seasoning to your taste.

• Remove giblets from a fat hen and boil with salt, pepper, onion, and celery until tender, and set aside. Boil the removed giblets (liver, gizzard, heart, neck) to use in gravy, or discard.

• Boil the hen until well done, and remove the meat. The rich broth is to be used in making dressing.

• Mix crumbled bread, 1-cup milk, and broth from cooked giblets. Add enough rich broth as needed to make a real thin batter, and add one or two eggs to the dressing mixture. Stir well and bake at about 350 degrees. When almost done, add pieces of chicken, or serve chicken separately. Umm-good!

• Make gravy from rich broth.

Dumplings East Tennessee Way

Aunt Minnie Sutton of Maryville, Tennessee, taught me to make dumplings the East Tennessee way. None of the little drop dumplings for her. She made them like this: roll out, cut, and cook in the chicken stock.

Some East Tennessee Biggs Recipes

I want to preserve these for your children and on and on.

When East Tennessee became my adopted home, and the Biggs family my adopted family, I inherited much of the East Tennessee kitchen customs. There are several old recipes that I want to preserve for both generations down the line. These came principally from the kitchen of "Mamaw" Sarah Biggs, Aunt Minnie Sutton, and Ruby Moriarty Biggs.

Shuck Beans
In the Fall, green string beans were gathered and strung on twine and hung in a dry basement for use in the cold winter.

Wash beans, soak, cut in pieces, and cook with pork until tender.

October Beans
East Tennessee may be their home, so if you can find them in the market, you are lucky.

Shell and cook as other shelly beans, and season with pork. Serve with cornbread and a slice of onion. Try them, they are good!

From a letter written to a cousin about his mother's cake. His mother's name was Ruby Moriarty.

Dear Joe Henry,

I enjoyed your mail about foods you remember. I have some I remember too. One of them is your mother's cake. I can remember getting to your house in the middle of the night, having been asleep in the car for who knows for how long. Knoxville was so far away from Sheffield. I couldn't comprehend the distance much less stay awake for the journey, anyway, on the kitchen counter ALWAYS was "the cake." We would have a piece no matter what time it was…then go back to sleep. Well, guess what! I have the recipe, mother had written it down and years ago gave me a packet with all kinds of family recipes in it, and this was one of them…so here it is.

Ruby's Devil's Food Cake

4 oz. bitter chocolate
1 cup boiling water
1/2 cup butter
2 teaspoons salt
2 eggs

2 cups flour
1 1/2 teaspoons soda
1/2 cup buttermilk
1 teaspoon vanilla

Place chocolate and butter in bowl. Add water. Stir until dissolved. Mix sugar, flour, salt, and soda. Add dry ingredients to liquid gradually. Beat well. Add buttermilk, eggs, and vanilla. Bake in layer pans at 350 degrees for 35 minutes. This makes two layers.

White Frosting

2 1/2 cups sugar
1/2 cup light corn syrup
1/2 cup water
1/8 teaspoon cream tartar

Few grains salt
2 egg whites, beaten stiff
1 1/2 teaspoons vanilla

Cook sugar, salt, syrup, and water to soft ball stage—240 degrees. Pour 1/3 of this mixture over egg whites, beating constantly. Cook remaining mixture until it forms a hard ball in water—254 degrees. Add to egg whites. Continue beating. Add vanilla. When cool spread on cake.

Hope you make this and enjoy!
Love Becky

Annapolis Avenue Church

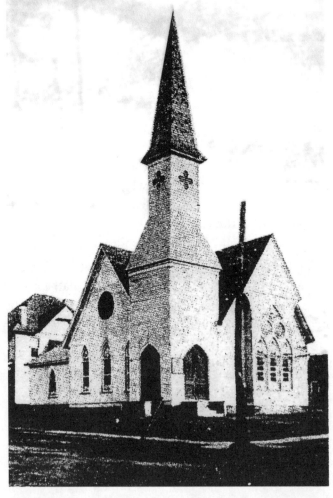

The First Christian Church on the corner of Seventh Street and Annapolis Avenue was built by the Northern Presbyterian Church. In 1895 it was sold to the Episcopal Church and in 1903 to the Christian Church. It is now the Annapolis Avenue Church of Christ. This congregation still holds regular services in this building, which has been remodeled and enlarged. LJW

My Church Home

A ray of sunshine came to all of us when we decided to make a move to Sheffield, Alabama. However, one of our major concerns was, "What about the church?" Grand Pa had already answered that question. Our house was located right across the street from the Annapolis Church of Christ.

This became our church home from then on. With all the goings and comings, we always found ourselves at the front door every Lord's day. For your future church history, I am printing the history of Annapolis Avenue Church of Christ.

Many of our ancestors were married here, many were baptized here, and several family funerals have been conducted here.

History Of Annapolis Avenue Church Of Christ Sheffield, Alabama
(Taken from the May 1985 Centennial Edition)

About the turn of the century, the congregation had a small beginning, with meetings being held from house to house and later in a frame school building on the site of what is now the playground of the W. A. Threadgill Elementary school. In 1904, a building that had been used by the Episcopalians on Annapolis Avenue at 7th Street was purchased. There were no seats, no class rooms, no baptistry, and certainly no central heating and air conditioning. To keep warm in the winter, a large heating stove was placed in the middle of the room and chairs were set around the stove. Each member was asked to buy a cane bottom chair, which cost 50 cents each. In the summer, the doors and windows (stained glass windows in the present building) were opened, and individual cardboard fans were placed on the seats. When there was a baptism service, everyone went down Alabama Avenue to the river. For a night service, lanterns were carried to light the way. In time, a baptistry was built underneath the rostrum (hinged doors were swung open), and pews were purchased.

In the early days, the work was slow in showing improvement. The following names were among those who gave material and spiritual aid to the work: Hamm, Hagler, Latimer, Baker, Harwell, Hanlin,

Moss, Foster, and Gambil. One person remembered by those interested in the work was Brother Lark Hagler, who was anxious to see that the big bell in the steeple was rung on time.

The congregation did not have regular preaching, but it did have meetings at times. Since the building was not large, tents were rented and were usually placed in a vacant lot close to the downtown area. People from all over town came to the meetings. The services, according to some of the old timers, were quite lengthy! Outstanding men of the brotherhood were invited to preach. I remember some of their names: Gus Dunn, Sr. and Jr., H. Leo Boles, Cled and Foy E. Wallace, Jr., and Roy Lanier.

Since 1912, preachers and their families have lived and worked with the congregation: John Hayes, C. E. Colemen, Ben F. Harding, John C. Graham, Jr., J. Frank Chambers, W. G. Hinds, C. L. Overturf, Sr., A. E. Emmons, Jr., Jack R. Hackworth, James E. Wells, Howard R. Allen, Chester A. Hunnicut, Berry L. Anderson, David Sain, Phil Hefley, John Weekley, and E. Leon Smith from Heritage Christian preached for several months. Currently, Annapolis Avenue has visiting preachers each Sunday. In 1927, G. A. Dunn was a visiting preacher.

In 1930, it became necessary to enlarge and remodel the building. Those were lean years; men were out of work. Some were allowed to work on the construction project and accepted pay for every other day. Even skilled workmen who did have jobs agreed to receive pay every other day. During the construction, the store building located at 113 North Columbia Avenue was used for worship services. This building was used until the auditorium was enlarged and the annex added in 1953.

January 21, 1971
Information Compiled by H.G. Hanlin

I began attending the Mens' Bible Class of Annapolis Avenue Church of Christ on September 27, 1958. Since that time the men whose names appear below have died. I have listed the last time they were in class and the time of the death of each.

	PRESENT	DIED
1. Wm. H. Pace, Sr.	June 29, 1958	?
2. George E. Sanders	Nov. 22, 1959	?
3. James B. Gambil, Jr.	Mar. 26, 1961	Apr. 2, 1961
4. S. Edgar Ingul	Jun. 13, 1961	Dec. 2, 1961
5. C. S. Landis	Apr. 2, 1962	May 17, 1962
6. S. A. Milstead	Oct. 14, 1962	Jan. 3, 1963
7. Joe M. Mills	Jul. 14, 1963	Feb. 7, 1964
8. C. M. Hopkins	May 24, 1964	Jun. 7, 1964
9. Terry F. Davis	May 10, 1964	Jul. 17, 1964
10. Robert M. Mitchell, Sr.	Jul. 4, 1965	Feb. 8, 1966
11. Roy W. Harris	Jun. 3, 1962	Nov. 20, 1966
12. Leland C. Biggs	Mar. 15, 1959	June 4, 1967
13. C. V. Carringer	Apr. 10, 1967	Oct. 4, 1967
14. John T. Ferrell	Jul. 17, 1966	Jan. 17, 1968
15. Ben Brenneman, Sr.	Feb. 11, 1966	Feb. 17, 1968
16. J. C. Mattox	Oct. 29, 1967	Aug. 22, 1968
17. Otho P. Green	Dec. 26, 1965	Apr. 6, 1970
18. Joe P. Lindsey	Nov. 16, 1969	May 9, 1970
19. Archie D. Frederick	Apr. 17, 1966	Oct. 27, 1970
20. W. Porter Pilkerton	Apr. 24, 1966	Jan. 12, 1971

Some who have visited the class and have died.

1. Grady Stewart	Jul. 3, 1960	Nov. 6, 62
2. George E. Sutton, Sr.	Jul. 5, 1959	Jul. 20, 63
3. William R. Lockhart	Mar. 25, 1962	May 15, 67

Annapolis has New Minister

Smith

SHEFFIELD – The Annapolis Avenue Church of Christ has a new evangelist. Sunday, September 2 was the first day for E. Leon Smith to serve the congregation which began in 1904 and is located at 610 Annapolis Avenue, Sheffield. Services take place at 10:30 am and 6 pm Sundays, and Bible studies at 9:30 am Sundays and 7 pm Wednesdays.

Smith holds a B.S. from International Bible College and a M.A. from Southern Christian University. He is Vice President for Institutional Advancement at Heritage Christian University.

For more information, call Annapolis Church of Christ at 383-1322.

2001

This is from the memory of Robert M. Mitchell, Jr. (Bob) about the Annapolis Avenue Church of Christ. Bob was born in 1921. He grew up attending this Church. This history was written to Shirley (my sister) in answers to some question she had about the Church here. Some people have asked about the history so this is a little of it. He says that as he thinks of things, he will pass them on.

Pat Mitchell Halley
10-18-01

Dear Shirley,

    It was good talking to you on the phone a few minutes ago. Here is some of the information that you said that you would like for me to write down. By the way, before I forget it, I'm sure that you can get a lot of history on the church building at the courthouse in Tuscumbia such as the date of the deed when it was purchased from the Episcopal Church when they acquired the property.

    You asked about an old wood burning stove. I am sure that was in the old Piney Grove building when we were kids. As you may remember, we would go out to the country sometimes and go to church with Grandmamma. As far as I can remember, the Annapolis Avenue building always had radiators. I am sure that they were hot water radiators and not steam. I remember the old boiler in the basement.

    When the building was purchased from the Episcopalians it did not have a baptistry. They would go to the foot of Alabama Avenue to the river to do their baptizing. I recall some of the older members talking about some of the walks to the river to baptize. Not too many people had cars back then. Daddy did not get his first car until after I was born.

    You asked about the church making a loan. I think it was Mrs. Cecil who let the church have the money when the building was renovated in the late 20s or early 30s. I am just not sure who it was who refused to lend the money.* Too, you asked me to be sure to mention that Sister J. B. Gamble was the church treasurer for many, many years. She was the treasurer while Brother Overturf was our preacher. When the depression hit, I remember that Brother Overturf requested that his salary be cut because of the low contribution due to no one working, and the payments had to be made on the building. He and Brother Frank Smith are the only two preachers that I have ever heard of who were willing to take a cut, or refused a raise, so that the work of the church could continue.

    The first preacher that I remember at Annapolis Avenue was Brother Frank Chambers. I can just see him now; he was a real jolly fellow. He had a son, Smith Chambers, who died in an accident--I don't remember the details of his death. I do remember Daddy talking about him, Daddy, and Brother Smith Chambers going over to Florence and starting the Sherrod Avenue congregation. Most of the time Daddy would lead the singing, and Brother Chambers would do the preaching.

    A couple of other things about Daddy that you may not know or remember. He never went to high school. He went from the 8th grade in a one room schoolhouse to college in Florence. UNA was the Florence Normal then.

    Daddy was at one time the youngest certified teacher in the state of Alabama, so I've been told. He was also the first mail carrier for the Sheffield Post Office and the first Superintendent of Mails. He tried to enlist in the army with Uncle Henry at the start of WWI but was told that he was too young, and they would not take him He went back home and got their family Bible and changed his birth date so as to make him old enough, took the Bible to the navy recruiter to prove his age and volunteered for the navy. He was in the navy the most of the war. Daddy was the first alternate for an appointment to West Point in case the first person did not make it. I don't recall his name just now, but the fellow that Daddy hoped would not make it through West Point did graduate, and after his military duty he came back to Sheffield and was one of the city's first civil engineers. I knew him but can't recall his name at this time.

I do very well remember Charles Lindbergh flying the Spirit of St. Louis over the town of Sheffield in 1927 and throwing out candy to all the kids. I had the honor and pleasure of meeting Col. Lindbergh one time when he was a guest speaker here in Birmingham. Willette and I were talking to him and mentioned the occasion when he flew over Sheffield. He said he remembered it and asked if we had gotten any of the candy.

Well, so much for the history lesson tonight. If I think of anything else, I'll write to you.

Love,
Bob

*(Mama told me that the woman who refused to lend the money lost her wealth in the Depression whereas the woman who lent the money was repaid in full.--s.c.)

About the stained glass windows in the church building, I doubt if anyone has the history on them. I do remember when the building was a wood frame building and had no basement. There used to be a steeple with a bell in it that had the most beautiful tone in town. This was originally the Episcopal Church, and when they moved to Montgomery Avenue a group of church members purchased the building from the Episcopal Church. This was before my time, but I remember some of the old people like Brother Hanlin and others talking about it. The windows were in the building then. Brother Lark Hagler, we called him Uncle Lark, was the bell ringer for the Church of Christ, and he would ring the bell every Sunday morning. I don't remember exactly when, but sometime in the late 20s or early 30s the church decided to remodel the building, and there was much discussion about what to do with the windows and the bell. It was decided that the windows would be removed from the old building and reinstalled in the new one. It was also decided that the bell would be sold to the foundry as scrap. Uncle Lark did not want to see the bell go because that was his job as a crippled man with very limited abilities. It was one thing he could do--Ring the Bell to let the rest of the church members know that it was time to get ready and come to church. There were other churches that rang their bells also, but ours had a very distinct tone. Daddy was a deacon then, and I remember he was the chairman of the building committee. All the church members chipped in with the work which was under the supervision of a Mr. Dudley who was at that time married to Mrs. Cecil, if I remember correctly. I was just a kid then, but I remember them digging the basement from under the existing building. We had classes in some of the rooms in the basement, but the most of the basement was used for our worship service while the upstairs was being rebuilt. I think I have a picture of the old wooden building here somewhere. If I can find it, I'll send you a copy.

Well, that is about the extent of my knowledge of the church windows. I do know that at today's prices those windows are worth a small fortune. They would run somewhere in the neighborhood of $10.00 per square inch at least, I am quite certain. While I was working, I had to appraise stained glass windows in several churches.

Love,
Bob

Whispers In The Wind
1923-1925
A Different Way Of Life

This whole business of moving—a new school, new church, no friends, and no hope of financial resources—made a deep impression on me and my way of thinking that seemed almost impossible to overcome. I did not want to talk about it, I did not even want to think about it, but I could not help myself because I had been a victim of a heart of darkness. I could not see a bright spot anywhere but knew I must try. The load must be pulled, and I was handed the singletree. I got knotty stomach pains with the dawn of each day, and I wondered if the pains and my frame of mind were a warning step toward a halfway house.

I grabbed at the chains that pull the load and put my shoulder to the wheel. I went to work after school at Elmore's 5 and 10 cent Store. Then after graduation in 1925, I secured a full time job doing general office work for Phillips Funeral Home on Raleigh Avenue in Sheffield.

Finances were at a low ebb and becoming lower everyday, but I had to keep on keeping on. I was paid seven dollars for a week's wages. This meager amount became our lifeline while my hands were reaching out to answer "whispers in the wind."

1925-1930

Since we had moved into entirely different surroundings and life style, I had had to learn or relearn the most descriptive word in the English language: poverty. I decided that there is nothing about poverty itself that is in any way disgraceful. "Water seeks its level" is an old adage. So my friends were naturally on the same level, and we in no way felt humiliated or hampered. Since all the others were also poor, we really didn't know that we were labeled as poor. I also struggled to disguise the fact of my economic condition. I remember draping a tablecloth around me and dancing on the green grass in the back yard. My state of mind kept saying, "You really are a princess, so grab a star and hold to the bright sunny clouds." There seemed to be at least two motivating forces in my life that served to mold the direction of all the years that followed: The first was "Keep on keeping on, ever pulling the load," and the second was "Never lose sight of the goal."

At my age then, I took it for granted that the world was this way, and it was not until the awakening years of adolescence and my teens that I became aware of the fact that the world is somewhat unevenly divided between the rich and the poor. I kept telling myself, "Don't stop. Keep reaching for the goal." It was about this time I convinced myself that, "Yes, there is a Cinderella-like life," and even I, with my head full of dreams, would have to stretch to the limits to *believe* all the lucky accidents and coincidences that lay in a life just ahead of me . . . *Could I be a Cinderella girl?* Such talent as I possess I will try to use well; yet, talent alone is not enough. Many gifted people flicker briefly and brilliantly and then fade into oblivion, despite their unusual gifts. But, I must keep on keeping on and reach the goal, somehow.

A JOB IS WHAT WE NEED!

When I stand before God at the end of my life,
I would hope that I would not have a single bit
Of talent left, and could say,
" I used everything You gave me."

– Erma Bombeck

1925
Sheffield

One of the first jobs I had after moving to Sheffield was as a receptionist at Phillips Funeral Home on Raleigh Avenue. Just through the alley from the funeral home was Spaldings' Drug Store on Montgomery Avenue. Bob Etheridge worked at Spaldings. I guess Bob and I had a lot in common. We both were from poverty-level homes. He was a very good-looking young man, with his jet-black hair, and his Elvis-slicked-down-middle-parted-hairdo.

I am sure romance made its appearance much before I realized what was happening. In the middle of every afternoon, without fail, Bob would emerge from the alley, carefully handing me a delicious treat such as a pecan-nut sundae, a chocolate soda, a nut-topped banana split, or maybe just a nut-filled butter pecan ice cream that was topped with a bright red cherry. Umm-good!

Bob and I spent much time together, just doing one thing and another that didn't call for much money. The Ritz Theatre always offered a show to our liking. We took advantage of all free entertainment in the Tri-Cities.

Bob had a family member who had moved to Michigan for better times—it was boom-days in the North. The call soon came offering Bob a job at one of the automobile factories at Pontiac, Michigan. He gladly accepted and left to try his luck at this opportunity. He apparently liked life in the North. We corresponded for a while, before other interests crept into our lives. I understand he married a girl there, and they made Pontiac, Michigan, their home. I hope he found the happiness that he deserved. He was a real friend, and I guess our relationship was just another phase of life for me. A short but sweet romance.

This was a fun time – especially being introduced to the perfect fizzing ice cream soda. There will never be more luscious goodies concocted and sneaked through an alley by a boy to a girl he thought he loved.

Alma sitting on the fender of the ambulance that belonged to Phillips Funeral Home where she worked for a while.

Our hopes were dwindling in Sheffield, and as far as Papa was concerned, nothing encouraging had been offered to him. Day after day would come and go, and his spirit seemed to be farther down hill each day. He would leave the house every morning and make the rounds, looking for a prospective, job, just any job. The only "open door" seemed to be the poolroom on Raleigh Avenue. The same crowd was there day after day, and it was a friendly group, all in the same boat. This was just about the daily routine. Then the next day was the same thing over again.

John L. Lewis started working in the coalmines at the age of twelve. He resolved that someday he was going to do something to alleviate the plight of the working man. He became head of the A.F.L. in 1911 and united the mine workers in 1919. Labor unions were organized all over the country, but there had been nothing to ease the hunger pains of the former self-employers who were caught in the recession after World War l. These people were completely left out of the plans, and therefore, they just gave up. They fell through the cracks, you might say, "Their plight was absolutely no fault of their own—they had no control." This is what my Papa was left with, a family of five to feed and clothe.

Mama used to say, "Things never get so bad but that they could be worse. When they get real bad, it's a good sign they are going to get better." But when? "Please, Joe, stay away from that pool room. There is nothing good that goes on in there." She hated it!!

The conversation each night at our supper table would be the same nagging, and I almost dreaded for that time to come. For one thing, our meal was dried beans, cornbread, and maybe potatoes and cabbage. As I glanced over toward Papa's place, he would be playing with his fork or spoon, and his shoulders would be drooped, almost touching the table.

Mama would say, "Look at him. He can't even hold his head up. He's a failure." We would never answer her. She at no time extolled his virtue or the fact that he once worked so hard. He was crushed by the world over which he had no control. She would sometimes end the contention, assuring him of his great ability, and that he must try harder to provide for his family.

About the middle of the afternoon, he would make his way back home from town, stop in the side yard, and settle down in his favorite straight chair, under his favorite tree, and start telling tall tales to all the school children who passed on their way home. Then he would start whittling. He once made a little oak chair for Bill, my son, which is still in one of our dormer rooms. Then he would smoke and cough, smoke and cough. Suppertime would come, and night would come, and he would cough and cough; then morning came and another day, no different from yesterday.

If I could say anything to my Papa, I would say: "Papa listen! I *know* you were not lazy, that you loved your family, and hated poverty, and I know it was not your fault. Maybe we didn't tell you or make you understand, but you were loved by your boys, by Mama, all of your grandchildren, and especially by me, your one and only Alma Lee!"

<blockquote>
The Chains are still being tugged and pulled
By the Singletree
From Tennessee,
And Prayers are still being answered.
</blockquote>

Whispers in the Wind

A circumstance may start out small, but with our human Minds,
It soon blows up just like a cloud and makes our spirits Blind.

For little things are what confuse and cause us to go wrong.
They lead our souls to mutter as they take away our Song.

The little cloud soon billows up encircled by a breeze.
We don't remember Who's our Lord, but see the swaying Trees.

The raindrops start, the clouds look black, the lightning Rips the sky.
We lean on others for our help as moisture Floods the eye.

The rain blows sideways; rivulets of water hit the street.
The whistling winds and driving rain the watery world Complete.

It blows into a hurricane—at last we listen right.
Through rain and tears His whisper comes and thunders Into might.

Our blurry vision clears, as now our fellowship is whole.
Through silvered clouds the rays of God suffuse the skies With gold.

Once more we see our smallness as once more we start to Grow.
And thank Him for His patience when our learning seems So slow.

Anonymous

This Anonymous poem assured me that "Whispers in the Wind" could be my hope.

P.S. I always wanted to be pretty, and I desired to have curly hair, but my hair was thick and straight.

Mama said, "Your hair is just like a mule's tail. We tried desperately to fix that. She would try rolling it up in kid curlers, roll it on stockings when it was long enough. Finally, we found some curling irons that were heated in the lamp chimney. All of this helped, but I still had thick, coarse hair. I was not transformed into a beauty, but I did try, and maybe it helped.

1927-28-29
My First Real Job

In the early part of 1927, I had an offer of a general office job. The business was owned and operated by Mr. A.G. Milam. Although not a step-up money wise, I looked at it as a step-up for later, perhaps. The business was a transfer and storage business that also serviced cars and trucks, and sold gasoline and other auto supplies. "Whispers in the wind," sounding loud and clear, gave me the thought that maybe this job was the right one for me after all.

Milam's was the largest general auto maintenance shop in the area. Therefore, many of the service companies depended on Milam's to keep their wheels rolling. A young man by the name of Loyd Carter (nicknamed "Little Man") did the clerical work, and I did most of the office work. We had been told that a dismantling company would be using our facilities very soon. The company had been awarded the contract to dismantle the old Sheffield waterworks project down on the Tennessee River. The word was that they would be arriving soon to do the job.

Sure enough on the morning of March 17,1930, several young men came knocking at our door. They were engineers employed to start the job. I remember one whose nickname was "Spud." He was still in college at T.P.I. (Tennessee Polytechnic Institute) at Cookville, Tennessee. We became good friends. Especially, I remember John Barksdale from the Corps of Engineers at Knoxville, Tennessee. John would pop in and out, overseeing the work. Several times we had nice visits, and maybe we would go to a show or just have a date. But when football time came—remember he was from Knoxville—he asked if I would go with him to the Alabama-Tennessee game being played at Birmingham's Legion Field. In my excitement, I decided to be an Alabama fan and, of course, he was for his Tennessee. When the day came, it rained and it sleeted and it rained some more! But as you can see from the ticket stubs, the game went this way: Tennessee 7 – Alabama 3. To this day, Alabama-Tennessee has been the football battle of the season. I am still for Alabama. "Go Tide!"

We made the whole trip with very little conversation. Then he reached over and took my hand and said, "The skin you love to touch." This statement was the nearest gesture toward romance that was made. I thought to myself, "He must have been listening to the Ivory Soap ad." Even with the rain, sleet, snow, and the fact that Alabama lost, I did enjoy being with him, and I will try to use Ivory from now on. Thank you, John.

Alabama Vs. Tennessee
October 15, 1932   Alabama Coach: Frank Thomas
Score: Tenn. 7 Ala. 3 Tennessee Coach: Bob Neyland

CAN INSURE GOODS, RESIDENCE TO DESTINATION, OR WHILE STORED

A. G. MILAM TRANSFER & STORAGE COMPANY
ALL KINDS OF HAULING—STORAGE WAREHOUSE
PACKING AND SHIPPING

AUTOMOBILE ACCESSORIES
TIRES AND TUBES
FOR ALL CARS

MEMBER OF NATIONAL FURNITURE WAREHOUSEMEN'S ASSOCIATION
MEMBER OF SOUTHERN FURNITURE WAREHOUSEMEN'S ASSOCIATION

515-16 MONTGOMERY AVENUE
TELEPHONE 14

SHEFFIELD, ALABAMA
December 24, 1928

A. G. Milam Transfer & Storage Co.
In Heart of Muscle Shoals
PACKING, CRATING, SHIPPING
Local and Long Distance Hauling
Sheffield, Ala.

Miss Alma Dukes
Sheffield, Alabama

Dear Alma:

    As we come to the close of another year, I wish to express my appreciation to you for your cooperation and interest, that you have shown during the year of 1928.

    With the spirit of the Holiday Season I extend most cordial greetings and hope that the New Year may hold for you an abundant measure of all the good things that make life truly worth while.

Yours very truly,
A. G. Milam

P. S.
Cooperation means Everything
See picture on cash register

*A postcard sent to Alma from Mrs. Milam
when she visited Cuba in 1928.*

Things President Woodrow Wilson Did For North Alabama

During the time of national mourning after the death of President Woodrow Wilson on February 3, 1924, the name of City Park in Florence, Alabama was officially changed on February 20 to become Woodrow Wilson Park.

It was this United States President who made the Muscle Shoals a household name around the world. He selected this area as the site for the massive World War 1 defense plants to produce synthetic nitrates for the munitions of war. To supply the hydroelectric power for these arsenals, he authorized the construction of Wilson Dam, which took more than seven years to complete. 1924 was the year my family moved from Tennessee to Alabama to an eventful, bustling economy.

Woodrow Wilson

Most of all, I remember Bill Hobson

Bill Hobson, Great Notch, New Jersey

Please turn the pages of this my story and read the most beautiful love story imaginable. It is all true, taken from pages where the ink is hardly dry.

I only knew him a short seven months . . . an eternity.

ADB

As the decade of the Roaring 20s neared a close, a chapter began in my life that held mystery and intrigue, which is unsolved to this day. My late husband and children, who of course did not come into my life until later, did not know about it for some time, but my children feel that I should relate it as a part of my life because it adds detail about emotions which forever became part of my being.

A young man came into my life unexpectedly in early Spring of 1929, and he left it as abruptly in September of 1930. He was daring and adventuresome, and, as you will learn from details to follow, he apparently thought I was as "special" to him as I regarded him to be to me at that time. Our relationship was as decent and honorable as any mother would hope for her son or daughter, even as our mothers did.

I was employed at Milam Transfer and Storage Company at the time. We became acquainted when he came from New Jersey as a mechanical engineer to dismantle the old Sheffield Water Works on the Tennessee River. In the seven months that followed, Bill and I exchanged many communications, by letter, telegraph, and phone. Although much of the detail is lengthy and does not advance the details of the story as it developed, I am including selected excerpts which will let you know how our relationship developed and eventually ended in tragedy.

*Alma Lee Dukes
as a young girl.*

William "Bill" Hobson

"Spud" a friend, and Alma at Alma's desk.

Alma Lee Dukes, a beautiful, ash-blond young girl had just graduated from Sheffield High School. Her foundation of morals and strength of character (that would give the stamina to survive and to be the singletree from Tennessee for her family) was already ingrained into her being by her conscientious, steadfast, devoted parents.

Life, even at this young age, had not been easy. Her father's country store, which had been their livelihood for sixteen years, had gone out of business because of the Depression. The family had moved to Sheffield, Alabama, leaving behind her childhood sweetheart, Charles Shea. Charles was Alma's first sweetheart. She remembers him as attractive and charming. They continued to be sweethearts after the move, but later the attraction begin to fade away as young romances sometime do: Out of sight, out of mind, as those with experience would say. They did have a mutual admiration society when they were together. Charles later became a Forest Ranger.

Alma, at the present time in her life, was the breadwinner for her family of five: Alma, Arlton, Lewis, and her Mother and Father. She was employed by Elmore's Five and Dime, part-time, and later by A.G. Milam, owner of Milam Transfer and Storage Company on Montgomery Avenue in Sheffield, Alabama.

As Alma sat working at her desk one Spring day, a group of mechanical engineers arrived outside the garage in a Mobile Oil Company car. The men stepped out of the car and came inside to do business with Mr. Milam. They had come from up North to dismantle the old Sheffield Water Works on the Tennessee River.

One of the engineers, a handsome bronzed young man, William Hobson, later described meeting Alma:

I met her one cold morning when she came running into the office with another girl who was older than she but just as cold. I was talking business. They went first thing to a large pot stove in the middle of the reception part of the office. At the time, I was talking to the big boss about a shipment. This transfer company ran the largest trucking outfit in that part of the state. The girls came in running and out of breath. I thought something was after them, but later I learned it was only "Jack Frost."

When they were sure the stove was in the right spot and had not moved over, they started to see if it had a fire in it. When they had warmed themselves, they began to remove their coats. Then, I was told by the boss that they were the office staff, and they had been looking for me since a few days before. I was introduced as Hobson of the car barn.

The first thing they wanted to know was where I was staying. That was soon straightened out. Then the girls were informed, "It was not cold outside." I have had people look at me before, but this girl had a look, that is, the younger one, that was straight in the eye. A look of wonder came on her face that was almost like a movie star would use. Still it was all very natural.

I had not said anything up until this time, had not had a chance, really. Then the boss told the girls I was teaching them some manners about wearing a hat. The little girl still had the same look of wonder on her face. I excused myself, saying I had to get some work done, and was off.

Three or four days later, I had to get a bill straightened out. There sat the little girl that I was referred to by the boss. This was the first time I had spoken to her. It was strictly business but in a most pleasant way. I received a receipt, and that was all.

The next day or so, I got to talking to a young fellow who was an operator for Southern Ohio. We were eating in a little jerk lunch room when he said, "Come with me to see a girl I am going to walk home."

"No, better go yourself, I will be in the way." I said.

"Don't be foolish," he said, "she might not be there. You are doing nothing else." So off I went, but made arrangements if she were there, I would go back to my room and study.

On the way over I said, "I think I know this girl," (after he made a statement about going to the transfer company). For the fun of it I showed him her name as she wrote it. We had a laugh, it was all in fun, but there she was when we got there. I was very much surprised by the greeting I got.

"Hello Hobson," she said, "Where did you find Spud?" Spud was a friend of hers and mine. Until the welcome, I thought she did not know my name. At first I was sorry I came, and then I was glad.

There was something pleasant about the whole atmosphere. I tried to get out in a nice way, but that was impossible. So I spent the afternoon there, and it was the most pleasant time I had had in a couple of weeks. We talked about everything and every place. A couple of nights after that we went to call on some friends. I had to stop in a couple of times during the week, and the next thing I knew it was a habit. I had more fun in that office in a couple of minutes than I would have all day. Several nights later The Girl, Spud, and I went to a show. We had a soda that we laughed about for sometime later and had a wonderful evening. At least, I did.

A letter written to Alma from Hobson, March 17, 1930; from The Cawthon, a hotel in Mobile, Alabama.

Hello Alma,

Just a line to show you I really went to Mobile.

The train ran along nice and fast, I was expecting it to go slow from what you had said about them. I saw more flowers and trees in full bloom than I have seen since last spring, even wild azalea. It looked very nice for the first time in a year.

I called the boss on the telephone this morning and told him as soon as I got the copper out I would go back to Sheffield, because I will not get this job over in a month and a half, otherwise.

It rained all day today that is a good start for a nice day.

Good evening, Bill

(Bill wrote rather long letters. The liberty has been taken to record what is meaningful to the story and to leave unimportant parts out.)

This letter was written from Alma on April 25, 1930.

Dearest Hobson,

It's just the time you usually came around the corner, for its now 12:20 P.M. Everyone has gone to lunch—you don't realize how much I do miss you, even tho you were here only a short time, you know we can learn a lot in a few minutes sometimes. Received your letter this morning and had really expected it before now, though I guess the time has seemed to pass so slowly that you haven't been gone as long as it seems.

... I was looking at those pictures we made, the ones that you have. Gee, we had a nice time that day even if we did tire.

What did your mother say about you going to see a little Southern Country girl?

Everything sure is quiet around the Tri-Cities now. I don't know what is going to happen, if something doesn't open up ... guess we have been living on Muscle Shoals hopes long enough and will have to get down to hard work, for I don't believe Congress will do a thing this time either. Things did look good for a while, but that has all died down now.

Well, Hobson, I must stop as it is almost one o'clock, and the others will be dropping in soon, and I am supposed to be working, you see—you know how it is.

Write me a long letter as before, for I am always anxious to hear from you.

Give my love to your Mother, for I feel that I almost know her, for you have talked to me of her so much.

Be good and don't forget to write.

Love,
Alma

Hobson had gone to Mobile to oversee a project to get copper and dismantle a mine there. In order to get back to Sheffield and Alma quickly, he had set a deadline. He said in his letter, " I want to get this job done in a month and a half and go back to Sheffield." He signed his letter, "Good evening, Bill."

April 27, 1930

My Dear Alma,

Well, this has been a big week. No rain, but plenty of cold weather. Saturday it got warm, and today is just the kind of weather you like.

By the way, how are you, kid? How is everything going on down there? It has been only two weeks that I have been away, but it seems longer, somehow.

William Hobson's parents owned a green house called "Roses" in Little Falls, New Jersey. Bill was back home working around his home business. His Dad wanted him to work on some machinery there in New York, but he refused. He wanted to get away from home.

"I think Monday night or Tuesday morning, I will start for Chicago. Then go on from there. I will let you know as soon as I reach a stopping place. I did not come out so bad on the job in the South (Sheffield). I gave my mother one hundred dollars, put one hundred in savings, and have eighty-five to work with. That makes seven hundred in my savings account. Every penny earned with my own paws.

The family doesn't know what is wrong with me that I don't jump at the first job offered. Mother asked me if I was going back down to my Alabama girl or what was up?

As some of Alma's letters were misplaced, we have to read between the lines to understand Hobson's answers. She asks about a former girlfriend of Hobson's. This is his answer.

"I saw Lea last Wednesday. She wanted to know why I did not write. I said, "When her mother started to kick, I thought it was time to forget it all." She wanted to know how the girl was down South. I told her, 'Great!'

Hobson refused to go to a dance rehearsal with Lea and broke-up his relationship with her.

"I told her things looked very bad, now. So I think I am all clear of that, and the ship will sail along smoothly."

"The sun just went down behind a mist. I could not see the mountains tonight, but they were wonderful every night this week.

"If I don't stop writing to you, I will have a chapter written. You will be hearing from me in a couple of days in another part of the country. Wishing you well and all the folks, too.

Good night. Will remain the same."

Bill

Hobson's plans did not materialize.

April 30, 1930

Hello Alma Dear,

    This is Wednesday, and I am still in Great Notch. I got your letters Monday and really have to apologize for not writing sooner.

    I wrote a letter yesterday and carried it all over New York today. Here is the low down on it, believe it or not:

    My Dad has been sick with a sore on his neck. Monday I had to go to N.Y.C. and see a man he had a date with. We were running here and there, looking for the man. The bird finally came in around two o'clock. You know how I felt. Then we went to inspect the boiler. I had to get state number, dates, size, and insurance reports, look in the boiler, and go through a list of things my dad wanted. The man who owned the boiler said he had never seen a kid go over a boiler and see so much in so little time. Well, that was Monday.

    Tuesday, I had to drive my dad to two jobs, which covered about 130 miles. We saw two boilers that we had put up last fall just before I went South. The people were very pleased with them. That was Tuesday.

    . . . Gee, Alma, that picture was nice to see. I have it in my second folder. That is the one I keep my money in. I guess you are there, watching it. The picture is you, and you are luck for me.

    Mother likes your picture fine. She said, "She is a bonny looking girl."

    She has tried to read the letters, but I have put them away in a book where they can't find them anywhere, and they are right there in the bookcase!

    Please take care of yourself. I don't know when I will get away, but have to go about one hundred miles north of Chicago. So that is not far. Good night, Kid O.

                Lots of love, Bill

In Chicago, May 5, 1930

Hello Dear Girl,

... How are you, still sitting on top of the world?

Well, Friday I drove Dad around with another man looking at hoists.

There was nothing in sight (no job) so Friday night, I got on a bus for Chicago. I told dad where I was going, so I will have a job Monday to find a man to collect some money.

This is Sunday night; I have been sitting watching the sun go down over the large buildings in the West.

Alma, I will go to the factory Tuesday, after I try to collect the money for Dad. I will call you Tuesday or Wednesday and tell you how we stand.

Don't write me at this address. I am leaving tomorrow.

Good night, Alma. I am tired and can't write any more or think either.

Love, Bill

P.S. The elevator railway runs down under me. I am on the tenth floor, but they make a noise that only a city boy would like.

May 10, 1930

(Part of a letter)

Alma, I am so tired I can't write at all, so I think I will finish in the morning.

Good night for now.

Well, here I am back again after a real sleep. I have a big day ahead: to get the garden all in. A dog killed two of our ducks. That is how things go.

There is a large hilltop farm here. I am thinking of buying some sheep and putting them on it. It was a dairy farm, but last year it burned down. It could be rented very reasonably.

We were talking of the sheep last night, so don't get worrying about that. I hardly think I will jump at the idea yet.

We have a thousand dollars. How can we make it work? You have to think too, now.

I will have to get this letter on the nine o'clock train, so I will have to close to make it.

How is everything down there? I will bet things are slow again. They did not do anything with Shoals again, did they? *(This was a reference to TVA.)*

Alma, I have thought how strange life is several times. I remember you saying we could not help who we liked. Well, I guess you hit the nail on the head.

Girly, don't call yourself a poor working girl again please. You would think I was somebody worth talking about. My Dad may have a couple of boilers to put up again, soon. That would be six months work at good pay. I hope it goes through.

Well, kid, the paper is short and so is time.

Love, Bill

May 19, 1930
Newark, NJ, 10:30 A.M.

I am here waiting for Dad and love the job, Yes! I waited last week an hour here and two or three somewhere. Today, I brought my pen and am writing on the wheel. It is a job for a contortionist. To make it pleasant, it has rained all day and is cold and raw.

Trolley cars, or streetcars as you call them, are back and forth. Buses, automobiles, and trucks make it just right to write. If you can read this, you are smart.

There is nothing new here. The Navy has been in the Hudson River for the past week and a half. At night, they keep their searchlights back and forth across the sky. I guess there are two hundred lights. Down the road a mile, we can see the lights in New York. The skyline and the Navy lights make it a dream in the distance.

I received your letter Saturday morning. It was a treat.

Thank you for your letter again. I will close now so I can get this letter off in the next mail out. I hope things are going smooth down in Alabama. They are here.

Have a good time in Chattanooga.

The same old Bill

May 23, 1930
11:30 P.M.

My Little Girl,

I received your letter tonight about six o'clock. I am almost as pleased to get one as to see you.

The time I was in Sheffield, I missed very few days that I did not have a little chat with you, Girly. Remember April Fool's Day? I said I would not stop in to see you, but I had to. The tractor made me.

Alma, I was sorry to hear you were having a blue spell, too. Please don't cry; it is so foolish. I say that because I hardly know what it is to cry. I get a pain in my chest or heart or wherever it is, there some place that almost stops my breathing. I wish I could cry sometimes to let it off, but usually have to do a lot of acting to keep it to myself.

Alma, if you only knew how I admire you for being so real. If you ever had anything to say to me, you said it. Do you know most people I ever have anything to do with say one thing and think another? More times than once I have been told about being too frank. With a lot of people, it doesn't pay nor do any good. But with you and me, it is something even deeper, much deeper than friendship. Call it what you like, but I think the little word covers it.

Girly, if I were to start to tell you all the things I admire you for, you would think I was twice the funny boy you do at present.

Well Girly, get this straight, we have done a little planning together, and I hope with a little help from the One above, we will do our plan together someday. You will always be my pal, whether you work it that way or not. I have always been a lone bird, always in my one wild love. I always love company, but never found it really 'till I went away down to Alabama.

You won't have to tell anyone about what I said, and I hope you won't think I have said too much. We have kept little secrets together.

Love from your Pal,
Bill

May 26, 1930
Newark, N.J. 9:30
My Dear Alma,

I hope this letter finds you in the best of spirits.
It is a cool morning with a right snappy wind. It was cold all day Saturday. I worked in the garden most all day.
Well, Girly, I will close short and sweet. Be a good girl or just be as you are. So long for now. I will write tonight.

Love, Bill

May 29, 1930
Thursday night, 9 o'clock
My Dear Alma,

Well, Girly, I feel like what was left of the straw heap after the windstorm. All gone off, little by little. For the last three days, I have been working on a couple of boilers of my Dad's. They had to be cleaned and painted.

You know when you work for your dad, it's just keeping the pot boiling. In other words, it is keeping the business on the go. But I don't get paid, so it always looks like a lot of work for nothing; although, it is really a way to get ahead.

Lots of love from the N.J. Pal,

Bill

June 2, 1930
Sunday Night, 9:14 o'clock
My Dear Alma,

As the Englishman says, "I say, old top, are you there?" I went to the airplane field today, had a charming chat with one of those fellows.

The roses are just starting to make large buds now. There is a hum in the air from the bees. The brook harmonized with a few little birds. How can people live in big apartment houses in the city and never know what old Mother Nature has just a few miles away in her garden?

I will say good night again and try not to knock the milk bottles down on the porch.

Love, Bill

June 9, 1930
Sunday, 10:30 P.M.
Dear Girl,
   Well, I sent you the roses, so if you get a box with a few in it.... Up here, they are all in bloom now, and you can't imagine how fine they are. I had to pick the ones which would last best, but my mother said she hardly thought they would last. If they don't, you can't say I did not do what I said I would. So will say, "Good night" . . .
Sincerely yours,
Bill

June 13, 1930
Friday night, 10:00 o'clock
My Dear Alma,
   Today was Friday the thirteenth, a good luck day for me, I got your letter! It surely was sweet, almost like stopping in and seeing you in the office. I would love to stop in just a minute. Gee, those days were wonderful... I would like to start the airplane up and see little you in nine or ten hours. *(An imagination game they played)*
   I was glad you got the roses OK.
   We understand each other in a very strange and keen way . . . Alma, I never have to tell you what I was getting at. When I spoke, you understood, and I think I understand you. I wish you could come up here. If you came walking in, I sure would be pleased. I will be walking down there when the next job is finished. I am half asleep now.
Yours with lots of love,
Bill

Monday, June 23, 1930
My Dear Alma,
   I received your letter this A.M. and was glad to get it. They always knock the gloom off the day.
   Bill had had a little fender bender, but was all right. Also in a previous letter Bill had encouraged Alma to go swimming and get the good exercise. He was considering going to South America to work for an oil company. He signed off . . . Good luck and so long for now . . .
Love, Bill

July 1, 1930

My Dear Alma,

Do you know it has been a year since I saw you last? Even though your picture always looks good, I like to hear your voice once in a while. How about a date? Write and tell me what night next week that I can call and what time or where. Send the number if it is a new meeting place . . .
                          Lovingly yours, Bill

July 6, 1930
Sunday

My Dear Alma,

The folks have gone to church and I am on watch, as we call it. Of course, I am a heathen and would not go anyway.

Alma, you wanted me to analyze your case. While I was in that little town in Alabama, I studied one little girl that interested me very much. The reason she interested me was because she seemed to be the girl I had a picture of in my mind.

In my stopping in at the office at noon, we got to talk of some things that I never have spoken about. It was like a couple of old friends talking about their past troubles. I tried not to show that I liked the kid, but every time I saw her, I would think twice as much of her. She did what stood out to me as I should have liked a sister to do, if I had a sister. She was a good sport, as I found out when we took a walk. Several times, right up to the last night when I left for Mobile not to return for awhile, I was taken with little things, but they showed the girl's character. The first thing I knew, I loved her very much and had to go off to another part of the state. That was the hardest thing I had ever had to do without showing any or as little emotion as possible! The evening I left, she was very sick but stayed up to talk to me for the last time in a while. We did not know how long I would be gone, and did not say very much. Both thought we knew what was ahead of us, at least as plans were.

The time came, I had to go. It was a moment that was dreaded by both of us. Up I got, I told her to stay, but she had to come to the door for the last good-bye. We shook hands, and that meant more to me than any handshake I ever had. It meant something to both of us, I will say. It was a moment I will never forget. No two ever parted that way before with the love we had for each other. Her last words were, "So long, Hudson, be a sweet boy."

Alma, you say that I should tell you what is wrong with that little girl:

She is so old-fashioned. If she ever is anything but that little girl I know down in Alabama, I would be a very sorry boy. That night she told me I would make the trip OK. This showed her concern for me.

Well, I have a book written for you.

Lots of love, Bill

July 9, 1930

My Dear Alma,

I received your letter of the third yesterday evening, but was so tired I could only enjoy it, could not answer it, so here it comes tonight.

I just watched the sun go down behind the mountain in the West. It has been a wonderful day, clear as a crystal. It was fairly warm but with a cool breeze.

I guess you hit it right the day you told me we couldn't help who we loved. I can't say I haven't been lonely even at sunset.

The boiler has not sold yet, but they are still going strong on one price and another. Dad wants to drive up to Northern Jersey, then across to New York where the boiler is (located) and see both the spot where it is, and where it is to be erected. That will be a big day for Yours Truly, over one hundred and fifty miles or more.

Will call you Monday on the telephone. Monday evening I'll call 539 somewhere about 7:30 your time; that will be 8:30 our time. Then I might know about the job for sure. Telephoning is not as expensive as a show, and it is worth it to hear your voice and to s "Hello".

Well, I will sign off and say, "Good night".

Lots of love, Bill

P.S. Did I fool you with that envelope? *He had sent the letter in an Austin Hotel, Chattanooga, Tennessee envelope.*

July 11, 1930

My Dear Alma,

You talk of me knowing what you think, but you were always right there when I had something on my mind.

Next summer will be a big time for both of us. I am going to start the ball rolling in that direction.

I will say good bye now will be seeing you soon.

Love, Bill

This is a part of a letter.
Little did he know what the future would bring.

July 15, 1930

My Dear Alma,

Mother was taken into the operating room at about 9:30 this morning and came out after 10 o'clock A.M.

Dad was there and told me she didn't look so bad. I will go to see her this evening. The next ten days are the dangerous ones. Her health condition was good, and she is one who recovers quickly.

I had a lot to talk to you about last night, but after all the commotion here I could not think of anything. At any rate, your voice did sound good. I wish I were down there, swimming. You have a real summer, there. We only have a short time of it.

When I got you last night on the phone, it was about fifteen after nine. It had been dark for almost an hour, and it was cool with a pleasant breeze all evening.

I will say, "So long for now." I will write more later when I am in a better mood.

Lots of love,
Bill

July 17, 1930
Wednesday 10 PM

My Dear Alma,

I was going to write you last night after seeing mother, but was really feeling bad.

Mother was still in shock. She was the lowest I have ever seen her. Gee, when you see your mother like that, it gets under your skin.

This morning, Dad saw her again, and she was back to her old self, quite normal, with just as much fun about her as usual. I have a big load off my chest, and I think she is on home stretch now.

We are having heavenly weather. The summer apples, currents, and berries are blooming. It is a good time to be alive.

I will be off to bed and say, "Good night".

Lots of love from the boy. Bill

July 18, 1930
Friday morning

My Dear Alma,

Dad and my brother saw Mother last night, and they said she looked good. The night nurse slept most all night, so they fired her.

I received your letter yesterday, and I don't know how to thank you. Gee, girly, you are a prince in plain English. I have had a week of acting, just keeping a smile, was work. Dad has a bad heart, at least when he worries. I keep him busy so he will not think of mother so much. Girly, I will close and say, 'Thanks again.' Be good, and tell your mother not to be sick. Gee, I hope she is well soon. I'll be off.

So long for now. Bill

July 19, 1930
9:30 PM

My Dear Alma,

Mother looks good and is herself again.

You mentioned the heat; it has been 90 in the shade all day. I mixed more cement, today. A good day for swimming to say nothing of work.

I'll bet I can make you laugh; go ahead, at my expense. Yesterday I made 25 quarts of current jam and 10 quarts of applesauce. I gave a little of the jam to Mr. Kameman, and he said it was good. A lady came to hear how mother was, so I gave her a quart of the sauce. She said it was very good, better than she could make. They have to say something. All hands have to make the work move here, so that is all I care about.

The apples last only a week, then they are all too ripe to do anything with. You have to make good sauce when they are almost ripe.

I think me and my shadow will be off to bed, I can sleep tonight without any help. Be good and good night.

Love, Bill

July 23, 1930
Tuesday evening

My Dear Alma,

Here I am again, believe it or not. How are you and is your Mother well? My Mother is coming on very well and in the best of humor. She put up a great front before she went to the hospital. She made a will and wrote other last requests before she left. She doesn't know I found them, and she will think no one has read them because I put them back just like I found them.

I will stay here until this storm is over, but then, after mother is home, I am off. I can hear you say, "Maybe," but please don't just laugh or smile like you did when you wanted to hide a thought.

Girly, I am off to bed and will see that sun up an hour before you will, and will start a good day before it gets to you.

Lots of love, Bill

July 29, 1930
Sunday Night

My Dear Alma,

I hope this note finds you well and your day as wonderful as this one was here.

The hospital called and said mother was doing fine and ready to come home, today. When we got to the hospital, she was still in bed and very surprised that the Dr. had said she could go home, as was her special nurse. We found out that there was another Mrs. Hobson in the hospital and got everything straightened out.

The nurses and mother started teasing me about you. They said you probably had three or four fellows by now. I said, "That is up to her." I was glad when Dad came to get me. Gee, they talked so much I about believed you had forgotten me, but I know different. Will say good bye now and hope you will sleep like I am going to.

Love,
Bill.

August 2, 1930

My Dear Alma,

I hope you are well and going strong.

Mother came home from the hospital today. The little brother was as pleased as if they had a million dollars. One fellow told me it was the first time he had seen me smile in a month. When I told him why, he was sorry. I could see his face change. He was a nice fellow, anyway, and we laughed it off.

Now I won't be telling you my troubles anymore, so that will be good news for you.

How is swimming? Is the heat bad yet? We have had a couple of wonderful days, not hot or cold, just a couple sent from heaven.

The sun is just going down now, a big red ball sliding very gracefully behind the hills. Something always happens to me when I watch it go down. I think of all the places I have seen it go down. When I am home, I think of some place far away. In Chattanooga, I saw some wonderful sunsets on the Tennessee River. One day when I was in Sheffield, I was coming from Florence, I had been looking for that copper that was stolen, remember? The trolley was in the middle of the river when the sun went down, and I shall never forget it.

The last day, when I was going to Decatur on the way to Mobile, the sun was a long time going down. I don't think I ever felt so lonely, I can't explain, I sure did not like to see it go.

Had better close. Good night, Girly. Write soon.

Love,
Bill

August 12, 1930

My Dear Alma,

    We have had no rain yet. A wonderful sunset was the sign for a good hot day tomorrow.

    I did not go on the fishing trip. We took honey from the bees yesterday and a little today. This is a thing that is very seldom done in summer, but they had it so we took it. We might get half a ton this year if things go well. We only have nine hives, but we keep them our own way, which gives results, and that is what speaks.

    It is a nice cool evening. I shall be in dreamland soon. By the way, I dreamed I saw you last night. You had a dress on that you wore one night at home when I was there. Everything seemed so real it made me wake with a start and spoil it all. I will be saying, "Good night."

Lots of love,
Bill

August 18, 1930

My Dear Alma,

    My brother has been given two weeks off. I will be able to tell you something by Tuesday or Wednesday. So until then, I can't say much.

    I went fishing for crabs this morning with a farmer and my little brother. We got up at 4 o'clock. There was not a sign of anything, and all hands were discouraged. By eight, we caught one on the side bank of the river. We netted from there, and I rowed, and we had good luck and caught one hundred by ten thirty. We went down the river bar four-and-a-half miles, then up the other side. We saw about ten other boats, but we were the only ones with any luck.

    When I came home and had dinner, it started to rain, so I got a good afternoon sleep in. Will go back to bed soon and be awake all night, I guess. I shall say good night and good luck.

Lots of love,
Bill

August 20, 1930
Saturday morning

Dear Girl,

I have been going like an engine that has not stopped for a couple of days.... Well, Girly, I am taking the job on my own back. Have been all week getting everything straight. Monday will be a day in New York with the Oil Company. The boat will cost something around $300.00 and the motor about $250.00. Then there will be $50.00 for tanks, gas, and other little things. I guess about another hundred for compass and logline, life preserver, and clothing. It looks like $700.00, but I am game. The fellow who never made a mistake never made anything. I think I will spend three days to a week around here trying things out. Maybe make a couple of little runs, and lift some records just for practice.

Well, girly, I shall let you know everything just as it is, so please don't think I am holding back anything. There will be no boating for at least a week. I don't think I am making much of a mistake on the boat or the engine. They are both the best, and I am getting one hundred and fifteen dollars off the boat; it is $415.00 new. The motor at about fifty off; it is worth $285.00 new. So it is as good as could be expected. Well, I shall say be good, and so long for now.

Love
Bill

Tuesday, September 2, 1930

My Dear Alma,

... I was running my motor on Sunday and Monday, so it will start back down the Long Island Sound, Friday, if it is a fair day. I have been swimming every day this week, and it is like old times. The boat was running like a dream. If you ever saw it, I'll bet you would fall in love with it.

I had it painted today and put in some lumber to carry the gas tanks. We will get them finished tomorrow and give it a run Thursday, to will be sure by Friday.

Will be calling you on the phone as soon as I get back to N.Y.C.

We have had wonderful weather for the last week, but for some heavy fogs.

Be good girly. I am and always will be just the same pal.

Lots of love,
Bill

Bill starts on his trip down the waterways on his way to a boat show in Miami, Florida.
He sends Alma a telegram at every stop on his way.

William "Bill" Hobson

WESTERN UNION

Received at 103 EAST THIRD STREET Sheffield, Ala.

24BM K 6

NEWYORK NY 344P SEP 9 1930

MISS ALMA DUKES
702 ANNAPOLIS AVE SHEFFIELD ALA

WILL TELEPHONE TUESDAY AT 7 PM

BILL

309P

WESTERN UNION

Received at 103 EAST THIRD STREET Sheffield, Ala.

13BM K 10

NORFOLK VIR 1058A SEP 13 1930

MISS ALMA DUKES
ANNAPOLIS AVE SHEFFIELD ALA

ARRIVED HERE LAST NIGHT AFTER BIG DAY ALL IS WELL

BILL

1025A

WESTERN UNION

CLASS OF SERVICE
This is a full-rate Telegram or Cablegram unless its deferred character is indicated by a suitable sign above or preceding the address.

NEWCOMB CARLTON, PRESIDENT   J. C. WILLEVER, FIRST VICE-PRESIDENT

Received at 108 EAST THIRD STREET Sheffield, Ala.

28BM K 11

WILMINGTON NCAR 320P SEP 16 1930

MISS ALMA DUKES

702 ANNAPOLIS AVE SHEFFIELD ALA

OK IN WILMINGTON NC HAD BAD WEATHER FOR LAST FEW DAYS

BILL

236P

THE BIRMINGHAM AGE-HERALD,

MISSING YOUTH SOUGHT

Radio Companies Asked To Aid In Search For William Hobson

NEW YORK, Sept. 26—(AP)—Assistance in searching for his son, William Hobson, who was last heard of in North Carolina on Sept. 18, was asked Friday by Russell B. Hobson, Great Notch, N. J., of government agencies and radio companies.

William Hobson, the father said, left New York for Miami on Sept. 10 in an 18-foot sea sled outboard motor boat with no name and no radio. The chief of police at Brunswick, Ga., notified the father that the boat had been found on the beach there on Sept. 24.

His son is 21 years old, Hobson said, five feet, eight inches tall and weighs 160 pounds.

RIVES PLANS ADDRESS

Democratic Drive In Pike County To Open Saturday

TROY, Ala., Sept. 26—Richard T. Rives will speak at Brundidge, Ala., at 3 p.m. Saturday in the interest of the Democratic party.

Mr. Rives' appearance at Brundidge will open a county-wide campaign of the Pike County Democratic Club. Members declared it is the intention of the club to carry the drive into every beat in the county in an effort to get voters to the polls in the November election.

WESTERN UNION

CLASS OF SERVICE
This is a full-rate Telegram or Cablegram unless its deferred character is indicated by a suitable sign above or preceding the address.

SIGNS
DL = Day Letter
NM = Night Message
NL = Night Letter
LCO = Deferred Cable
NLT = Cable Letter
WLT = Week-End L

NEWCOMB CARLTON, PRESIDENT — J. C. WILLEVER, FIRST VICE-PRESIDENT

Received at 103 EAST THIRD STREET

27BM K 10

GREATNOTCH NJ 435P OCT 1 1930

MISS ALMA DUKES S.O.S.

702 ANNAPOLIS AVE SHEFFIELD ALA

FIFTY NAVY AND COASTGUARD BOATS SEARCHING THINKING ALL IS WELL

MOTHER

412P

FIRST KNOWLEDGE OF THE TRAGEDY

Alma was attending services at Annapolis Avenue Church of Christ when a stranger arrived at the front door of the church building. He asked if Alma Dukes happened to be there. This stranger was a reporter from the Commercial Appeal out of Memphis. It had been reported to them that a capsized boat had been found floating near Charleston Port, a large Coast Guard station. The Coast Guard had secured the boat and found Alma's letters in a sealed, secret drawer. The reporter was asking for any information that Alma might have concerning this solo trip from Mayfall, Virginia, to Miami, Florida, to a boat show. Alma told him everything that she could tell him in a short time.

It was mentioned to Alma that the waters where the boat was found were shark infested.

The following article was taken from the Birmingham Age Herald after the boat was found.

THURSDAY, SEPTEMBER 25, 1930

FEAR HELD FOR BOATMAN

Craft Found Off Georgia Coast Identified After Wreck

BRUNSWICK, Ga., Sept. 24—(AP)—Authorities here Wednesday expressed fear that William Hobson, of Great Notch, N. J., lost his life off Sea Island Beach when his motorboat overturned. The craft was found disabled and overturned off the island Tuesday by fishermen, and was identified Wednesday as the property of Hobson. A suitcase was found aboard and papers in it indicated Hobson was en route from New Jersey to Miami.

WESTERN UNION

Received at 103 EAST THIRD STREET

27BM K 19 XU

TDFH GREATNOTCH NJ-728P SEP 24 1930

MISS ALMA DUKES

509 ATLANTA AVE SHEFFIELD ALA

REPORT BILL HOBSONS BOAT FOUND OVERTURNED OFF SEA ISLAND BEACH BRUNSWICK GEORGIA WIRE IF YOU KNOW ANYTHING ABOUT HIM

MRS HOBSON

723P

WESTERN UNION

Received at 103 EAST THIRD STREET

22BM K 33

TDFH LITTLEFALLS NJ 332P SEP 26 1930

MISS ALMA DUKES

509 ATLANTA AVE SHEFFIELD ALA

PLEASE LOAN US IMMEDIATELY BY REGISTERED MAIL LETTERS THAT WILL THROW LIGHT ON THIS TRIP YOUR NAME MUST NOT GET MIXED UP IN THIS AFFAIR WILL RETURN LETTERS NO NEWS YET WRITING LOVINGLY

MOTHER

313P

Letters and Correspondence After The Accident

Letters to Alma from Hobson's Parents

RUSSELL B. HOBSON

THE HOLLY GRAVITY RETURN SYSTEM
THE STATIC BOILER FEED REGULATOR
STEAM BOILERS AND ACCESSORIES

TELEPHONE LITTLE FALLS 659

GREAT NOTCH, N. J.   9/26/1930

Miss Alma Dukes
    Sheffield   Ala.

Dear Miss Dukes

       I was deeply grateful for your prompt telephone message about Bill.

       I wonder if you could tell us what you know about this trip which seems to have cost the boy his life, for the reason that we are trying to discover if he was in the nature of an employee of any of the 3 parties, the Oil Co or the Engine Co, or the Boat Co.

       We have wired the Chief of Police at Brunswick Ga to keep the effects intact. We presume also that he has the custody of the Boat.

       If there are any of his letters which would throw light on this matter, and you send them, we shall be careful to return them.

       We have been hoping that there might be a chance of his having been picked up and carried to some distance by a boat, but inasmuch as he was in Wilmington on the 16th which is 10 days ago, the chance is becoming most remote.

       We suppose that there is still the hope for his body to have been found along the coast between Wilmington and Brunswick, and maybe this might never come to our attention. It is hard at the distance to see what best to do. It would be difficult to advise the different places where he might be found, or ask them. And he may have been blown out to sea.

       At first we were too stunned to have the thing sink in, but as we comprehend more, and as hope seems to wane, it assumes its true aspect, and we feel that we have lost a good kind brave and ever loving boy.

                Respectfully yours

                          Elizabeth Hobson
                          (Mrs Russell B Hobson)

Letters to Alma from Elizabeth Hobson
William Hobson's Mother

RUSSELL B. HOBSON

THE HOLLY GRAVITY RETURN SYSTEM
THE STATIC BOILER FEED REGULATOR
STEAM BOILERS AND ACCESSORIES

TELEPHONE LITTLE FALLS 653

Oct 14 1939
GREAT NOTCH, N. J.

My dearest Alma:-

Many thanks for the letters. There is no more news except that a Mr F P McClellan and Family Box 905 Charleston 8 C. entertained Bill in the night of the 19 and that he saw him leave on the 20 also that a Standard Oil man the name of Hopkins saw him leave Charleston harbor on the 20 and Bill told him that he had a lot of time to make up and that he would have to do some night driving and that he was going on the outside route. This would mean tha that he was about 25 or more miles out. The fisherman found his boa boat with the stern down in the water and the weight of the engine held it down so that there was only two inches of the bow above water and Dad thinks that a big sea swamped it and that Bill thought she was a gom gonner and swam for shore and that it was twenty miles at least etc etc I have been wondering why he did not write to you on the twentyth as he was in Charleston two days with engine trouble. I hope you willl forgive my saying so also burn this letter be sure - could he have abandoned the trip boat etc when he woke up and saw that they were usig him for a good thing, and might he not be suffering from chagrin. His boat may have drifted away or been stolen and in desperation he may have disappeared, tell me what you think. If that is the case he might be ashamed that you might know etc or us either. If I hear or know of anything I will wire you you must know that.. We are trying not to talk about it or say anything that will remind Dad of it he has taken it so hardly that we hope we will get off with only loosing Bill.

and you dear girl must put him out of your mind as it might easily be t
that you would fret about that so long that it might ruin other and
better chances of happiness.. Bill was always riding a sky hook
and when I got iup on the table to be operated on I realized that I
was not taking any bigger chance than when I got in the car to go to
the hospital. Those sort of fellows are very charming and it may
be that marriage is the only way that dame nature can tame them and
keep them on the earth.

       Write to that man if you like and tell him who you are
etc he is so nice and all this false modesty gives me a pain in the
neck. I hope that you will have a little more confidence in your old
folks opinions even if they are like Bills oldfashioned so that your
days may be long in the land etc.

       With much love Your devoted Mother

RUSSELL B. HOBSON

THE HOLLY GRAVITY RETURN SYSTEM Oct 30 1930
THE STATIC BOILER FEED REGULATOR   TELEPHONE LITTLE FALLS 653
STEAM BOILERS AND ACCESSORIES

GREAT NOTCH. N. J.

My Dearest Alma:-

I feel that I have been neglecting you frightfully and wonder why I am so slow about writing. I always have to wait till all the family are gone so I can drop you a line. First we are having a trying time with Dad all he cares to do is cry and cry and some one of us has to stay with him all the time so that he will not feel too lost.
He has been in to see the oil men and they are so disturbed at his distress that they are glad to be rid of him? Many of these stops are mistakes and they will do well enough, you will know what construction to put on them.
The oil men showed Russ a clipping showing that Bill was last seen by two men employed by Dr Torrey at Ossabau and he told them that he was going to the island of Sapelo for fuel. They were in Savannah on the night of October third and had never heard of this thing as they had seen Bill on 20th of Sept. I wired the Navy when I got this letter also I wired McClellan and he wired back that he was investigating the report and that he was going down there Nov 1st and that he would find out what he could etc., Dad is sorry that he can only think that Bill was swept out to sea.
I am sure that you cannot believe how truly gratefull we are to you for sending the letters and we will return them as soon as we get to it.   I thioughtvthat it would be a goodplan to get the other letters from friends etc that bear on the subject and make a sort of book out of it and send you one at least. Bill spoke of all of you so very nicely even Dimple, and I have wondered if hw would make for her place. It seems that it cost him $150 for the gasoline to get to Charleston the Oil man told Dad so as he only had $200 we dont have to worry about the holdup. It looks to me as tho the holdu holdup was in New York. .   Arthur who is Twenty Oct 15 is his Birthday and Bills 17 and Russell jnr 28 of Oct feels very bitter about the whole thing he feels that it was very inconsiderate etc and he is so loving and nice to both of us. They are out now delivering a boiler that they sold and I hasten to close before they return I have had to leave it to answer the phone get lunch etc With much love and assuring you that all the news etc is open to you and hoping that htere may be more to tell truly thy Mother

Letters to Alma from Elizabeth Hobson
William Hobson's Mother

January 21, 1931
Great Notch, N.J.

My Dearest Alma,

You will be wondering why I don't write and send on your letters etc. and also reply to the others – Just laziness – I keep putting it off. Today is nice and quiet (Arthur is home doing his studies), the twins and Russell are at school, and the two cats are quiet – the twins have been home with chicken pox, and one had sore eyes after, so I have been doing a lot of nursing, and it is very monotonous. I called up Leonores mother and asked her about Bill etc., and she said Leonore was married on Labor Day, and she had not seen Bill since April last.

You promised to copy McClellan's letter and send it to us, but I suppose you are waiting to hear from me. Your Christmas card was very pretty. I don't know whether I sent you one or not, because Dad was disgusted at the cards I got. He thinks those Madonna & Child pictures are—to say the least—disgusting—Selah.

The motor boat show is on in N.Y., and I would like to go to see it and talk with a few of the people and look at the life belts. I think I feel worse as time goes on, and as for Dad he does not care whether school keeps or doesn't.

Business is gone to the Bow Wows, and we are all broke. Arthur is very nice and kind now, and I hope he will be able to keep at school. He is going to N.Y.U., taking the night course in English.

Did any of the roses take root that your mother was trying? What is that little blue flower that Bill said grew wild all around there?

Do you think there is any possibility of his still being alive and wishing to keep quiet—I often wonder, let's hope so. With very much love, hoping to hear from you soon again.

Lovingly,
Mother

March 13, 1931

My Dear Alma,

Tomorrow is Friday the 13th. I suppose there is plenty more misery up misfortune's sleeve waiting for both of us.

I have copied one of Bill's letters and enclosed it. I shall send them all back that way. I hate to part with them but realize that they, like the writer, were only loaned to me. I must be glad to have had that good fortune.

I am torn between the desire to write you and the wish to have you try and forget it all. I came across a few letters you wrote him, I suppose the were hidden away very safely till he would return. I seem to feel the misery of it more as time goes on and Dad says the same. We go out to plan what can be done in Spring, and there are so many things that he did around the place that the thought of going on with the job seems impossible.

There is still to my mind a chance that he is alive. But Mrs. Numgerser also thinks that her son lives – so I suppose it is a sign I am all off. I cannot feel as some do that it is the Lord's will, etc. My misery is that we just let him slip through our fingers. Still I am glad to have you left to me out of the wreck. You can have no idea what a comfort you are to me.

I won't be satisfied until I go down there and look the land over, or rather the water—Dad thinks that is all rot and that there is not a chance in the world that he got away. According to Mr. McClellan, there are many islands around there. Thanks so much for the letter you copied. He went to quite a lot of trouble.

I see by tonight's paper that Ford is going to make a car that people can drive on land or water. Of course, when I read the letter he wrote you about his trip from Mystic, I can only wonder or fear that he did the same thing that night of the 20th. If there was only proof that he survived that night, I think he could have easily been so unnerved he would not want to see his boat anymore, or us. I should be very happy to learn he was. I don't know where we are lifted to draw our own conclusions—the boat has not come up yet.

Jack has a very bad boil on his neck and I wish it would cure up. Very much Love from all.

Lovingly, Mother

Alma's Closure After The Tragedy

The skies are weeping.
It's vain to wait for clearer sky.
I must run for shelter
And live a normal life,
Thinking perhaps someday he will return.

Poem written by Hobson's Dad

TO BILL.

Beloved Boy, with eyes scanning the skies,
        And o'er the waters deep to distant lands
Rich colored with the hues of youth's romance
        As one, even solate to manhood come,
Enamoured of life, intent to explore its deep significance,
        And fill some forward rank in earth's advance;
Eager to break a lance with destiny,
        And deaf to caution, or to turning back
            from thy far faring quest.

As if irked by the somberness of this slow moving scene
        Which seemed to imprison thee,
Planning thy liberty, and looking forth from thy close cell;
        Did'st study how thou might by some fair fete
Burst from thy bounds, and find thy way to some far fairer realm
        As was thy right.

And so thou chose thy venture on ocean deep, as though
        Sensing thy new found power, and all thy fair endurance;
Still, what dire spell could so divert thy course
        Into such unaccustomed element?
And yet the turbulent sea, with restless surge,
        Matched well thy ardent soul,
But, Alas; rising tumultuous, didst engulf thy tiny skiff,
        And overwhealming thee, didst take thee to itself,
And there doth hold thee, beyond 400 leagues,
        Tired boy, at rest.

But where; Oh where, dear boy, sailing alone into the night
        Didst thou last see the light of God's fair day?
How many friendly eyes have peered into the deep,
        And searched through every cove for trace of thee?
We only know that tis His ocean too,
        And all His world is consecrate,
And none 'ere lost, but all subject at last to His own will,
        Whose everlasting arms are underneath.

Dear son: on that so recent morn, departing from thy accustomed place
        Amongst the hills and woods, which so well thou didst love,
And were the well thumbed volumes of thy love,
        Thou didst withold from mother thy accustomed kiss,
Giving but promise of a quick return;
        And so didst go, casting but a furtive glance behind,
And hiding thy resolve, lest she should know, or guess.

We know not, but with what prescience inspired,
              Thou didst detect some sign of a more distant voyage
Beyond the fogs and mists of measured time, or undimensioned space,
              And wouldst at every cost have hid it from her.
T'were a vain hope; for she who nurtured thee, and tended all thy ills,
              More truly knew how tenuous the veil
Between the uncertain now, and that insistent then,
              What fragile webb spanning twixt life, and death,
Dreading that thou wouldst tread,
              And so was torn for fear of harm to thee.

How strangely intertwined are joy and anguish
              Within this vale of tears
Where flowers do charm, and thorns do tear,
              And every smile close followed by a sigh.
What beauteous flower, torn from thy mead,
              Lies scattered wanton on that distant sea,
Where crossed the convergent lines of thy young hope
              With the insatiate toils of fate's dark infamy.

Brave boy; honoring thy wish that not a ripple of fear
              Should mar thy going
So shall we never bid thee a farewell,
              But here upon this hearth shall await thy coming.
And as we wait, the memory of thy great gentleness
              And of thy gifts of warm humanity, shall ever keep it warm.

And in this home of memory,
              We shall dwell with thee more intimately than before.
Here we shall listen to thy abounding laughter,
              And still shall know the support of thy strong arm
And all thy winsomeness from childhood on.
              And if we sleep while still awaiting thee,
We shall awake to know thy warm embrace,
              And thou and we shall travel on together
In that fair realm, where love makes life complete.

Oh blessed realm of love, God's realm
              With many mansions dight, and lit by love,
And here beloved boy, we are at home,
              Dear heart, sleep well: good night:
And soon the morning light: Good night: Good night.

              "Dad".   10/25/30.

UNITED STATES ENGINEER OFFICE
CUSTOMHOUSE
P.O. BOX 905
CHARLESTON, S. C.

Oct. 25, 1930

Miss Alma Dukes
702 Annapolis Ave
Sheffield, Ala.

My dear Miss Dukes:—

I have your letter of Oct 21st and regret that an up state appointment on Hydro-Electric work taking me out of the office for several days (I leave in an hour) prevents me from answering your inquiries in detail today but upon my return I will be glad to give you the whole story. Am sorry to say that no trace of him has been found & time has forced me to give him up as lost but I have traced him to within two hours of the time when disaster could have overtaken him and am sure my story will be of interest to you.

Sincerely
E. R. McClellan

FILE _____

UNITED STATES ENGINEER OFFICE
CUSTOMHOUSE
P. O. BOX 905
CHARLESTON, S. C.

Oct 29th. 1930.

My dear Miss Dukes:-

          Your letter of inquiry into the fate of Wm Hobson reached me on the 24th and it is a pleasure to submit the details of this awful tragedy if such information as I have will be of any consolation to you. From the statement that you received a wire from him at Wilmington, Itrust that I am not wrong in surmising that there was a deeper feeling than mere friendship between you for it is upon this assumption that I feel that I am rendering a sad but true service in the concluding chapters of one of the saddest tragedies that I have ever known.

          I met him at the Standard Oil Marine Filling Station and after an acquaintance of about an hour - during which time I had learned of the trip he was undertaking - I inquired as to where he expected to spend the night and he said he intended to go back to the Y M C A. (He had spent the previous night there) Having by this time sized him up as a young man of good breeding, intelligence and the courage of a Lindburgh and seeing the opportunity to learn the adventures of his trip so far, as well as to save him the expense of another night in the city, I invited him to go over to Castle Pinckney and spend the night with myself and family.

          Castle Pinckney is a small, Government owned island in Charleston Harbor about three quarters of a mile from the city, and is now a National Monument, having been made so by proclamation of Ex-President Coolidge. It is under the care of the Engineer Department and is used by them as Storage Base for Materials and Supplies and as a residence by myself and family. I have no connection with the operation of warehouses - being employed in the office as district cost accountant - but having an ungovernable love for the Sea you will readily understand why I should elect to live on an island and why I should be so anxious for Bill to spend the night with us and hear the wonderful story of his trip.

          He accepted the invitation upon the condition that no trouble or inconvenience would be caused by his stopping. Assuring him that this would be OK we boarded his sled and went over. After making the sled safe and fast for the night we went up to the Castle and met the family. While supper was being prepared Bill, Mrs McClellan, Ruth (12), Edward Jr (8) Carolyn (5) and myself (the entire population of the island with the exception of the servant and the night watchmen) all sat on the front piazza and listened to his story. He was not as talkative as I had hoped he would be but I rather admired his conservitiveness though we all hoped that he would go into more detail.

          Supper was announced and during the meal I was a back number. Between his enjoyment of the wife's hot biscuits and the conversation that Carolyn had drawn him into about Santa Claus he was busy, so I talked little. I was surprised to find that he would neither drink tea or coffee though we offered him both.

          After the meal was over I took him on a walk around the Castle explaining the historical details and finally wound up at a place where I was outfitting a small power boat of my own. He was thrilled and enthused and here again we talked "Boats and the Sea" untill darkness fell, then again repairing to the front piazza we all sat and talked till about 10 PM, when he retired for his night's rest before the start in the morning.

UNITED STATES ENGINEER OFFICE
CUSTOMHOUSE
P.O. BOX 905
CHARLESTON, S. C.

FILE_____

At day-break we were up and down to the sled. Bill packed everything in its place, fastened down the cover over the foward hatch, tested his motor and made ready to get under way.

Breakfast was announced and after the meal the customary "Good-Byes", his expressions of appreciation of our hospitality (when in truth we enjoyed his visit a thousand times more than he did) andagain down to the sled, lines unfastened, the purring motor, his promise to send us all cards when he reached Miami, and Bill was on his way. He headed for the open sea and passing the front of the wharf he stood up in his sled, strapped his Life Jacket around his body, waved a last "Good-Bye" and sat down.

I watched him untill all that I could see was the wake of his sled appearing as a silver streak against the rising sun. He had passed historic Fort Sumter.

Nothing was heard from him again untill the 24th when the evening paper reported that his sled had been found, up-turned, on the beach at Brunswick, Ga. By the time that this reached me his father had appealed to the Navy Dept at Washington, and Radio Companies to assist in the search for him. A Coast Guard picket was dispatched from St Augustine Fla to the scene and after two days of fruitless searching returned to its base with nothing to report. In the mean time I had been in touch with the finder of the sled and learned that the news paper report was erroneous for instead of the sled being washed up on the beach it was picked up five miles out at sea - the finding of it being the merest accident - it was caught in the net gear of a schrimping trawler, having been swamped and the engine holding down so that it was floating in an almost vertical position with only about five or six inches of the bow above water. The Captain of the trawler said that it is very doubtful if he would have seen it at all had it not caught in his net gear. His tool kit was unopened, indicating no engine trouble or the fact that if he stopped on account of engine trouble that he swamped before he could get out his tools. His anchor was let out about 25 or 30 feet indicating an attempt to anchor as when he left me the anchor was securely fastened by the fluke to the foward bit and could not possibly have washed aloose. His tanks contained about 25 gallons of fuel and his water bottle was full indicating that he had stopped and refilled his bottle at least since leaving me for it is improbable that he would gone all day on an open sea with out a drink of water.

The next report that I had was a wire from his mother stating that two men, employees of Dr Torrey on Ossabaw Island, had seen him on the afternoon of the 20th going to Sapelo Islands for gasoline. I have not been able to get in touch with any one on either Ossabaw or Sapelo Islands but have letters of inquiry out and if I do not get some reply by the end of this week expect to make a trip down there by auto to satisfy myself and his mother that there was no foul play. (I received the wire from her the same day that I received your letter and while I do not suspect foul play I cannot understand why these men that saw him have waited so long to say so).

This makes me believe that he stopped at Sapelo and traces him to within 25 miles of where his sled was found and to with in two hours of the time when disaster could have overtaken him. Foul play is ofcouse possible buy very higly improbable. Suicide is out of the question for no man with the pioneering instincts and the love of adventure that Bill had ever gave suicide a second thought.

As to his future plans, I know no other than that he expected to

UNITED STATES ENGINEER OFFICE
CUSTOMHOUSE
P. O. BOX 905
CHARLESTON, S. C.

FILE_____

better the record made by Frank Moreley (see October 1930 issue of "Motor Boating"), and that if successful he would again set out with a new sled and motor to establish a record from Miami, Fla. to Seattle, Wash. via the Panama Canal.

With his father's permission I expect to send Bill's story to Motor Boating along with his picture and it is possible that it may be published. However if it does not appear do not be surprised for by this time you must have realized that I am a poor writer.

To hold out further hope is futile, as hard as this may be, but from my knowledge of boats and the sea and the study that I have made of every angle of Bill's case , I have concluded that the made a stop at Sapelo or some near by island and again got under way and after about two hours run he stopped for some reason and attempted to cast anchor and that the sled swamped and sank from under him leaving him to the mercy of the wind and waves and those hideous man-eating demons that infest our Southern Coast and Coastal Waters.

We had nothing in the line of entertainment in our humble home to offer Bill but I do know that he enjoyed his night's rest at Castle Pinckney, whose peaceful serenity is unbroken save by the cry of a wandering sea gull and the wash of the waves against its jettied shores, and could he again come and spend a night with us I am sure that he would he would say with me:

"At Castle Pinckney I love to be
When twilight veils the magic scene
And Sea Gulls flying lazily above the shielding green
Of Castle Pinckney.

In sheets of tranquil indigo,
Oleanders in their varied hues
Reflect their faces, ere they go
Up Slumbers dim lit avenues.

And tress ! Old China-Berries
Clothed in dreams, bow to a distant Angelus
While in Sunset's sea there gleams
A phosphorescent Hesperus.

Perchance the Blessed Mary's Son
When in the garden of His doom
Yearned for such benison
As cloaks at dusk the peaceful boon
Of Castle Pinckney".

Thus Miss Dukes have I attempted to describe to you Bill's visit, his impressions and mine and I leave you with the sad but solemn pride that must be yours at having won the love of a man who so heroically laid down his life, a veritable sacrifice on the altar of adventure.

Sincerely yours,

UNITED STATES ENGINEER OFFICE
CUSTOMHOUSE
P. O. BOX 905
CHARLESTON, S. C.

11/13/30

FILE_____

Miss Alma Dukes
702 Anapolis Ave,
Sheffield, Ala.

My dear Miss Dukes:-
      I have your letter of the 10th and assure you that it will be a pleasure to advise you if I am able to get Bill's story to the press. In the mean time may I ask a favor of you? Possibly you can tell me off hand, or maybe you will be able to find out; at least I should think that you are in the better position to find out.

      I want to know if Bill was related in any way to the Lieut Hobson that sunk the Merrimac in the entrance to Santiago Harbor during the Spanish American War.

      My idea is to weave a thread of inherited courage and fearlessness into Bill's unfortunate adventure and feel somewhat constrained to ask his father. If I can find that he was related to the Lieutenant and in what degree, I am sure that I will be able to get at least a small tribute to Bill before the public.

      In justice to myself and a profound respect to Bill himself let me assure you that the story will not be commercialized though I have been approached by two men and each representing a different literary organization for the copy-right of the story when finished. I must say tho that this caused me to condense my original layout, but I am determined to get, as I have said, some tribute to his courage before the public.

      May I hear from you,?

      Sincerely yours,

      E. P. McClean

P.S. In the little poem in my last letter: 4th verse, 2nd line - change the word "peaceful" to "shadowed". The word "peaceful" should appear only in next line.
      EPM

Charleston, S. C.
Feb 4th. 1931

Miss Alma Dukes,
702 Annapolis Ave,
Sheffield Ala,

My dear Miss Dukes:-

I have definately given up the idea of publishing Bill's story for the reason the "World will little care nor long remember" anything that I might say as a tribute to him.

Our thoughts of him if confined to the immediate circle of those who felt the greater interest will make our chain that encircles his memory more sacred.

Mr Hobson has written a poem about him that is and will forever remain an undying tribute to the boy and as an expression of a father's love will never be surpassed.

The following verse or stanza selected from his poem:

"What beauteous flower, torn from Thy mead,
Lies scattered, wanton, on that distant sea,
Where the convergent lines of Hope
Crossed with the insatiate coils of Fate's dark infamy".

No doubt you have received a copy of the entire poem but if not and want one I shall be glad to make a copy from mine for you. In the mean time I am enclosing my attempt at a tribute to him.

Our whole family, with the exception of Caroline, has been ill with Influenza but all are on the mend now and will be out in the next few days.

I have been given the refusal of what appears to be real position in Washington. Am investigating and if it proves to be what it looks like it might be, it will good bye to my beloved ocean for a while atleast for we will all have to move to Washington - but its going to take some attraction to tear me away from Castle Pinckney--"Where I love to be".

Sincerely,

William Hobson

When to the treshold of the Great Recess
      His frail boat came,
He knew that death was on him.
         Yet a little while and ere it fled,
He resigned his high and holy soul
      To images of the majestic past,
That paused within his passive being now
         Like winds that bear sweet music
Through some dim-latticed shutter.

With strong arms he clutched his frail bark,
        Upon her deck reclined his languid head,
His limbs rested - diffused and motionless.-
        And thus he lay - on the brink
Of that obscure chasm - surrendering
        To its final impulses
The hovering powers of life.
        Hope and Despair - the torturers - slept;
No mortal pain or fear marred his repose.
        The influxes of sense
And his own being unalloyed by pain,
        Calmly fed his stream of thought,
Till he lay breathing there,
        At peace and faintly smiling.

His last sight was God's beautiful moon
        Which over the western line of the wide world,
Her mighty horn suspended,
        And with whose dim beams interwoven
Darkness seemed to single.
        How upon the distant shore-line
It seemed to rest
        And as the divided frame
Of that vast meteor sunk,
        The Boy's heart, that ever beat
In mystic rythm with Ocean's ebb and flow,
        Grew feebler still,
And when two lessening points of light
        Gleamed through the darkness,
The alternate gasp of his faint respiration
        Calmly stirred the darkening night;
Till the minutest ray was quenched
        The pulse yet lingered in his heart
It paused - it fluttered.

But when Heaven became utterly dark,
        The Ocean waters revealed an Image,
Silent, cold and motionless
        As her own voiceless caverns.
Even as a vapour fed with golden beams
        That ministered on sunlight,
Ere the west eclipses it,
        So now was that boyish frame:
No voice, no thought, no motion.
        A fragile lute over whose harmonious strings
The breath of Heaven had passed.
        A bright stream, once fed with many-voiced waves,
A dream of youth, that Fate and Ocean had quenched forever.

                      by E. L. McClellan

Letters To Mrs. Hobson From Alma

Heart broken, Alma tossed the letters into the fire. Then she reconsidered and retrieved them. Here they are, as she expressed to Mrs. Hobson the sorrow she felt. Even though they are difficult to read, she felt they would be more meaningful as originally written.

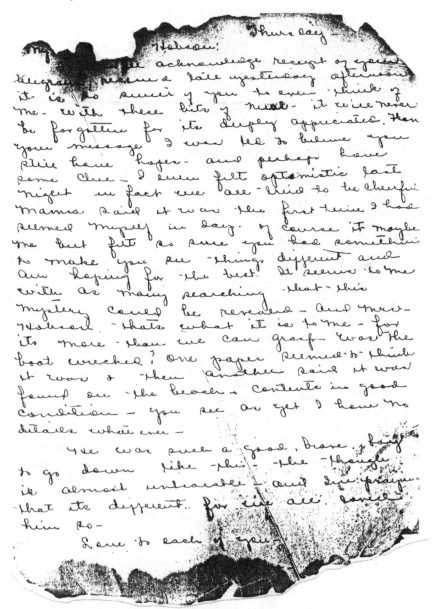

OPERATING MOTOR FREIGHT LINES
O AND FROM BIRMINGHAM,
NASHVILLE, HUNTSVILLE,
DECATUR, DOUBLE SPRINGS
AND ALL INTERMEDIATE
AND LOCAL POINTS.

ALL KINDS OF HAULING — STORAGE WAREHOUSE
PACKING AND SHIPPING
MEMBER OF NATIONAL FURNITURE WAREHOUSEMEN'S ASSOCIATION

SHIP

5|5-16

SHEFFIELD, ALABAMA
Sept. 24, 1931

Dear Mrs. Hobson:

  Just these few lines to let you know I am thinking of you. It has been some little while since I heard from you, but I know you are busy as the children are going to school. Then in the Fall it seems that household tasks are always heavier, especially where anyone does canning and preserving. We have had an abundance of fruits and vegetables all this season, and the farmers have sold their products almost for a song. Ihrum has all her cans filled and some dried fruit.

  It certainly has been hot for the last month, in fact its given up as being the hottest September on record, and there is no relief in sight, tho we did have a shower of rain since noon.

  Are business conditions any brighter there? It seems things steadily grow worse here. Of course we have Muscle Shoals to look forward to when Congress convenes in December, tho sometimes I think we would be better off without it. If something does'nt turn up I don't know what people are going to do this Winter.

  I am still working for the same people as when Hobson was here, tho have been working one-half day all this Summer for our representative in Congress, Congressman Ed. B. Almon, whose home is in Tuscumbia, a distance of about two miles. I have enjoyed the work so much, for it has at least been a change from the usual run. Of course, that will end when he goes back to Washington in December, and I will be back here all day.

  How is Mr. Hobson getting along now? And the children. Sometime when you have a spare minute would appreciate a note from you. I think of you so often. A whole year has passed and it seems that time has made no difference.

    With kindest regards to each of you, I am

       Lovingly,

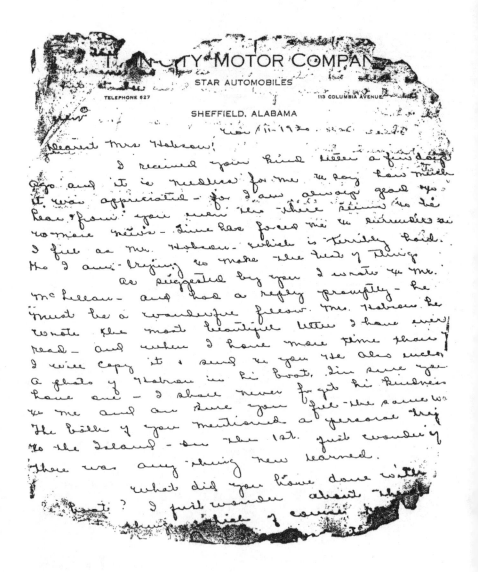

TRI-CITY MOTOR COMPANY
STAR AUTOMOBILES
TELEPHONE 627   113 COLUMBIA AVENUE
SHEFFIELD, ALABAMA

Jan /11-1930

Dearest Mrs Hobson,

I received your kind letter a few days ago and it is needless for me to say how much it was appreciated – for I am always glad to hear from you even tho there seems to be no more news. Time has forced me to circumstances as I feel as Mr. Hobson – which is terribly hard. Tho I am trying to make the best of things.

As suggested by you I wrote to Mr. McLellan – and had a reply promptly – he must be a wonderful fellow Mrs. Hobson. He wrote the most beautiful letter I have ever read – and when I have more time than I will copy it & send to you. He also enclosed a photo of Hobson in his boat. I'm sure you have one – I shall never forget his kindness to me and am sure you feel the same way. The letter if you mentioned a personal trip to the Island – on the 1st. just wondering if there was anything new learned.

What did you have done with the boat? I just wonder about that

Mrs. Hayes and wished there would be some news by this but as yet I have heard nothing — talking with you. Maybe we are to the dark side — as quickly "live-it," all will be well yet, you know possibilities even now, and so me new encouragement. I know [...] is terrible but Mrs. Hobson, please try to be brave, think of your self — for I know you are weak & have not fully recovered from your recent illness — so try as best you can to stand up.

Hobson had been planning this and other trips for some time. I begged him to tell you what he was trying to do — and he always said "no use to worry her." I tried every way to make him give up these ideas — but he only explained that he had been studying, saving and working to that end since he stopped school — and would never be satisfied until he tried putting it over. And I believe that this happened while he was trying to do that one thing — That was the way I found him — if he determined to do a thing he would be found trying — Of course you, his mother, understood him better than anyone else — tho the short time he was here I think I learned to know and love him almost as you. Hobson one of the sweetest boys I have ever known absolutely clean & a gentleman — in the meaning of the word —

you [...] want it
is not [about] it for its much [...]
than [the] one I had —

Mrs Hobson I really do want
you to return the letters, of course
it just merely the feeling that I
have toward them — otherwise I
wouldn't mind. But some time
at your convenience I would appreciate your mailing them to me.

I, like you cant seem to get
away from this thing, even last night
I dreamed of him returning — its been
on my mind all day. Mrs. Hobson
please write to me as often as you can
for I know you're one that dont
understand — and I hope some day
it will be ours to know each other
better.

Every one I meet that has been
out to Sea, is questioned by me as to
their opinion as to what happened. I dont
know. sometimes I feel that its all a
scheme of some kind then again I dont
know — we dont know that all there
is to be said —

I must stop now — and hoping
to hear from you soon
Love
Anna

My ... thanks for your letter received a few days ago. Am always so glad to hear from you.

We're having some beautiful weather now - is just like real spring time. Speaking of the flowers - I don't know what Bill had reference to - unless its the wild Sweet William, that blooms early in spring - Mrs Hobson we really have a beautiful country - of course as you know this is known as Muscle Shoals. Wilson Dam is out of Sheffield about seven miles and that is a gigantic plant, is more than I'm capable of grasping. Bill went all through the power house + all - of course he was at home there and seemed to understand every phase of the thing - (Ill send you some pictures of it soon). The Tennessee river divides Sheffield and Florence - Then Tuscumbia and Sheffield City limits touch - so you see we have a Tri Cities really one city - and would be a real place if this Muscle Shoal question could ever be settled.

Financial conditions here are very bad and cant see the end yet. We hope this depression ...

Alma's Thoughts 40 Years Later
The Return of Hobson

There was every reason to feel nostalgic that cool, rainy late afternoon of September 25, 1968. Thus far, today had been much the same as many other autumn days long past—a busy one, with the usual demands that come from caring for an invalid mother, appeasing four children (three married), the youngest son in college (and in love), plus keeping tabs on five beautiful grandchildren.

My husband had fallen victim of the dreaded disease of cancer and had died June 4, 1967, approximately two years ago. Since that time, I had sought ways and means of filling this tremendous gap in my life. The only answer seemed to be: Keep busy. I doubled my efforts toward this end, teaching Bible classes, visiting the sick and shut-ins, and at the same time endeavoring to run the home in the same efficient manner as when we were a complete family unit. So as this September autumn day came to a close, I was tired, but at the same time I felt that at least I had kept busy and was perhaps useful to those around me.

Suddenly, jarring me from my sober reflections, the phone rang. Mary Agnes, a secretary from the office of our family business, now being operated entirely by our two sons, said, "Mrs. Biggs, can you run over to the office, please? There is a young man here, asking for you. He says he is Hobson from up North. I checked his license plate, and it's a New Jersey tag. He insists that it's important that he sees and talks with you, having made this long trip for that express purpose. I asked him his name and he only said, 'Mr. Hobson.'"

Did I understand her correctly? My heart began to beat faster and faster, and my mind raced as never before. "Oh! Stop it, I told myself. It can't be. Bill Hobson was lost in that tragic sea accident. He is dead, and everyone knows that. I have all the details regarding this and the final conclusion from the Government Officials that he was lost about five miles out from Brunswick, Georgia. Come to think of it—it was 38 years ago today. The name surely must not be Hobson. But Miss Agnes had just plainly told me that the visitor's name is the same as his. This young man is waiting over there right now to see me. Who can it be? And why, after all these years, would a name which at one time was so meaningful to me—but which was now only a memory tied with a faded yellow ribbon into a bundle of letters—be suddenly reappearing? Trying to calm my shaking knees and trembling hands, I let my mind drift back to the yellowed letters, pictures, and various other contents of a small trunk tucked into the far corner of the attic. I climbed the stairs that led to one of the several dormer rooms, pulled the little trunk into an open space near a window, and with the opening of the lid which was covered with an accumulation of dust, a bright patchwork quilt appeared. This quilt carried me back far beyond the name of Hobson. It was still so beautiful, yet so worn, that it caught my special attention. I picked up the quilt and stood clutching it, holding it close with the feeling that I did not want to let it go. It was so faded and threadbare that apparently its only use was to incite my memory back, back to my early childhood. As I stood there in the semi-darkness, it seemed as if a curtain was drawing and the stage slowly emerged, all set for "My Story." It was not that the picture unfolding was so unusual, but the detailed mental arrangement was mine, sealed until this day to be presented to my children, my grandchildren, my great-grandchildren, and on and on.

I soon realized that the picture being revealed to me was that of Mama, Maud Milstead Dukes, just finishing the last stitch on the very quilt I had rediscovered. She appears worn but gives the impression of the kind of tired feeling one has who is secure and has completed a labor of love. The quilting frames are by her side, supported by four of our slat kitchen chairs. In the picture, she is slowly spreading the quilt out over her lap as if appraising her work of art.

I gathered my thoughts and glanced over the letters that had been tied with the yellow ribbon. Then I rushed to powder my face, comb my hair, make myself presentable, and hurried to the office to meet Mr. Hobson.

It turned out that Mr. Hobson was Bill's younger brother. When going through the house after his mother died, he had found the letters that I had sent Mrs. Hobson after "Bill" was in the accident. My daughter "Becky," myself, and Mr. Hobson went to lunch. We visited for about two hours, going over all the details of what I had known and remembered about Bill. Bill's brother left with a smile saying, "Sheffield is a much more attractive place than I expected."

Sunshine

Next Comes Washington
November of 1931

The 1930's were hard times. The average per capita income for sharecropper families was $28 a year, federal relief checks amounted to $12 a month for white families, $8 a month for black families, and cotton prices in 1932 were five cents a pound. Even our personal problems and pleasures were always secondary to our economic concerns.

I could hardly believe the calendar. It showed November 1930. After all known methods of searching were made in an effort to gain more information into the disappearance of Bill Hobson, it was hard to leave the sea with any a ray of hope. The professionals agreed that more time spent in the effort would be to no avail. They were very clear in their determination that Bill had met a tragic death. We do not know the details of those last few hours or even minutes, and perhaps it is God's providence that we were spared further heartache. I said that I had made feeble efforts to console the family, especially Bill's mother. This was something he "HAD TO DO." I carry no personal guilt, because even though I supported him I did not encourage this venture. He was a strong-willed young man and was determined to take a chance on this adventure. He was a loner.

I said that time is the great healer, and I was praying it would be so in this case. I was taking one step at a time, one day at a time, not knowing what the answer for me would be. It had been almost a year since the accident, and I was still trying to adjust.

September of 1931

Some notes in my private journal records events of the time:

"I am still working at Milam's. I also worked this summer one-half day during June, July, and August for our representative in Congress, Mr. Edward B. Almon. Mr. Almon's residence and summer office is located in his home in Tuscumbia, Alabama, about two miles from Sheffield. I have enjoyed this work break, for it is a real challenge and entirely different. It is politics in action.

The Almon's will be returning to Washington when Congress convenes in December 1931. Then I will again be full time at the Storage Company." (I thought!)

However, fate works in mysterious ways, and to my surprise one morning Mr. Almon came to our establishment to have his car serviced. I looked up, and he was walking toward my desk. Then out of the clear blue sky he said, "Alma how would you like to come with us, (his whole family) to Washington?" Mrs. Curry (Mrs. Almon's sister) and Miss Lottie (Mrs. James A. Ryder, his daughter) had been his office staff for twenty years. They were tired: He had been in Congress from 1913 to 1933.

I was so excited I could hardly talk when I got home. But I finally broke the news to Mama and Papa. Mr. Almon said to Mama, "If you will consider this offer, we will assure you that she will be cared for as one of our own. The salary would be good, even great, and the experience wonderful."

So it was decided that I would be leaving with them in December 1931. I went into my room jumping up and down trying to CONVINCE myself that—

I AM TRULY THE CINDERELLA GIRL
From Tennessee.
Hitched to the Singletree
Ready to pull.

1929, 30, 31, 32, 33
Washington

In the meantime, Herbert Hoover was elected president (1929-1933). Hoover promised us, "I will put a chicken in every pot and an automobile in every garage." They were false promises that did not happen, and the economy only grew worse.

In 1928, Herbert Hoover said, "We in America today are nearer to the final triumph over poverty than ever before in the history of any land." Yet within months, the stock market crashed and the nation spiraled downward into the Depression. Our country became the scapegoat of the Depression, and Hoover was badly defeated in the presidental election of 1932. Hoover was perhaps unfairly painted as a callous and cruel President. He was born in 1874 and died on October 20,1964, at 90 years of age. He lived a long life.

In the midst of America's Great Depression, which began in 1929 with the stock market crash and ended within a decade, everyone was frightened. I was working at Milam's Transfer and Storage Company at the time. I was coming back from the bank and heard some one say, "The Stock Market has crashed!" I didn't really know what the Stock Market was or the consequences of what was happening. I asked, "What is happening?" I was told, "Oh, you would not understand." I didn't understand. But later on everyone understood what had happened to "our world."

On October 24, 1929, "Black Thursday" appeared and the economy collapsed. This was the worst slump in U.S. history and it spread to the entire world. Stocks fell so low that at times during the day, no buyers were available at any price. There were many men who jumped from office windows, committing suicide, because they were unable to pay their debts.

This financial catastrophe could not have had much of an effect on our family, because we had already reached bottom in the earlier big recession. I might say that things were looking a bit brighter for me and mine due to my increased salary. Arlton still made a little spending money from his paper route, and Papa finally got a job at Hardy Motors. Lewis didn't seem to be too concerned, since he was in school. He was a charming young fellow with lots of friends, both girls and boys. He became head cheerleader for Sheffield High football team, and he turned many heads when dressed out in his uniform.

I had counted the days, and almost the hours, before I would be leaving the Tri-Cities. Finally, the day came and departure time arrived. Word got around that I would be leaving, and the people, our church friends, and many others were so anxious to help me. Of course, I had to start from scratch. Mrs. Lydia Hanlin and Mrs. Didi Brenneman from the Church announced, "A Shower for Alma." Presents came from every direction: petticoats, panties, bras, gowns, and things everyone thought I might need. This was the kind of love and hospitality I needed to help me leave with optimism.

The departure day arrived, and Mr. Almon's chauffeur, John, drove up in a big black Buick to my front door. The Almons were already packed and sitting on "go." With goodbye to everyone and promises made to keep in touch, I left with John at the wheel of what seemed to me to be a real "glass slipper" on a quest to find "Prince Charming." We drove over to Tuscumbia and, with last minute instructions, we took off. I remember what Mama said, "Behave yourself, remember who you are, and No Catholic." These were her last words to me as the wheels turned for our destination: Washington, D.C., Capitol of the United States of America!

Franklin D. Roosevelt was elected president in November 1932. In 1933 he proposed a program to bring recovery to business and agriculture and relief to the unemployed and to those in danger of losing farms and homes. Also, he promoted reform, especially through the establishment of the Tennessee Valley Authority. Roosevelt led the nation through the Great Depression and World War ll. During one of his famous "Fireside Chats," he said, "The only thing we have to fear is fear itself."

While still in the grips of hunger pangs and empty pocketbooks in 1933, Roosevelt was our hope, as our new president. He promised, "Peace and prosperity." He created the CCCs (Civilian Conservation Corps) that kept workers busy building scenic highways, parks, and the WPA (Works Project Administration), and as mentioned before the great Tennessee Valley Authority. Attitudes were changing, and we heard hope from what we thought was hopeless. On the highways and byways, people were saying, "We are going to make it," and we did make it. People were actually seen with dinner pails "going to work." The days, the world, had taken on a rosy hue. The song of the day was "Happy Days Are Here Again." Roosevelt was the man of the hour, and America once again was a land of plenty. On June 27, 1936, Roosevelt was nominated for the second time, and then he was nominated again for third and fourth terms.

When it finally sank into my feeble mind that I would actually be going to work in our nation's Capitol, I thought of some of the history lessons I had learned during school years. Will I actually be able to visit at least some of these historical sites? My head began swimming. Maybe I could really stand where our forefathers stood and shaped history and gave us the freedom we enjoy today.

Our majestic monuments are recognized all around the world. The Washington Monument can be seen from almost anywhere in the Capitol city. Then there were the historical monuments located in and around this part of our nation. All the experiences stretching before me created history. The historical information almost dormant in my mind had been achieved from teachers and books; now they would have a concrete place in my experience and intellect.

This now will be shared with you and yours and yours. I am stealing precious time from the short seasons of my life, and I hope you enjoy these experiences to the fullest.

December of 1931

I had just gotten settled in at 1330 L Street N. W. in a brownstone building named The Evangeline, when I approached the desk and asked the clerk for help in locating the Church of Christ. The weekend was fast approaching. As usual, the girl at the desk was not aware of any Church of Christ. She tried to direct me to the Christian Church or the Christian Scientist. I kept turning the pages of the phone book and finally spotted Church of Christ, 14th and Meridian Place, Washington, D. C.

I knew instantly that this was the right place for me. On Sunday morning, bright and early, I caught a bus and asked the driver to stop at this location. The congregation was small. It was Sunday school time and classes were in session. I was immediately greeted with a gracious "Welcome!" I noticed several young girls in the class and was told that they all worked for the government and were from various states.

I immediately felt secure and among friends. I am listing several special names because we became "bosom buddies" far beyond 14th and Meridian. Artelia Humphries from Tennessee; Gwen Humphries (White), Tennessee; Bonnie Lee (Williams), Arkansas; Ruby Lee, Arkansas; Evelyn Moore (Parrish), Tennessee; Alma Dukes (Biggs), Alabama; The Ed Ensors, Washington, D.C.; and the Bingham Family, Washington, D.C.

I attended this congregation faithfully as long as I was in Washington. Later the congregation moved to Alexandria, Virginia. Years later, Lewis my brother and his wife Pearl, attended there.

Mch 16.32

Excerpt Lewis' letter —

We went to church today in Alexandria, the preacher's name is Hugo McCord, rather young, has good delivery speech, — Ulma would be happy in church work there also as they are in almost the same position as Fountain City, trying to get started and build — The services are now being held in the basement of one of the hotels in Alexandria. "Lewis."

— then back to Arlington   *Pearl*

Christmas In Washington

I do not remember much about Christmas in Washington. We were on the go all the time. Christmas there was not like the Christmases in Pocahontas, Tennessee.

This card kept me from being just a little bit homesick.

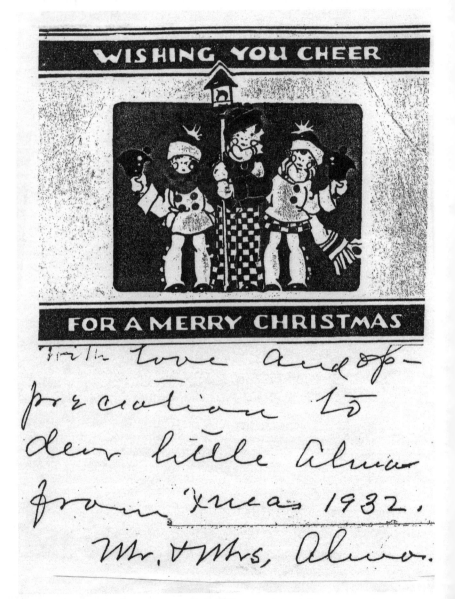

January of 1932-33
Congress Convenes

We will call this the first day of work at the House Office Building. I am living at the Evangeline. I am up early to face the sunrise at the beginning of what could have been "just another day," but everything is so different. I am wondering what they are doing at Milams, so far away in Alabama. The offices here are beautifully furnished. My office joins the big spacious office of Mrs. Curry. They all seem so anxious to help me get adjusted to this "new way" of life. I still had not come down to earth. I felt I was still wearing the proverbial "glass slipper."

The office routine had been the same year after year for the past twenty years. The social invitations that fell from their mailbox seemed almost to be a carbon copy of the ones the year before. Their answer, as they handed the invitations to me, was, "Here, you go. We have been there and done that so many times." So I was wined and dined, entertained and coddled far beyond the "call of duty."

Today, I am trying to stretch my imagination to the fullest extent in order to create a mental picture of a little scared girl from Alabama being caught up in a "social whirl-a-magig."

The first week, I met several young people from various states: Michigan, Wisconsin, Louisiana, and even from right here in D.C. Most of them are here with their representatives and are in offices right down the hall. The next several weeks will be spent learning history. I will try to take advantage every day after I finish my work to walk the several blocks to the Evangeline. I can almost touch the many historical sites along Constitution Avenue and then on down Pennsylvania Avenue. Springtime is near. I have been told about the famous Cherry Trees along the Tidal Basin. Words fail me; it is just something to be experienced.

As I walk along, I am suddenly right in the middle of Washington's shopping district. Even though I do not feel financially secure enough to do much shopping, I still like to look and look. Lerner's store seems to be a drawing card. Lerner's caters to juniors and small sizes. That's me, I only weigh 98 pounds. The big stores are also in this area where the politically affluent seem to find merchandise to their liking. These stores are Hechts' and I can't forget Garfinkles. My sister-in-law, Pearl, saw Mrs. Coolidge shopping there for the "just right" corset.

One of the first young men I met on a social basis was Terry McPhearson from Louisiana. We seemed to enjoy some of the same "handiwork's of God and man," so we joined hands and interests and took advantage of the opportunities offered. Terry was a charming young fellow, full of life and fun. When he said, "Go," I was ready.

January of 1932
The White House

Since arriving in Washington, I did not seem to have much time for social activities. However, as I recall, I was not a wallflower, and I said, "Let's go, this time."

On January 26, 1932, an invitation was delivered to the office, an invitation to a reception at the White House. This reception was for all the representatives of the United States. As promised, Mr. Almon handed the beautifully engraved envelope to me. I was so excited, for I knew this was one of the most coveted parties of the year. Of course, my first thought was, "What shall I wear?" Mrs. Almon and Mrs. Curry helped me select the dress of the night. It was floor length of white chiffon, and sleeveless. Then they said, "Long white gloves are a must."

The gloves reached from my shoulders to my wrist. I just had to look my best, remember who I was, and be appreciative of all favors both great and small.

When I showed the invitation to Terry, he said, "Let's go together!"

We planned for him to be my escort, if he could manage to contain his excitement. He was a very chubby, short guy and had a hard time finding a tuxedo that said, "One size fits all." His shoes were like mirrors, and his tails touched the floor. But he had a grin from ear to ear. So we went, a little girl from the hills of Tennessee and Alabama and a young fellow from the Bayou country of Louisiana.

It was required that we have the correct credentials ready to show. I was afraid to trust Terry, so I tucked them inside my gloves for safekeeping. As we passed through a series of doors, we were finally there. Another big door opened, and a booming announcement sounded forth:

Congressman and Mrs. Ed. B. Almon
Eighth District of Alabama
Tuscumbia, Alabama

The long reception line was headed by none other than the President of the United States.

Imagine me, in line to be presented to the President of the United States of America. Terry was about as nervous as I, and he came away missing a few fingernails. I have often wondered what Mr. Almon's co-workers thought. Perhaps he has found the fountain of youth, and could he have acquired a new young wife? Oh! Well.

The White House was clean and shining for a visit from and with all of us. We had come home to a welcome greeting. I asked myself, "Who owns this beautiful building anyway?" We the People do. The House is so beautiful, especially during times like Christmas.

Everyone had a big laugh over the fraudulent couple moving slowly down the line. I thought I heard someone say, "Somebody goofed." But this will be long remembered by two very young people known as Terry McPhearson of Louisiana and Alma Dukes of Alabama, representing the Bayou and the red clay of Tennessee-Alabama. We had come to town.

Our Admittance to the White House

The White House

Admit at East Gate

NOT TRANSFERABLE

January 26, 1932

DISPLAY ON WIND SHIELD OF CAR

THE WHITE HOUSE

February 4, 1932
Strayer College Commencement

The next invitation came out of the clear blue. It was not one of the political black tie events but a night long to be remembered as mingling with the rank and file.

Fred Hall and I had become very good friends, and with a smile on his face he handed me the card which had to be presented at the door of the Grand Ball Room at the Mayflower Hotel. Of course, I had heard of the beauty and grandeur of the Mayflower, and I would have appreciated just a peep inside the door. That alone would have been a great treat for me. Yet, we were actually going to be guests of the gala affair on February 4, 1932 at 7:15 P.M.

Since neither of us danced, we wondered how we could gracefully stumble over the floor that was so highly polished that one step might have been our last.

Again, what would we wear? However, since these people were mostly strangers to us, it really didn't matter. So I donned my white chiffon and my long gloves, and I slipped on my "glass slippers" again, and was ready to go.

Fred had graciously remembered to send me a beautiful orchid corsage, and it looked great on the white chiffon. He, like Terry, had to make the rounds for a tuxedo his size. He was a charming, handsome young fellow, and I was sure we made a fetching pair.

I hope that some day, far down the line, while visiting Washington, my grandchildren and great-grandchildren will say, "Oh! Look! The Mayflower. Our grandma danced a "jig" in their ballroom. Do you really believe she did? I do."

This entire evening was right out of the storybook CINDERELLA! Thank you, Fred, wherever you are, and I hope you are still dancing your nights away. You are a great guy.

RENAISSANCE.
MAYFLOWER HOTEL
WASHINGTON, DC

1127 Connecticut Avenue NW
Washington, DC 20036
USA
Phone: 1-202-347-3000
Fax: 1-202-776-9182
Toll Free: 800-228-7697

Washington DC's largest luxury hotel, this National Landmark hotel is a member to Historical America and is located in the heart of Washington's business district. We are conveniently located just four block from the White House, minutes away from Smithsonian museums and National Monuments, and just steps away from the city's finest restaurants and shopping. In addition, there are three metro subway lines within two blocks offering our guests easy access to all points of the nation's capital.

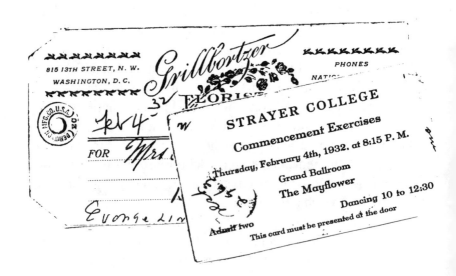

February 21, 1932
Blossom Time Operetta And Easter Matinee

*There are silver ships and there are golden ships,
But the best ships are friendships.*

Lois McKean and I had become good friends in the short time we had been in Washington. Lois was a beautiful blond from a small town in Northern Michigan, just about as "Yankee" as they come. When her family learned that she had taken up with a girl of the deep South, they were horrified. They cautioned her to be careful of the southern drawl. They said, "Please don't acquire a taste for soul food, particularly cornbread and turnip greens." I really don't think any of my traditional ways rubbed off on her, and I know I maintained my identity.

We attended many shows, games, and special events together. We really looked forward with excitement to the world-acclaimed operetta, Blossom Time. We decided we would attend the matinee on February 21, 1932, because it was less expensive than the evening performance. This production would be on the stage of the famous Shubert-Belasco Theatre.

Shubert-Belasco Theatre
Direction Messrs. Lee and J. J. Shubert
L. Stoddard Taylor, Manager
Twenty-seventh Season

Beginning Sunday, February 21, 1932
Matinees Thursday and Saturday

The World-Acclaimed Operetta 25th

"BLOSSOM TIME"

CAST
(In the order of their appearance)

Kupelweiser ... Donnelly
Vogl ...
Von Schwind ...
Binder ... Harry Rabke
Erkman ... vrence Wells
Domeyer ... Edgar Hunt
Greta ... n Selwood
Bella Bru... ACT I ... an Gaige
Co... Greta, Kupelweiser, Von Schwind, Vogl ... Leonard
 and Chorus ... Justice
Opening ... Mitzi, Fritzi, Kitzi, Vogl, Kupelweiser, Bella Bruna ... Powers
Melody Triste ... Schober, Schubert, Vogl, Violinist ... ertora
Three Little Maids ... Schober, Schubert ... ilbert
Serenade ... Von Schwind and Mitzi ... eece
My Springtime Thou Art ... Kupelweiser, Von Schubert ... ner
 Ensemble ... er
Song of Love ... ACT II ... n
Finale ... Schubert, Violinist and Mitzi
Moment Musicale ... Schober, Blader, Erkman, Kitzi ... Fritzi, Kitzi and Schober
Love Is a Riddle ... Bella Bruna and Schober
Let Me Awake ... Mitzi and Schober
Tell Me, Daisy ... Ever Fills the Heart, Schubert and Schober
Only One Love ... ACT III ... Greta
Finale ... Bella Bruna, Vogl, Von Schwind
Opening ... and Kupelweiser
Keep It Dark ... Mitzi, Fritzi, Kitzi, Vogl, Greta, Vogl
Lonely Heart ... Schober, Schubert
Finale ... Ensemble
ACT 1. Prater Park in Vienna. An afternoon in May, 1826.
ACT 2. Drawing Room in the House of Franz. Three months later.
(Intermezzo Serenade, Schubert-Romberg) Two months later.
ACT 3. Franz Schubert's Lodgings. Shoes by Weldy, of Paris, and executed by La Ray Boot Shop.
Costumes designed by Mode Costume Company. Fred W. Jordan
Business Manager ... Harold Hevia
Company Manager ... Walter Wahl
Stage Manager

STIEFF PIANOS used exclusively in this Theatre

Gaiety and lightness of plot distinguished the Blosson Time Operetta. The costumes were beautiful, and the lighting effects were unbelievable. Though we were not of the polished opera set, and the overall story begged to be understood, we appreciated the music, and the costumes will long be remembered. The afternoon at the Shubert-Belasco Theatre, which was their 27th season of performance, was one of the highlights of my stay in Washington D.C.

March 27, 1932
Easter Sunrise Service

Lois and I decided we would make ourselves get out of that bed and attend the Easter Sunrise Service at the Garden Theatre at 7:30 A.M. on March 27, 1932. This was not easy, but we did it. We both had new outfits for Easter. It was really chilly, but the weather cooperated as far as rain was concerned.

I had shopped several times after work and finally found a white linen three-piece suit. It was a fit, and I really liked it. So Lerners made one more sale just before closing time. I believe Lois decided on a baby blue dress that was just right, for it matched her eyes. She was a natural gorgeous blond. I had a hard time always being a few steps behind her. "Oh, well," Mama always said, "If you act as good as you look, you will be alright." "I'll try," I always said. The service was inspirational, and, of course, we enjoyed the Army Band. Walter Reed's grounds were overflowing. The entire audience was asked to stand while the U.S. Band and Chorus sang, "Christ The Lord Is Risen Today."

After the service was over, I called a taxi to drive me several miles over to 14th and Meridian Place, and attended the service there. Then we all met and had lunch together; afterward, each went their own way. I am sure Lois made it home all right. It had been a beautiful day, and I prayed that many more Easters would come for all of us.

Easter Sunrise Service

Garden Amphitheater

7:30 A. M.

WALTER REED GENERAL HOSPITAL

Living Cross

Army Medical Center

Colonel Albert E. Truby, M. C., U. S. Army
Commanding

Chaplain R. Earl Boyd, U. S. Army
Chaplain

Washington, D. C., March 27, 1932

March 29, 1932
Monticello

Early on the morning of March 29th, 1932, Terry and I drove over to Monticello. This estate is located near Charlottesville, Virginia. This is the home of Thomas Jefferson, the third president of the United States. Thomas Jefferson was born in 1763 and died July 4, 1826. He is buried on this estate. Monticello means little mountain. The mansion was planned by President Jefferson, and all the material used was prepared right on the grounds. The estate is made up of many houses and, during his day, was practically an independent community behind its serpentine walls.

The U.S. Government gained control of the estate in 1923. It is now a national shrine for the enduring inspiration of the American people. President Jefferson's ideas of civil liberty, religious tolerance, and universal education were left for our children and their children. It was a beautiful day for us.

The many historical trips were such a pleasure and were also very educational. I was glad to have this opportunity. This, plus the many friends who came my way, made my tenure in Washington a great part of my life.

April 10, 1932
Barbara Fritchie House

Fred Hall and I made another daylong trip to historic Frederick, Maryland, when we visited the Barbara Fritchie House. John Greenleaf Whittier wrote a poem entitled "Barbara Fritchie," in her honor. Barbara was the aged woman who picked up our battered flag during the Civil War. Stonewall Jackson led the Confederates through this little town. So many interesting tid-bits of our history slip by us when we are in school. It is good to have a renewal course; don't you think?

I have this day visited MONTICELLO, the home of Thomas Jefferson, whose Ideals of Civil Liberty, Religious Tolerance, and Universal Education are our priceless heritage.

Toward the purchase of MONTICELLO and its upkeep, as a National Shrine for the enduring inspiration of the American people, I contribute the sum of

Date Mch 29 1932 $ 1.00

A 24393 Name _____

Address _____

AUTOGRAPHIC SYSTEMS
HAMILTON, OHIO

"THOMAS JEFFERSON MEMORIAL FOUNDATION,
National Headquarters—115 Broadway, New York City."

Welcome to Historic Frederick
VISIT HER SHRINES: Apr 16 1932

CHIEF JUSTICE TANEY HOUSE   BARBARA FRITCHIE HOUSE

VISIT THE WINE CELLAR
SEE THE SLAVE QUARTERS

"SEE THE FLAG
SHE WAVED"

April 1932 —

Sheffield Ala
April 1st 1932

Dearest Alma

I received your card and am so glad to know you thought of me. You were the only one to send me anything. I am so glad that you are having a pleasant time and seeing so much and making good with your work. Nothing new here only Emma and Maud went a fishing yesterday eve. only caught about 6. Well Alma I am sending you one of my pictures I had made this A.M. I was 65. Hope you like it. Well as your mother keeps you posted on the news I will quit.

Oodles of Love   Your Grand Pa
S. A. Milstead

S. A. Milstead (Grand Pa)

April 20, 1932
Washington Tidal Basin

The cherry trees that grow around the tidal basin in Washington and bloom in the Spring each year were given to the United States by the Government of Japan. This happened during the presidential term of President Taft. Mrs. Taft accepted this gracious gift. The original gift was made in May, 1912. 3,000 trees were planted and provided two miles of unbroken beauty. The basin is truly one of the most beautiful spots of our Capitol, especially when the trees are in bloom.

Cherry blossoms outline the Tidal Basin
With heavenly pink froth.
Joggers liberated from their cubicles
Stretch pale legs in the midday sun.
Tour buses parade up Constitution Avenue.
It is April in the Capitol. A sight to behold.

Friends of Washington Days

Alma and Terry

Fred, Elizabeth, Alma, and Terry on a Sunday afternoon stroll through the Tidal Basin. The cherry trees were in their prime.

Fred, Liz, Alma, and Terry

May 1, 1932
Alma's Visit To The Metropolitan Baptist Church

Terry M. McPherson invited me to go to the Metropolitan Baptist Church for an evening service on May 1, 1932. Terry was the First Vice President of the Student Union. The Student Union's motto for 1932 was, "The grass withereth, the flower fadeth, but the Word of our Lord shall stand forever."

The "Welcome" on their church bulletin was a beautiful invitation to all. The thought was to all who need a church home, who mourn and need comfort, to all who are friendless and want friendship, to those who are lonely and need companionship, to all who pray, and to all who do not but aught, to all who sin and need a Savior, and to whomsoever will: this church opens wide the door and makes free a place, and in the name of Jesus the Lord says, "Welcome!"

May 11, 1932
Frank Loomis

During the regular workday, I had become friendly with Frank Loomis, whose home was in Wisconsin. His representative from the State of Wisconsin employed him. He teased me about my slow Southern way of doing everything, and of course I came back with, "All you know is how to make more and better cheese." We would often go places together after the workday was over. He was a devout Christian Scientist, and he practically dragged me to one of their services. I learned that they call their Teacher or Preacher their Reader. Frank had climbed up their religious ladder to become a Reader.

He invited me to go with him on Wednesday evening, May 11, to a program, the Cantata "Washington" by Massed Chorus at Constitution Hall. Captain Taylor Branson was conductor of the Marine Band. This was a beautiful tribute to George Washington. We both enjoyed the evening as well as other times and places we visited.

Frank Loomis and Alma
Right front, on a visit

May 22, 1932
A Romantic Decision

Now, you all listen, for this is a true romantic story. I did not make it up. His name was Bob McClellan, born and reared in Washington, D. C.

Soon after my arrival in Washington in February, 1932, I met Bob McClellan, who was then a young struggling artist. Much of his time was spent on the Hill, trying to persuade the right people that his talent should be used. He was particularly talented in postage stamp designs. Mrs. Roosevelt became interested in the stamp world and encouraged Bob. There was to be an upcoming exhibition where artists would display their work. One advertisement read, "Plans are being perfected for a great international stamp exposition to be held in Washington D.C. in October or November." Bob's work is similar to the Whistler's Mother stamp of some time ago. He was very, very good.

If you asked me to describe Bob, I would be at a loss for adjectives, but here goes. He was tall, dark, charming, neat, smart, mannerly, and then some. He was just as handsome as can be. What else can I say? He almost swept me off my feet.

We spent much time together, but I was surprised at what happened on the night of May 22, 1932. He suggested that we drive out to a quaint small restaurant just over the Maryland line. I agreed that the drive should be nice and maybe not too much traffic.

We left home fairly early and drove out of D.C. toward the state line. After some time, I was beginning to feel that he had lost the road map. He said, "We are almost there. It is just around the corner." We parked in front of a small cottage type house. When he started fumbling in his pocket nervously, I asked, "What is the matter?" Then it happened! He held up a small white box, like a ring box. "Please, open this," he said. I was flabbergasted, and then my world started spinning round and round, but all I could think of was my mother's request as I left her doorstep. She said, "Remember who you are, and No Catholic." And I thought, "Here I am, sitting by the most handsome man I have ever seen, and he is saying, 'Here, take this ring! Marry me now, tonight, right here.'" But he was

Catholic. Of course, he said that made no difference to him, because he was not a good Catholic. The sound in my ears became louder and louder. No Catholic! No Catholic! No Catholic! I was trying to find an acceptable answer for him, but all I could do was cry. Then I said, "I am sorry." The answer finally came, "I can't!"

From that time on, we were together less and less frequently. I advised him, "Find a sweet Catholic girl who thinks the same way you do. Marry and have a nice family. Your family will be happy, and you will be too, I hope. Work hard on your stamp paintings, and win at the exhibition in the mall."

Sometime later, I heard Bob had found the right girl, married her, and had a beautiful family. I have kept this story until now, so that you will understand it is sometimes necessary to just say, "No." My life went on, and the tug of the singletree pulled tense as the loads became heavier and heavier.

Bob McClellan

May of 1932
Traditional Tourist

I soon became a traditional tourist again. Time flies, and a summer recess would quickly be coming to all who worked in Washington. I tried to use the short time to visit as many historic sights as possible. It seemed like cramming for an exam.

Several of my co-workers took a little time off and visited as many interesting spots as could be crowded in. Their first stop was Washington's birthplace, Wakefield. Some went to Mount Vernon, Washington's home. Later they visited Washington's memorial at Alexandra, Virginia.

On May 25th, 1932, a memorial exercise was presented in honor of three Senators and sixteen Representatives who had died between March 1, 1931, and April 31, 1932. The Honorable William B. Bankhead from our own state of Alabama gave the main address. The Navy Band preformed, and the chaplain read scripture. The entire program was excellently and seriously performed.

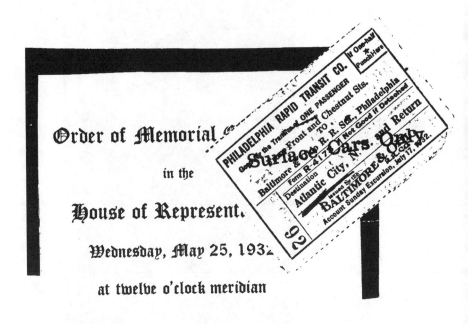

Places We Visited In May 1932

Wakefield, birthplace of Washington

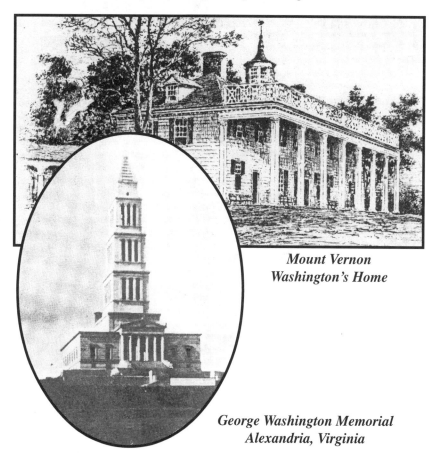

*Mount Vernon
Washington's Home*

*George Washington Memorial
Alexandria, Virginia*

1932
Back at Home

The Congress recessed in August of 1932. That was homecoming time for me. I was so excited, because I guess I was just a bit homesick, as this was my first time away from home. It was so good to be back in Alabama with my family and friends. I would work for Mr. Almon during the summertime.

Financially, things were running smoothly. The Dukes were still eating the same food, not because they had to but because that was their way of life, and mine, too. My birthday came up October 26. The only Washington friend who seemed to remember was Terry. He telegraphed me and even said he was anxiously awaiting my return to Washington. That was nice.

After our summer in Alabama, it was time to make the trip back to Washington. Through the Smokies, up the East Coast, and on and on, until finally we reached the city limits of our Capitol, Washington, D.C.

The Almons went far beyond the call of duty in taking care of me. They are of the old school in everything, and that is how my life is geared. Thank you is so inadequate, but thank you so very much.

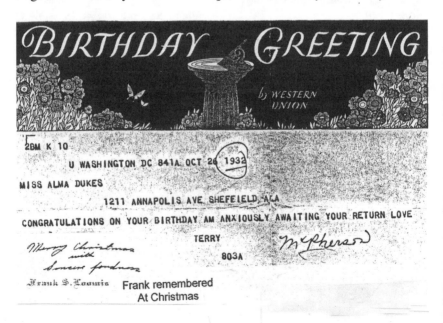

Frank remembered At Christmas

February 6, 1933
Memorial Service Of The Late Calvin Coolidge

On February 6, 1933, the Congress of the United States issued invitations to the Memorial Service for the late President Calvin Coolidge.

My seat was Number 32, Row C, and Gallery 10. Of course this invitation was sent to Mr. Almon, and he so graciously handed it to me. Thank you, again!

March 4, 1933
Roosevelt Inauguration

On March 4, 1933, I was presented a press quest card Number 1190, which stated: "The bearer to Platform B, Outside of and on the House side, but not to the Capitol Building."

An Invitation to: Inauguration Ceremonies Of Franklin D. Roosevelt

This was a great experience for me, especially since I had been an admirer of Mr. Roosevelt for many years.

SEVENTY-SECOND CONGRESS

EDWARD B. ALMON, ALA., CHAIRMAN
BOLIVAR E. KEMP, LA.
LINDSAY C. WARREN, N. C.
WILBURN CARTWRIGHT, OKLA.
O. H. CROSS, TEX.
CLAUDE A. FULLER, ARK.
WILLIAM M. WHITTINGTON, MISS.
WRIGHT PATMAN, TEX.
ROBERT RAMSPECK, GA.
CLAUDE V. PARSONS, ILL.
EUGENE B. CROWE, IND.
CHARLES H. MARTIN, OREG.

CASSIUS C. DOWELL, IOWA
CHARLES BRAND, OHIO
JOE J. MANLOVE, MO.
DON B. COLTON, UTAH
JOHN M. NELSON, WIS.
ROBERT H. CLANCY, MICH.
CONRAD G. SELVIG, MINN.
C. MURRAY TURPIN, PA.
J. ROLAND KINZER, PA.

CHARLOTTE R. CURRY, CLERK

House of Representatives U.S.
COMMITTEE ON ROADS
Washington, D. C.

March 4, 1933.

To Whom It May Concern:

    This will be presented by my secretary, Miss Alma Dukes, and I will appreciate any courtesies you may extend her and her friends. They are reliable in every way.

    Thanking you in advance, I am

        Yours very truly,

        Ed B Almon
        M.C.   Alabama.

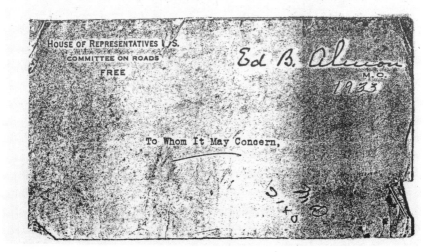

July 15, 1933
A Taste of Mexican Food

One evening, several of us thought it would be nice to eat some Mexican food. There was a popular Mexican Café just down the street from the office. It advertised, "A bit of Old Mexico in the

Capitol." I was so hungry for some of Mama's cooking, but I knew I would have to settle for this: "So, pass me the chili beans, please."

July 18, 1932 was the last day I lived at the Evangeline. After recess at home, I returned to Washington in December of 1933. My friend, Lois, and I had thought about finding a room together. We looked at many of the places, and we finally decided to check out a room on A street near the office buildings.

Miss Coffee answered our knock on the front door. She was a tall, gray-haired, business-like woman who posted her house rules and regulations up front: Curfew at 10 P.M. and No Male Visitors. Our bed was hidden in a section of the wall and was called a Murphy Bed. There was not much conversation because there was not much to be talked about: The price was right, and the location was ideal. So we signed Miss Coffee's contract and assured her that we would abide by her rules. The rules were a rigid collection of "Do's and Don'ts."

This living arrangement proved to be fine, and we shared these close living quarters until I had to come home. We were good friends, and we made many pleasant memories to share with others. Miss Coffee finally accepted us as "what you see is what you get."

Perhaps I have neglected to mention many places and times enjoyed, but in this account I am trying to make you aware of my busy time in D.C. Remember, I had a job from 9 A.M. till 4 P.M. each day.

I was excited when the day came for the inauguration of Franklin D. Roosevelt. This was a great day in history for us.

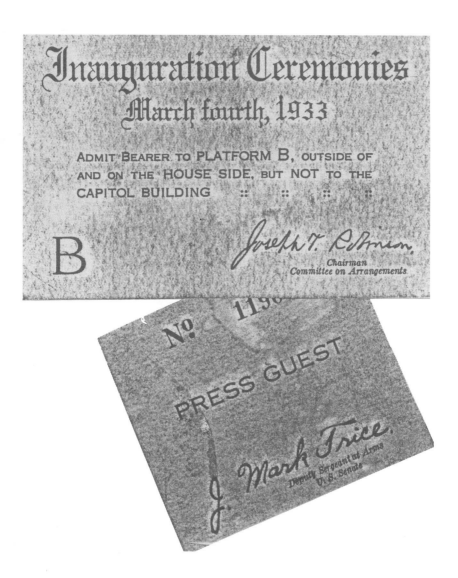

Alma & Lois, Roommates

Lois and Miss Coffee

Alma and Miss Coffee Homeowner

Mr. Almon Dies

On Thursday, June 22, 1933, Mr. Almon died of a massive heart attack at his hotel home in Washington, D.C. He was 73. This was a heart breaking blow for all of us who were part of his active life, and especially for me, for he had transformed me from a shy, poverty-stricken young girl to a Cinderella who wore glass slippers and dreamed big dreams. I would be leaving Washington the next day, going home to Alabama. The greatest tug at my heartstrings would be leaving my special Washington friends.

As I tried to say, Good-bye, I felt my world come crashing down around my shoulders. Of all the words I had written on paper, as a secretary to a wonderful man—a Representative sent to Congress by his friends—goodbyes cramped all the facets of my life and created a dead weight in my heart. Good-bye hurts so much that I will just wave goodbye to you.

Friday at 3:30, June 23, 1933, Mr. Almon's body was placed on a train, and he left his beloved Washington for the very last time. On June 24, his body arrived at his home, 201 Almon Avenue, Tuscumbia, Alabama. He remained in State until time for the funeral service at the First Methodist church at 5 P.M. Burial followed at Oakwood cemetery in Tuscumbia, Alabama.

REPRESENTATIVE ALMON,
—Harris-Ewing Photo

He Died On the Heights

The following tribute is taken from an article in our own local *Times* newspaper, and it is so fitly said. I am borrowing this information for my children, and my grandchildren, and all will understand why I feel close and appreciative of this great man. He apparently finished his course and made our own area aware of just what one dedicated person can accomplish.

He Died On The Heights

This District and the Tennessee Valley are paying their last tribute to their late Congressman, Ed. B. Almon. The death of no man in this Valley, in this generation, has been so deeply mourned by so many people as that of Congressman Almon. Men and women by hundreds feel that they have lost not only a public servant who was always true to his trust, but a friend who would do whatever he possibly could to help them in any way in his official capacity as their representative in Washington.

The death of Congressman Almon at this time is peculiarly poignant;—he did not live to see the fruition of his work and his hopes for the Muscle Shoals District. Yet, to his family and to his constituents, there is this deeply comforting thought;—that he passed away when his life had reached its climax. After all, there is something glorious in this, Henry W. Grady, one of the finest tongues and noblest hearts that the South has ever produced died a few days after his immortal address in Boston on the "new South." That address was the pinnacle of his career. If he had lived there would have been an anti-climax in his life; as it was, he died on the heights. It has been very much the same with Judge Almon. He died at the height of his career, leaving behind him accomplishments that will bring greater and greater benefits to the people as the years go by.

If he had lived, the people of this District would have sent him back to Congress continuously until the end. They felt a deep gratitude for the years of labor he had put in at Washington for his District and they probably would have given no consideration to anyone who might have opposed him for re-election. And yet, it would have been anti-climax. Nothing he could have accomplished could ever have equalled what he had done in the decade and a half previous to the visit of President Roosevelt here and the subsequent enactment into law by Congress of Muscle Shoals legislation, for which Judge Almon had worked tirelessly year after year and through one Congressional term after another, against odds that would have discouraged any man. But he never became discouraged. He never gave up. During the Harding, Coolidge and Hoover Administrations, with overwhelming odds against him and against his District, he kept right on working and striving; making one effort after another along one line after another, in order to bring into reality the hopes of his constituents for the full use of the rich resources of this Valley for the benefit of the people. When the Muscle Shoals Bill was passed, Judge Almon's life work was done. Just before he returned to Congress for the last time, he said to the writer that he would be satisfied to live long enough to see the big job of his life completed, by enactment of the Muscle Shoals Bill by Congress and its signing by the President.

In paying this last tribute to him, we feel that the people of this District should secure all of the speeches that Judge Almon made on Muscle Shoals during his long career in Congress, and that these should be bound and put into circulation as a memorial of one of the most consistent, continued efforts for a truly great objective that has ever been made in this Country. It is not going too far to say that Congressman Almon did more for his District in this effort than any other Congressman in Alabama has ever accomplished for his District. The present generation and generations to come will reap, increasingly, the rewards of his faithful work. He fought a hard fight; kept the faith and he won a great victory. He leaves to us an untarnished name whose brightness is enhanced because he died on the heights immediately after the winning of the long, hard fight he had made for his people in a great cause.

The people will remember Judge Almon; his name is deeply engraved on the Tennessee Valley. He reflected its spirit and its hopes; he gave himself to it completely; he lived nobly and he died in a noble cause of service.

The tribute being paid to him now is from the hearts of the people who loved him and by whom he cannot be forgotten.

Leaving Washington

We all left Washington with bowed heads and heavy hearts. June 1933 was a bittersweet date. What the future held for me would soon be revealed. Would I get to keep the glass slippers?

June 24, 1933	Saturday	Mr. Almon's Funeral
June 25	Sunday	Home
June 26	Monday	TVA
June 24, 25, 26,		Home in Sheffield, Alabama

Yes, my wonderful experience came to a sad abrupt end. The Representative for the Eighth District of Alabama changed overnight. The fruit basket turned over, and Mr. Carmichael of Tuscumbia filled the vacancy. His office personnel quickly claimed their respective positions. This is when it seems I heard a small voice saying, "Don't worry. A job is waiting for you at your own home, at Wilson Dam."

The Norris Bill which Mr. Almon so untiringly guided through the political ups and downs of Congress—day by day, month by month and even through years of hopes and dreams—was finally approved and signed by President Roosevelt. This, in my opinion, was the departing heritage that Mr. Almon left for his people. Due to that heritage, I became one of the very first employees of TVA.

Yes, it seemed I was trying very hard to pick up the pieces, redeem the time, and again wear the fairyland slippers. My path really took a turn, and at this point it seemed a door opened with opportunities far beyond my dreams. I am trying to paint a word picture of my life just for you. It seemed that all I needed was encouragement, for someone to say, "It's worth the effort." Thank you, especially thank you my grandchildren, for those words, "You can do it."

Yes, I visited the "johnny" in the cold weather. Yes, I walked to school in rain and in snow. Yes, I colored the white blocks of "oleo" with a package of yellow something and transformed it into almost real butter. I lived through the make-do years and learned lessons of economy and other ways and means to survive two depressions. Yet, I was just a normal girl living a normal life as it was presented to me.

In looking back, it seems that "memories turned into memoirs" creates a big business. Maybe someone knew that my story deserves space on the shelf to be read by generations to come. As I crawled out of my own bed this morning, I thought, "I am the luckiest girl in the whole world." Someday, maybe I will stop long enough to call my children, their families, and even the great ones to my knee and tell them about my struggles and encourage them to have the determination not to give up but to keep the chains of the singletree pulling the load.

Knoxville Days

A Job With TVA

Monday morning, June 26, 1933, I was up bright and early and made my way out to Wilson Dam to claim my new job with TVA. I was immediately introduced to Mr. Lillienthal. He had just arrived from up East, I think, to become manager of the Wilson Dam office. Mr. Lillienthal would be my boss.

My job description seemed fairly simple, that is if one could count. He said, "We are counting nuts and bolts and similar small items that add up to a tremendous inventory. Since TVA is newly created, each item must be counted, piece by piece, in order to be transferred from the United States Engineering Department to TVA." I was happy with my lowly position of counting, recounting, and packing these small items.

My family called Sheffield home, and I had come back to home base in order to work. This five-day a week job became very dull, but it was my job and my home, and I wanted to be with my family. Then one day I was called into the inner office to answer a phone call. The voice came through strongly, and I immediately knew that I was being transferred from Wilson Dam to Knoxville, Tennessee.

The TVA Bill stated clearly that the main office would be located at Wilson Dam, Alabama. But I soon understood that "Politics" had entered the picture, and TVA was laying foundations for the office to be permanently located at Knoxville. This did happen later.

The person who called was Miss Irene McCauley who had recently been appointed Director of Personnel. She was very firm in her demand that I should make this move without protest. But I immediately tried to explain why I wanted to stay at Muscle Shoals.

She said, "Miss Dukes, if you want to work for TVA, you must report to the Knoxville office immediately."

Of course, this was the end of that, so I just started packing, actually repacking from my Washington move. The next morning, I boarded the train for Knoxville, Tennessee.

TVA In 1933

Maybe you youngsters don't really know what TVA is or how it has benefited us. Of course, TVA is an abbreviation for Tennessee Valley Authority. It was created for a threefold purpose: to control flooding, to produce electricity, and to make the rivers easy to navigate for shipping.

The first dam, which was Wilson Dam at Muscle Shoals, Alabama, was constructed during World War I and is located in Northwest Muscle Shoals, Alabama. There is a succession of rapids in the Tennessee River at that point. The government developed enormous waterpower at this site. Wilson Dam was finished in 1925. It is a monumental structure that was built from concrete under the supervision of the U.S. Engineering Department. This development includes the entire Tennessee River Valley system.

After the war, the project was virtually forgotten and was at a partial standstill under the oversight of the Engineering Department. However, on May 18, 1933, the TVA bill was passed into law by Congress and took effect immediately. The bill emphatically stated that the principle office would be Muscle Shoals, Alabama. This never happened, and I suppose politics got its way, and the home office is still located in Knoxville, Tennessee.

The bill called for the development of the Tennessee River and its tributaries in the interest of navigation, and for the development of electrical power. Also, the development of new fertilizers and other plant foods have been of great benefit to our way of life. The TVA system of dams takes its place among the major engineering projects in world history. This great agency has been a blessing to the whole world and especially the southern part of our country, which includes our area. We now enjoy electric push-button everything.

Original funds for the project amounted to $260,000,000. A board of three directors administer the activities of TVA. As I told you previously, Mr. Almon will always be remembered as one who would not give up on the project. He kept pushing and pushing until TVA finally happened. And I had the honor of being one of the very first office employees of TVA.

August 1, 1933

I arrived by train at the station in Knoxville around noon on August 1, 1933. As we pulled into Knoxville, I didn't know whether to laugh or cry. Then I realized that a big door of opportunity had just opened for me. Yes, I was lonely, but I decided to take one step at a time.

At the station with my bags of worldly goods piled around me, I motioned for a taxi, and one immediately stopped and began loading my belongings.

"Where to, lady?"

"To the new Sprankle Building, please."

"Lots of people going up there. Many folks going and coming."

He was so friendly, I thought, maybe this is not so bad after all. In a few minutes, the cab stopped and my things were unloaded on the sidewalk in the front of the Sprankle Building.

I climbed the big open stairs to the second floor, stopped to get my breath, and noticed a sign, that read, "Typing Pool." As I opened the door, I stood awed at the big office where many people were typing. In just a few minutes, I was overwhelmed when three or four girls greeted me. "Who are these people?" I asked myself. Then I recognized them as friends from my days in Washington. They were happy to leave their old government jobs and start new careers with TVA. They immediately said, "We have a large apartment at Sterchi's."

Already I was feeling better about everything. I had enjoyed my ride on the train, which was equipped with a diner and beds in the Pullman that had been stacked to the ceiling of the sleeper car. I felt good about my job, and these special friends made me feel that this experience with TVA was going to be great, almost like being home.

The young ladies lived at Sterchi apartments. Artelia, was the "mother hen." She was a little older and much much wiser than the other four.

The next morning I reported for work and was told I would be in the typing pool for a few days. I was glad the promise was for only a few days. This pool was under the supervision of a Miss Churchill. I had heard through the gossip channel that she was homosexual.

Well, that scared me to death. I was told she maintained a home in Washington for her counterpart. Anyway, she was a very large masculine type person, and I believed every word I was told.

As promised, I was soon assigned a position in the Purchasing Department. Mr. McGarity was head of this department, and he was a very nice person. His secretary was Miss Alice Shea. I came next in line, and I immediately responded whenever the intercom called, "Miss Dukes."

The Smoky Mountains

Working for TVA in the early years called for dedication and loyalty. It was a tedious job and demanded long hours of almost manual labor, sunup to sundown. I suppose I was considered a loyal employee, as I tried to follow all the rules.

Up until this time, my life in Knoxville had seemed to be harnessed to chariots of time and consumed with work, work, work, with no end in sight. Every day was just another day of the same.

I thought I was coming down with something called the flu, but it turned out that I was only home sick and over worked. Mr. McGarity noticed the slow pace I had fallen into and called me into his office.

"Alma, what is your trouble?" he asked.

"I don't really know." I answered.

"I know you are just worn to a frazzle, and we can fix that. I have broad shoulders, and if a good cry would help, I'm here. But go home and rest, take as long as you need, and come back a new person. Forget TVA."

I did as he advised, and after about a month I was back carrying my load, and fully fit for the task ahead. New friends came my way, and I felt that I was entering a new way of life.

I have told you all of this so that you will understand that I was vulnerable and ready for some new diversion, but I surely could not have seen the new turn about to occur in my life that would affect me for the duration.

Artelia came home from the office and excitedly told me about a new young man being assigned to her department, the Finance

Department. And the nice young man had asked her to introduce him to an employee in the Purchasing Department, who happened to be one of her roommates. This young man turned out to be Leland Calvin Biggs of Fountain City, a suburb of Knoxville, and he wanted to meet me. When I met him, I learned that he had been a student at the University of Tennessee and was now ready to go to work. I was not financially able to attend college, so that put me a notch ahead of him in the business world.

Artelia served as our line of communication. Then a little later he asked her to see if I would be his date on a weekend party up in the Smokies. It seems young people from First Christian Church would make up the group. I took her advice and said, "Maybe." I wanted to think about it, for I had heard about the popular parties in the mountains, and I hesitated to say I would go.

It seems that the Smoky Mountains were a part of the Bigg's heritage. Their roots ran deep in and around Sevierville, Tennessee. I had heard about Leland's family tree, and I had been looking forward to a trip to Gatlinburg. It was said that Colonel Biggs was one of the last to turn the latch on the family's cabin door. The great Smoky Mountains were fast becoming America's playground. Families who had cabins in the mountains when the government took the property over to make it a National Park were allowed to stay there until all the family died, but they could not pass it down.

Now, about the weekend party, I was told we would be chaperoned, and Artelia said, "You need a break, so go!"

I did go. Leland met me in uptown Knoxville. He was dressed for the occasion: Knickers, a baby blue turtleneck, and a U.T. sweater. He really looked sporty. We met Jack McAmy, Leland's best friend, and his girlfriend, and we took off. By now it almost seemed too late to go, for I think it was about a thirty-mile drive.

When we arrived, we parked the car in the parking lot. After walking for miles, we finally reached the cabin at the top of the mountain. The cabin had not been used for many months, and the spiders and roaches had taken over. Jack said, "My Uncle and Aunt planned to come, but at the last minute could not make it." So there was no chaperone anywhere around.

A roaring fire greeted us with its warm, flickering flames. Several of the groups had come ahead of us, and they were busily unpacking and unrolling bed mats. It was at this time that I realized they were making beds for couples to sleep in front of the fireplace. I instantly became aware that I needed a guardian angel. Leland immediately knew by the expression on my face that I would not be a part of any of this. So I asked him to take me home. He said, "Everything will be alright, we will go home in the morning. Jack and I will make our beds just outside the window, and Jack's girlfriend and you can sleep in the house just inside the window." Then he added, "Just be patient, and we will leave in the morning." This was our first date, the beginning of many more.

One of the girls who had known the Biggs family said to me, "I hear you had a date with Leland Biggs. You had better leave him alone, I think he is engaged."

Now, Children, I think you have been properly introduced to:

Leland Calvin Biggs

Leland later became your Father, Grandfather, Great-Grandfather, and for even some of you a Great-Great-Grandfather.

Alma & Leland
First Date (Smoky Mountains, November, 1933) I weighed 98 lbs.

1934
Living At Sterchi Apartments In Knoxville, Tennessee

Our group of girls enjoyed living together. At the end of the day, we would come home and pull off our work outfits and put on something comfortable. Sometimes we would eat out, but most of the time we took turns at preparing our night meal. After dinner there would be a jam session discussing and exchanging the happenings of the day. "Did you talk to Leland, today?" This was one of the big subjects of discussion. "How are things going?" they would ask. Most of the time, there was nothing of interest to report. But then I did tell them everything in the courting department was O.K. "I am going to the football game with him Saturday."

Football was an ingrained, looked-forward-to, event. Season tickets were always purchased far in advance. We would go to the game rain or shine, sleet or snow. Win or lose, Tennessee was our team. At that time Kentucky, Alabama, and Tennessee were at the top of the list. I think I tried to be an Alabama fan, but I soon realized that if I wanted to be in the good graces of the Biggs clan I could not utter a squeak for Alabama. "Oh, well," I said to myself, "I guess I can be half Tennessee and half Alabama."

Religion was another big concern with me. Leland's family had been Baptists for generations. So there I was trying to make another romantic decision. I tried to tell my conscience that a charter member of one of the largest Baptist churches around would not be as hard to convert to my way of thinking as a Catholic.

Since Leland did not own a car, travel was limited for us. Mr. Biggs (Papa) was very generous, and he allowed us limited use of the family car on most weekends. Mrs. Biggs (Mamaw) was like a mother hen, providing delicious Tennessee country meals for her family. She convinced me that she really enjoyed "putting the little pot in the big one" and dropping one more potato into the stew. Her table was always loaded with real vittles, and I know I was lucky to have a chair waiting for me.

There was not much exciting in our lives for the month of November. I planned to spend Thanksgiving in Sheffield with my family. Financially, they were status quo and waiting for the mail the first of each month. I was still attached to the tug of the singletree, and to tell the truth this small monthly benevolence never occurred to me to be much of a drain on my income.

February 14, 1935

February 14 happened to be Leland's birthday and, of course, Valentine's Day. I have been able to find only two messages from him to me before we married. The first one was mailed to me at Aconda Court Apartments, where I had moved from the group of girls in Knoxville. This apartment was located on or very near the University of Tennessee Campus. I hope you appreciate this beautiful Valentine message, which has been preserved for all to enjoy.

Proposal 1934

On November 29, 1934, Leland mailed the one and only love letter I ever received from him. He mailed it to me when I was at home in Sheffield. I guess for that reason I tied a blue ribbon around it and tucked it into a drawer for a time such as this. The following February 14, he sent me a sweet Valentine card. It still brings tears and feelings of nostalgia when I read it.

1935

"Work, Work" seemed to be the name of the game. Everything at the office appeared to be running smoothly. "How are you and Leland getting along?" Fellow workers constantly asked. The native Knoxvillian friend, who first told me that Leland was "taken," cornered me one day and unloaded his past romantic activities. It seemed that this girl, a school teacher, was a long-time friend of Leland's sister, Ruby. Ruby and her friend had carefully planned Leland's future, and I was told that marriage was definitely around the corner. However, sometime before Leland and I had been introduced, things between him and Ruby's friend had run into a romantic pitfall. Ruby did not approve of me in any shape, fashion, or form. The rough times were blamed on the "new girl on the block." Yet, I had absolutely nothing to do with his break up, for I had never heard of her, and I didn't even know Leland until he began to inquire about me.

Ruby was a very unhappy, self-willed person, and she immediately marked me off the prospective list for her future sister-in-law. She was a hard person to please, and actually her whole life was far from being happy.

Home
Thanksgiving Day
November 29, 1934

Dearest Alma:—

Wishing you a very pleasant Thanksgiving Day with your family and friends.

There are so many things I would like to say that it is rather hard for me to find a place to start. First tho I hope your trip home was ~~made~~ safely made, and that you were not so tired when you arrived. ~~Hmm~~ It was too bad the weather couldn't favor your trip home, but maybe it wasn't so bad after all.

After I left you yesterday I came back to the office, intending to stay only a few minutes, but it turned out to be otherwise. Mr Robertson began to talk to me alone and when we were thru, it was almost 4:30.

There was so much said that it would be hard to tell everything, but during the past few days you know what ~~has~~ the talking has been about. So it was yesterday, tho the entire talk was not confined to the office. In short he gave me a brief outline of his life and various experiences. It was very interesting. We then had much to say about us. It was very favorable as you might guess.

From the way Mr Robertson talked we do have everything in the world. He said he would give anything in the world to have our ages. I think tho we realize to a certain extent the opportunity we have, dont you. Will make the most of it, wont we. We just mustn't do anything but make good and we will.

It is hard to tell all, so when you get back I will tell you in brief our talk.

But for awhile I'll start writing about something else.

Yes, as I promised, I went to church last night. The service was very good, tho the rain kept the crowd down considerable. Several of the old gang were there, but after the service I walked up in town to see what things looked like. The city wasnt in such a turmoil as I had expected, but guess the city will be very gay today. As I am now writing it is almost 1:00, and in a few minutes I am going to have to leave for the football game.

I would like to write more, but if I am to mail this letter today I'll have to get ready. Again wishing a pleasant thanksgiving.

I love you,
Leland—

I thought I would have to close a few minutes ago, but it has turned out otherwise so, I will continue on for awhile longer.

It will not surprise me greatly if you fail to read the first part of my letter with any coherence. I was trying to listen to a football game over the radio and write at the same time. As it turned out I listened to the game very well but the writing? The game was between the Chicago Bears and Detroit Lions, Chicago winning 19-16. Chicago is the team which Feathers of Tennessee plays. What would you say or think if I should tell you that in a few more minutes the football game between Kentucky and Tennessee will be going on, and here I am still writing. After I got ready to go a few minutes ago, I decided that I didn't want to see the game, so here I am. Ruby and the rest of the family couldn't believe it, and when they saw that I intended to stay, they tried to persuade me to go. I haven't any reason, except, I just didn't want to go.

Jack called me up this morning about 11.00 and talked awhile. He was wanting to know if he could see me this afternoon at the game. At the time I thought so, and was going to meet him where they fire the Cannon, but of course now I won't. He asked me if I wanted to go up in the mountains after the game. He said, "I know you won't go, but I am asking you anyway". He wasn't sure tho whether he was going — a chance that he might. I asked Jack to come on out home and have dinner with us tonight. Edmond will be here, and if only you were here too. I hope you are getting some very good rest if that could be possible with the few short days you have home. I am making the most out of today, getting up about 9 this morning.

In a few minutes I am going to town and mail this letter — so you'll get it tomorrow. Can you give me Lois's address from your home.

Give all your love to your family for me, you should have seen mother when your flowers came this morning — just like a child again. She was very happy. May I say, again only

you I have,
Leland —

Leland and I finally reached the time that serious decisions had to be discussed and made. One afternoon, we were on the campus steps at the University of Tennessee, and he finally got up courage to say, "Will you consider marrying me?"

I then replied with the same answer I had given at another time to another proposal. "I can't. I am the financial source of my parents. This small amount is necessary to keep their rent paid and food on the table."

"I know that," Leland said, "and I promise that things will not change. I will never upset your way of life. Will you trust me?"

"Let me think," I said, "but right now the answer has to be, No." Really, I cared for him, and finally, with much persuasion and many promises, I said, "Do you actually understand what I have said?"

Leland answered "Yes!" And he never broke his promise.

Ruby later married Edmond Morarity, and they had two sons, Joe Henry and Charles.

The Ring

The next date we had was filled with excitement, on my part especially. Leland had a friend on South Gay Street, Knoxville, Tennessee, who owned and operated a pawnshop. A time was arranged for us to meet him, for we were ring hunting. Of course, price was a big consideration. We were welcomed at this store as lookers. I started looking on the shelves and in the cases, and I decided it must be "raining diamonds." I had never seen as many pieces of jewelry at one time. He pointed out several different shades of color, which he said designated the quality of the stone. Many sizes were brought to our attention, from the size of a pinhead to what I would call a whopper.

We browsed around trying to decide if any would fit into our meager and depleting budget. Finally a second clerk came through a door curtained with what might have been a sheet. He said, "Leland, I want to show this beauty." This is the first time it has been offered for sale. The size was a little more than one carat, its color was perfectly clear, and it was priced in a range that we might be able to handle. Anyway, after considering the shower of diamonds shown us, we decided this one was it. The diamond would be set in a plain gold solitaire setting. This beautiful ring became the seal of our love and a promise of "till death do us part." We appreciated all the help we received in making this very important decision.

Then we really started making serious plans. I found that promising to marry someone unleashes a long list of things to think about and do. We decided to make our vows on February 24, 1935, but we had many other important decisions to make about the following:

Things to Think About And Do

1. Our Religion?
2. Would we have a family?
3. Where would we live?
4. How would we handle our bank accounts?
5. Who would we select as our attendants, as our preacher?
6. How would we word our wedding vows?

7. Where would we go on our "honeymoon," for how long, and how much would the trip cost?

After all the disagreements and agreements were ironed out, it was wonderful to look into Leland's eyes, and without fear be willing to trust him, not knowing what the future would bring us. Truly, that has to be Love. I asked myself, "Did I make a mistake?" And I answered myself, "I guess time will tell." We set the date for February 24, 1935.

My big concern was where would we live? Leland promised me we would find a small apartment, and then later maybe build our own house. I was not aware that he had a "thing" about paying rent. So that plan seemed all right to me. But I never heard anymore about what our new address would be. Again, I trusted.

We both agreed that a couple of little Biggs would be a welcome addition. But later I thought, "Alma you are so naïve." I had been so sheltered in this department, since these subjects were not discussed around our dinner table. Sometimes I had wondered where my brothers and I had come from. I had not seen any storks flying around. My mother was as Victorian as the queen herself. She would not think about going to bed "until all the shades were drawn down tight," not a streak of light showing. Well, in looking around I decided that Mother Nature must have had her hands full finding a peep hole at our house.

I finally got up enough courage to ask Marie, my aunt, to give me some advice. Her information of "just trial and error" didn't seem quite like some of the stories I had heard from the "horses mouths" at the office. Marie said, "Oh Alma," and she then gave me a lesson on the birds and the bees. Just don't believe everything you hear. I will add, believe it or not, Leland was just as uneducated as I. Our marriage vows would say "until death do us part," and this we heeded.

Alma Lee Dukes was married to Leland Calvin Biggs of Knoxville, Tennessee on February 24, 1935. The ceremony was held at the Annapolis Avenue Church of Christ in Sheffield, Alabama. Leland is the son of William Henry and Sarah Sutton Biggs of Fountain City, Tennessee.

William Henry, Leland's father, was born in Jefferson County, Tennessee, on September 28, 1882. He died on June 24, 1958, in Sheffield, Alabama. Sarah Sutton was born on May 10, 1887, in Sevier County, Tennessee. She died in 1963 in Knoxville, Tennessee. Leland Calvin Biggs was born February 14, 1910, and he died on June 24, 1967, in Sheffield, Alabama. At the time of his death, he was in the Coffee Hospital in Florence, Alabama.

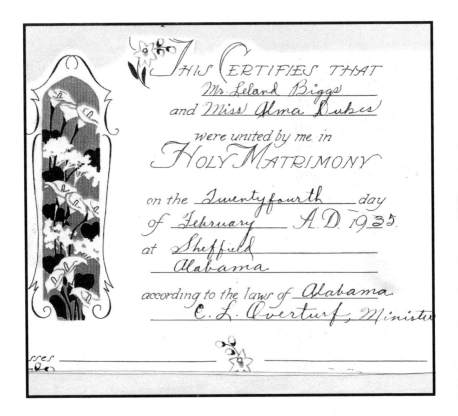

The daily papers ran the following story about Alma's and Leland's wedding:

> Mr. and Mrs. Joe F. Dukes of Sheffield, Alabama, announce the marriage of their daughter, Alma, to Leland C. Biggs on Sunday, February 24, 1935, at the Church of Christ in Sheffield.
>
> Mr. Biggs is the son of Mr. and Mrs. W.H. Biggs of Fountain City, Tennessee.
>
> Immediately after the ceremony Mr. and Mrs. Biggs left on a Southern trip and reached New Orleans in time for Mardi Gras.
>
> Mr. and Mrs. Biggs will live in Knoxville, where both are employed by the Tennessee Valley Authority.

Alma's and Leland's Wedding Announcement

Mr. and Mrs. Joe F. Dukes

announce the marriage of their daughter

Alma Lee

to

Mr. Leland C. Biggs

on Sunday, February the twenty-fourth

Nineteen hundred and thirty-five

Sheffield, Alabama

Leland and Marie

ALMA LEE DUKES BIGGS

LELAND CALVIN BIGGS

Our Honeymoon And After

Our Honeymoon In New Orleans

The small wedding was performed at Annapolis Avenue Church of Christ, with Brother C. L. Overturf officiating. The wedding was followed by the Sunday morning Service.

I wore a light blue suit trimmed in gray fur. Marie Brewer was my maid of honor, and Jack McAmy from Knoxville was Leland's best man. Several out-of-town visitors were present, including the Biggs family and others from our offices in Knoxville. After the ceremony, the wedding party and guests enjoyed a brunch at the Cardiff Hotel in Tuscumbia, Alabama.

We left by train from the Tuscumbia Railroad Station about 1:30 P.M. for our wedding trip to New Orleans and other southern points. When we reached New Orleans, we found ourselves in the middle of their Mardi Gras. All the motels, hotels, and private homes had "No Vacancy" signs fluttering in the wind. Finally, after knocking on many doors, a lady opened her door and said, "We do not take guests."

I think Leland put his foot in the door and said, "Lady, we don't want to be your guests. We have just gotten married and need a place to stay one night."

She looked us over and said, "Alright, only one night, come in."

We had no idea what Mardi Gras meant, or what was going on. The sidewalks, streets, roads and lanes were swarming with people in all kinds of garb and costumes. Our landlady explained to us, "This is an annual festival, a Catholic holiday, having to do with Lent."

Right after noon the next day, we started packing to leave. Our landlady came in and said, "Since you are such a nice couple, you may stay another night." Of course, this pleased us. We got out, and walked up the street, and became a part of the frivolity. We became acquainted with many of their dishes, especially the French cuisine.

I told Leland I liked most everything, but I didn't even want to taste the cute little lamb chops. He said, "Okay with me."

As we started preparing to leave, I wondered how much money we had left; for we surely had been what I would call extravagant. I said, "Leland, don't you think we had better pool our money?" The amount we had would determine our plans for the next few days. As we counted the nickels and dimes, I sort of panicked and said, "What will we do?"

Leland remembered a co-worker who lived in Birmingham, Alabama, Jerry Brown and his wife, Betty. "I'll call him," Leland said, "Maybe he will be home since this is the weekend."

Leland, while on our honeymoon.

We found his number in Leland's notebook. Leland asked me, "What do you think?"

"I am sorry, but I can't think, right now," I replied. "If you feel comfortable sending him an 'SOS,' then do. We can't just sit here."

Luckily, Jerry was at home and answered the phone. He seemed pleased to hear from us and extended us a gracious welcome. Together we had just enough money to buy tickets from New Orleans to Birmingham. Leland explained to him how we had overspent, and that our salary checks would be awaiting us at the office. We assured him that the money would be a short time loan, and he trusted us. Of course, he became a real friend in our time of need. I will never forget our trip to New Orleans or Mardi Gras, February 1935.

We rushed to the bus station and found a bus showing a big BIRMINGHAM destination. When the driver said, "Where to?" we said in unison, "Birmingham." We finally caught our breath and said, "Actually, we are going home." We arrived in Birmingham in the late afternoon and, peeping out the window, we saw Jerry waiting for us. After greetings and the handling of luggage Jerry said, "It's a little drive from here. We live on Red Mountain."

We remembered and said, "Oh, yes, that is where the Iron Man Statue is located." The Vulcan has long been the symbol of all the iron deposits in this area.

Jerry's wife was named Betty. She was a pretty wife and homemaker. She was a charming hostess and had prepared a delicious meal. We were so appreciative of all the hospitality they afforded us. Since our noontime meal had been hamburgers and chips, we thought we were starving. We were ready for anything, and her selection of good, almost Tennessee food was a welcome sight. It looked good, smelled good, and was good. Our plates were piled high with creamed potatoes, green beans, creamed corn, and a crisp garden salad. Then Jerry picked up the big platter of golden brown chops, and he said, "This is Betty's specialty." We all ate until we said, "We have had a gracious plenty."

Then to make conversation I said," Betty, tell me how you fixed those delicious pork chops." She said, "Thank you, but they were lamb chops." I smiled and said, "They were so good. You are a wonderful cook."

Our trip was cut short because Leland's brother, Everett, was to be married on March 9. He was marrying Elizabeth Dooley, and it was to be a "big" affair. Her family went many generations back in Knoxville circles.

Our Bank Account

First, the decision was made to pay all of our bills, and then we would be concerned about other matters. After our bills were paid, there was little to be concerned about. However, I do think we did very well with our mite. The rule, "What is yours is mine, and what is mine is yours," was practiced without exception.

Mr. and Mrs. Everett Biggs and Wedding Party

Mr. and Mrs. Everett Biggs and members of their wedding party are shown above. They were married Saturday, March 9, at First Baptist Church. Mrs. Biggs was Miss Elizabeth Dooley.

In front row, left to right, are Mr. and Mrs. Biggs and Mrs. Myrna Marks, matron of honor. The bride wore a Molyneaux model of white satin fashioned on princess lines. Mrs. Marks wore turquoise blue and carried Acacia, gold standard roses and calendulas.

The bridesmaids on the second row, left to right, are: Miss Janie Galbraith who wore orchid and carried orchid sweet peas and gold standard roses; Miss Sarah Thackston, who wore rose and carried blue delphinium and Talisman roses; Miss Mary Elizabeth Keister, who wore yellow and carried blue sweet peas and Joanna Hill roses; Mrs. Audrin May, who wore green and carried Briarcliff roses and pink sweet peas; Miss Ruby Bigg who wore peach and carried Talisman roses and sweet peas.

The groomsmen in back row, left to right, Charles Dooley brother of the bride; Eugene Mynatt, Leland Biggs, brother of the groom, Kenneth Parry, John Dooley, brother of the bride and W. E. Matlock.

March 9, 1935
Everett and Elizabeth
Married

Everett, Elizabeth,
and Alma

The next morning we were up bright and early, as the bus was scheduled to leave at about 7:30. Upon arrival at the terminal, we called Papaw to please come and pick us up. We were loaded down with our luggage and our souvenirs. We were on the last leg of our journey, and it was so good to see the two-story, white house at 701 Maple Avenue, Fountain City. Fountain City was really a suburb of Knoxville, Tennessee. I knew then that the Biggs' house would be my home for quite a while.

After greetings and much ado, we were told that we would be making our residence in the third floor attic. It had been scrubbed squeaky clean, and on the table was a bowl of fresh flowers out of Mamaw's yard.

I thought to myself, "Is this my small apartment?" And I then knew I could no longer have my way about everything. We settled down at the Biggs' home.

Our First House

Leland and I both worked for TVA in Knoxville, and since we lived a distance away and had no transportation except the city bus, we had to leave early and usually got home late. This was the year 1935. The time swiftly passed, and we called our attic room our home much longer than I realized. Then one night, Leland said, "I have found a place for us that maybe we might like. Tomorrow, let's get off the bus at Woodrush Avenue and look at some lots."

It seemed that a new subdivision was opening up, and Leland thought we could be interested. That was music to my ears. This sounded like "my way" after a long long wait. We both fell in love with the location. It was so convenient to everything except the church. The Laurel Avenue Church was located in West Knoxville, and getting to church would be hard to manage. But where there is a will, there is a way.

We decided to make payments on a lot at Woodrush Avenue, Fountain City, Tennessee, and we were forced to "pinch pennies," but we were determined to own something of our very own. We had decided on our location, now what was the next step in building a house? We were so inexperienced in ways and means that we decided to listen to the advice of those who knew.

M. F. WILLIAMS
GENERAL CONTRACTOR
109 Empire Building
"For Good Workmanship and Dependability"
Telephone 3-0312
KNOXVILLE, TENNESSEE

May 30, 1940

Federal Home Savings Bank
Knoxville, Tennessee

Gentlemen:

    I hereby authorize and direct you to accept this assignment of my account number *1286*, in your bank in the amount of $*301.56*. This assignment is made by me for the purpose of securing payment of a note for $1,000.00, made by me to the Morris Plan Bank of Knoxville. In case of non-payment of this note the Morris Plan Bank of Knoxville shall have full authority to withdraw the balance of said account number *1286*, and credit same to above mentioned note.

                              Leland C. Biggs
                                Leland C. Biggs

WITNESS:

M. F. Williams

LFB/lh

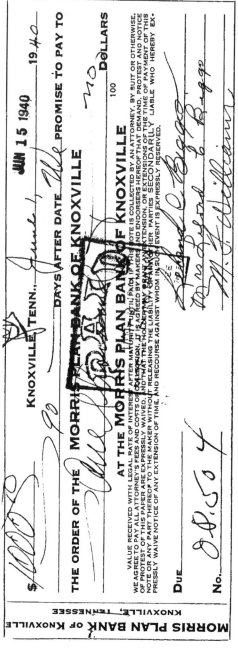

Several of our friends had used a contractor by the name of M. F. Williams. A small local contractor, he did much of the work himself, but he hired bricklayers to do the masonry work. We were in total agreement with Mr. Williams's ideas and work. He knew the best grade of every material used, even to the copper awning over the bay window. Our new address would soon be a reality.

Records show that we borrowed $1000 to help in our financial struggle while building the house. The Morris Plan Bank of Knoxville loaned us the money, and security was with Home Savings Bank. Somehow we managed and thought we were ready for the future come what may.

Congratulations

One day near Christmas of 1937, I was on the "puny" list. After much complaining and ill humor, Leland insisted that we see a Doctor. "What kind of Doctor? I have never been sick, and I don't know anything about the Doctors here." Leland decided to check the telephone directory. Then he blindly selected some help. Together we decided on a Doctor McElwayne, and he called for an appointment.

The appointment day came, and after the office visit, the Doctor made the diagnosis. He said, "Mrs. Biggs you do not have the flu, but you are very much pregnant, and you are having what we call baby morning sickness. You are going to have a baby, and don't argue with that, come back to see me in about three weeks." At that time, the Doctor had no idea how many visits this one opened the door for. He had many, many calls to answer questions from this young bride's inquisitive mind. I was later told by neighbors, "You are lucky to have Dr. McElwayne. He is one of the best. He is particularly popular with the young people."

"What do I do for nine long months?" I asked the Doctor.

"Would you consider going back to your job with TVA? That would be my top advice." This was the Doctor's expert opinion.

I returned to the office with the great news and congratulations from my good friends. However, I was still wondering just what I would do after the blessed event. Mamaw, Leland's mother, quickly worked out the solution. She did not wait to be asked but immediately applied for the baby sitting job.

Bill Is Born

The months moved quickly enough. Then the night of August 8, I experienced unbelievable pains. Leland called Dr. McElwayne and with panic in his voice asked, "What do I do Doctor? Alma is driving me crazy and has wet the whole bedroom!"

"Meet me at the hospital right away!" was his quick reply.

Fort Sanders Hospital was about eight miles away. I knew absolutely nothing about baby birthing or hospitals. I had heard that once admitted, especially for a baby, food was not allowed. "I am starved," I insisted that we make one little pit stop at Regas Café. Leland was very nervous, but he did not deny me this last request. I enjoyed a delicious full breakfast.

Then we proceeded to the hospital where Dr. McElwayne waited. That is all I remember until it was over. Then a nurse came in and said, "You have a fine baby boy. He is 23" tall, lean and lanky with black curly hair, standing defiantly straight up. All the patting and setting was to no avail." His hair finally gave up and left him with beautiful black waves. A cap was permanent attire when anyone asked to see the baby. I was sound asleep before I could count fingers and toes. I just breathed a "Thank you, Lord. He is beautiful."

At dinnertime, a full meal was brought to my bedside. "Food fit for a king," I thought. The meat was fried to a golden brown on the outside, and was white and tender on the inside. I asked, "What is this?" I couldn't believe the answer when they replied, "Rabbit." It didn't seem to matter. I was hungry after all that work.

The Doctor came in and sat on the side of the bed and said, "I must ask you about circumcision." This took us by surprise. We thought only Jewish boys were circumcised, and then as a religious rite. He explained that this was advised for health reasons. The minor surgery was performed and forgotten.

A nurse came in the room and said, "It's naming time. The hospital requires this be done before you leave the hospital." I had thought for sure that Leland would quickly say, "Leland Junior." But for some reason he said, "I do not want a junior." That was that. Then what? William is very much a Biggs name; so it would be William Duke. Somewhere in the naming process, the "s" was dropped from my family name "Dukes," and his name was recorded as William Duke Biggs. He is known at schools, businesses, churches, and by the U.S. Government as Bill Biggs.

After about a two weeks stay in Fort Sanders Hospital, Dr. McElwayne sent us home with tender loving instructions. I thought Bill was a contented, good baby. There was no crying or walking the floor at night as I had expected. I tried to be the trusted "tried and true mother."

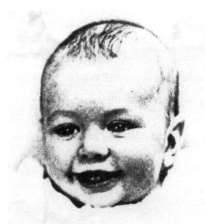

William Duke Biggs

I had noticed that our baby did not seem to be gaining weight as described in Dr. Spock's books. I kept the Spock "bible" by my side, and I was determined to note every whimper or squirm.

Leland and I had asked Dr. Hill, our friend and Elder at the Laurel Avenue Church of Christ in West Knoxville, to be our "Guardian Angel" during the early learning days. On the baby's first check-up visit to Dr. Hill, I asked, "How are we doing?" He answered, "Listen to me, this boy is not getting enough nourishment. Breast-feeding is not sufficient to appease both appetite and promote growth." So I asked, "What do I do now? I practically stand on my head at feeding times." The Doctor explained to me that my nipples were inverted, and this did not permit the natural flow of milk. He added that a supplement would have to be added by bottle feedings. The supplement he suggested was Similac, which had proven to be very beneficial.

I took his advice, and sure enough Bill began to gain weight and was really a happy and smiling baby. But I personally had to sterilize everything and watch my diet, along with other demanding duties. I made the big decision to bottle feed only. And it worked!

Looking back, I suppose since Bill was the first born, more attention was given to the details of his early learning days than to the other three children yet to come. Someone has said, "Every child is a success story waiting to begin." So Bill was our beginning. Our children are our most precious resources.

When Bill was born on August 9, 1938, his father, Leland C. Biggs, wrote this letter (for Bill) to my Mother and Father. He signed the letter "William Leland Duke," which is not correct. As mentioned, I had hoped for a "Leland C. Biggs, Jr.," but Leland had said, "No." Then we agreed on the name "William Duke Biggs." Maybe false pride stepped in. Anyway, here is a copy of the original letter to my Mother and Father. Notice the letter is dated August 11, Bill was two days old, and it was written on letterhead from the Hotel Farragut. Why? I don't know.

L.M. WAITE, MANAGER

HOTEL FARRAGUT

FARRAGUT OPERATING CO., PROPS.
DIRECTION ROBERT R. MEYER

300 ROOMS EACH WITH INDIVIDUAL BATH
AND ELECTRIC CEILING FANS

MODERN　　　EUROPEAN　　　FIREPROOF

"DIRECT CONNECTED GARAGE"
"LOUD SPEAKER RADIO IN EVERY ROOM"

KNOXVILLE, TENN.

August 11, 1938

Dear Grandma,

I guess you are getting anxious to hear from me and mother. You know this is the third day I have been with mother but I like it so well I am going to stay forever. I didn't know I would like the place so well; everyone has been so nice - and mother tells me she is going to take me to a permanent home in a few more days - tho I haven't complained of being here - there are so many nice girls handling me - you should see the attention I receive.

ROBERT MEYER HOTELS
HOTEL STACY-TRENT, TRENTON, NEW JERSEY
HOTEL PATRICK HENRY, ROANOKE, VIRGINIA
FARRAGUT HOTEL, KNOXVILLE, TENNESSEE
HERMITAGE HOTEL, NASHVILLE, TENNESSEE
WINECOFF HOTEL, ATLANTA, GEORGIA
WINDSOR HOTEL, JACKSONVILLE, FLORIDA
HOTEL SIR WALTER, RALEIGH, NORTH CAROLINA
HOTEL ROOSEVELT, JACKSONVILLE, FLORIDA
HOTEL EMERSON, BALTIMORE, MARYLAND

HOTEL FARRAGUT

FARRAGUT OPERATING CO., PROPS.
DIRECTION ROBERT R. MEYER

300 ROOMS EACH WITH INDIVIDUAL BATH
AND ELECTRIC CEILING FANS

MODERN   EUROPEAN   FIREPROOF
"DIRECT CONNECTED GARAGE"
"LOUD SPEAKER RADIO IN EVERY ROOM"

KNOXVILLE, TENN.

L. M. WAITE,
MANAGER

I bet you are wondering how mother is? I can tell you that in just one word — splendid. Mother and I are ready to eat any time they bring something around. You should see mama eat — why if they didn't bring her rabbit yesterday.

You know they thought they were fooling me for the first two days. They made me think mother was feeding me — but I knew better, tho I didn't say anything. I decided to wait until the third day before registering a protest. But I haven't anything now to complain about — they have stopped fooling me.

It is very nice and cool in our room, one of the nicest rooms in the building — you know we are staying at the Fort-Sanders.

This is about all I have to say this time — I am a good boy, weighing 6-9 and have brown hair thus far. I haven't cried any so far but wait until I get home & there I will have a dad to walk the floor with me — tho he has told me he wouldn't.

Mother said she would write you a little later and said to tell you and Grandpa she was feeling just "swell".

When are you all coming up to see me — I'll be home by then waiting for you. You know there are quite a few relatives I haven't seen.

So be good and come and see me.

Your Grandson,
William Leland Duke

Now we had a new house and a new baby boy: William Duke Biggs who was our pride and joy. We were all set in our house, but we owned very little furniture, and I had no idea about a style and design that would be appropriate. I thought a bed was a bed, a table a table, and a chair a chair. Did our house have a particular style? Our neighbor directly across the road was a blessing in disguise. Mrs. Kranz, her daughter, Louise Vangilder, and her young son, Jack Vangilder, told me that their furniture was brought over by families from Germany and were now considered to be antiques. Right away we fell in love with this type of furniture.

At this time, Leland's work covered the Norris Dam area. The whole Tennessee countryside was flooded with water from Norris Dam. People were forced to abandon their ancestral homes, and many sold their heirlooms to avoid destruction by floodwaters. Mrs. Kranz gave me some good advice about furnishing our home.

One morning Mrs. Kranz came to the side door with a basket full of Christmas goodies and said, "These are all good, but my favorite recipe from my childhood is Scotch Shortbread."

Scotch Shortbread

- 3/4 lb butter
- 6 tablespoons powdered sugar
- 3 cups flour (all-purpose)
- teaspoon vanilla

Cream butter, add sugar and flour gradually. Press into pan about one inch thick. Prick with fork. Bake 35 minutes at 350 degrees. Easy and delicious.

* * *

During the next three years, my and Leland's life took on the glow of family pride and happiness. Bill was getting to be a big boy, and he would soon be entering the terrible twos. I clearly remember two or three episodes that are typical of this age.

First, every time he could catch me in a prolonged telephone conversation, he would enter the picture just for attention, I supposed. Our house was an open runway from bedrooms, dining room, kitchen, and breakfast nook. He would catch the rightment and raid the kitchen for anything, especially a box of Tide. He would enter room by room, pouring Tide in a full stream through each. Try sweeping up Tide—well, you know it doesn't come up easily.

Second, many words came into his vocabulary at the proper age, but some were just his words. For instance, shoes were "Ooshies" to him. Airplane was "airtane." He picked up an imaginary playmate during this time, which happened to be a pug puppy. We listened to his conversations and wondered what would come next.

Then, one morning, when we were at the breakfast table, Bill's highchair faced the door that led straight down to a concrete basement. He made known that he wanted the door open. Then the dog, and more chatter began. "I am tired of this!" Leland said, and made a big kick through the door toward the basement. Then he added, "Dog, get out of here, and stay where you belong."

The girl who helped with the housework came in about the time of all the commotion and immediately picked up her things. She said, "I'm leaving. All you Biggs are crazy, talking to things that do not exist." After much explaining, she decided to stay. We assured her the "dog" was gone. This broke hearts all around. But the dog disappeared, and it was supposed that another playmate took its place. That is our dog tale, believe it or not. Sometimes we all let our imaginations run wild, and I know our friends and neighbors have labeled us all crazy at one time or another.

From this date on, our life was as normal as could be. We were taking one day at a time, wondering what the war troubles in Europe would do to our economy. Perhaps another World War? When the time came for Bill to start to school, my eyes filled with tears. But the decision had to be faced, and we decided on a small school nearby. A small vicinity called Smithwood Community was a short distance from our home on Woodrush Avenue. This is where we decided to send Bill for his first two years of school. His first grade teacher was Mary E. Foster, and a Mrs. Davis was the second year teacher. Both his cards were marked excellent, of course. "We were very proud of such a good student." The years were 1944-46.

Warnings From Young Parents

Bill was born on August 9, 1938. Other young parents had come to us with gentle warnings to share and to help prepare our little family for what might be called age-old problems.

When children arrive and reach the one-year old stage—which some may call toddlerhood—which is soon followed by the terrible twos, be prepared for surprises! Development and changes are made at a rapid pace. New words are sputtered and uttered daily. There is one word that dominates during the fifteenth to twenty-fourth month.

NO! NO! NO!

1. They refuse to eat their cereal.
2. They will not accept any toy created for amusement.
3. They refuse to take a bath.
4. They refuse to go to bed.

Also add that they spill everything, destroy everything, fall off everything, and try to flush everything down the toilet. Yes, and all this is nerve wracking and really awful to deal with, but this too shall pass, I promise.

Wouldn't it be nice to roll the pages back? This applies to one and all. This little poem was found glued on the doorpost in a bedroom. The door jam was covered with birthday dates, tooth pulling dates, the children's height and weight, and many other important dates. When I found this poem and the dates, I was sure Leland kept these records.

> I stood the children, straight and tall,
> By last year's marks upon the wall.
> Another year! How soon they go.
> And see how fast the children grow!
> But then I thought how God's Word says,
> "Grow in peace and in the Lord."
> And as I knelt with God alone
> He asked me gently, "Have you grown?"
> When you look back and understand
> How sun and rain came from my hand?
> And trials, which my love decreed,
> Did they not prove me real indeed?
> Or would you change a single hour,
> And miss the knowledge of my power?
> Do I seem nearer when you pray,
> Than just a year ago today?
> And does your zeal for lost men die,
> Or greater grow, as years go by?"
> The deep and searching questions these!
> They kept me long upon my knees;
> Where His gaze my soul must own,
> How very little it had grown.
> Oh Lord, this year may all men see,
> That I grow daily more like Thee.
>
> Anonymous

Winston Is Born

Leland Winston Biggs was born November 16, 1941. There was three years difference in Winston's and Bill's ages. With a new baby and a new house, my time was very full. All I seemed to know about babysitting was what I remembered a long time ago, when my brothers were young, especially Lewis. During this time span, things became more modernized. I pretty much relied upon our Doctor Hill and the *Baby Book*.

In March 1941, I diagnosed my own feelings that things were not exactly normal. I became irritable, snappy, felt unloved, and finally, yes, experienced morning sickness. I announced, "Maybe we should call our Dr. McElwayne, just anything to make me feel better and to fortify my thinking for the next nine months," which would be from March through November 16, 1941.

I have said that Bill made it by the hardest of the schoolhouse doors. Mamaw, Leland's mother, was great to help me out, especially when in March I found that I was expecting again.

Dr. McElwayne said for me to go back to work for awhile. Mamaw was just waiting to open her door to Bill. She was so gracious and loving to spend time with Bill, and we were so blessed to have her help.

All the time between Bill and a new baby seemed to pass without big incidents. I worked, sort of kept house, cooked a little, and waited from one Friday to another. During the week, Leland's job kept him out of town dealing with TVA offices, and he came home for weekends. I would take special care of the household chores at the end of the week. I would even polish the floors with the best help (wax) and manually rub them. They turned a golden sheen with oak overtones. I soon learned it does not have to be that way.

Weekends were wonderful. Our house was in the middle of other similar houses, owned and occupied by families with young children. It was comforting since we all seemed to be in the same boat.

From August 9, 1938, until November 16, 1941 was a blur in my mind. I do remember that the talk of war was the main topic. Even President Roosevelt tried to assure us that we would remain neutral. But by November, it looked like we would be forced to take a stand on World War II. Germany and Italy declared war on the United States of America.

We were blessed with our family in WWI. No one was drafted as I remember. But this time, both of my brothers (Lewis and Arlton) were the right age. Much worrying crept in, especially with many of our boys looking toward unfriendly visits to foreign neighbors.

Our household continued normally enough. I had gained and gained weight. One of our neighbors, Carl Sandberg, came by one day to sit on the porch and gossip. Getting ready to leave he said, "Alma, you should stay pregnant. It becomes you."

The trips to the doctor, the pills, diet, and some of the bad humor was near the "freedom day." I had to be different about my yen for certain foods, and believe it or not charcoal was Number 1 on my list! Poor Leland searched far and wide for someone who burned wood fires that left a residue of charcoal. Really, he did not know what he was looking for or why. But he ended up victorious! An old time drug store had "powdered charcoal" in a jar. Leland was so glad to have this crazy request behind him. But when I opened the jar, the powdered stuff flew everywhere like black snowflakes. So the stuff was deposited on a shelf in the kitchen, and it was still there when we moved from that location. I lived without the calcium I must have needed. The next time, I hoped my craving would at least be easily obtainable.

The date finally appeared on my calendar. We made a repeat trip and appearance at Fort Sanders Hospital, and we called again for Dr. McElwayne to make "haste." I was sure this was it. Sure enough, everything went fine, and they announced to me that we had another fine baby boy. They did not say a word about circumcision. After worrying about this surgery, I was told that this was taken care of along with delivery. Oh, yes! His name. Since we had not used Leland Jr. before, I still wanted that name to be attached to our family. So we came up with Leland Winston Biggs, still no junior, but I think Winston is a nice name, and not because of Churchill, but just because we liked it.

We stayed the prescribed number of days in the hospital, and then we left for our home. Incidentally, things are not the same when the little ones start taking over.

Wynn was a beautiful child, ringlets covered his head, and he didn't seem to have a neck. His head seemed to sit firmly on his shoulders. He was blond, chunky, and cuddly.

Leland Winston Biggs

On or about Sunday, November 12, we had special company. Curious to see our new addition, Leland's cousin, Wilfred Sulton, his wife, Daisy, and their little son came over from Maryville, Tennessee. They were oohing and aahing about our new baby when someone said, "Listen. There is news on the radio." The news spot expressed growing concern over the Japanese and their involvement in the war.

The Japanese attacked Pearl Harbor on December 7, 1941. President Roosevelt had tried to remain neutral but was forced into conflict with the attack on Pearl Harbor.

After adjusting to an all male household, we wondered what other Blessed Event the stork would deposit at our door!

With Leland's work being out of town so much, I coped as a single mother for about five years, until the end of World War II.

Winston and Bill visiting at Grandma Dukes' house in Sheffield, Alabama.

Leland Biggs' Father

Leland Biggs' father, Henry Biggs worked on the Civilian Conservation Corps (CCC) in early 1942. This was part of the New Deal, President Franklin Roosevelt's system of programs designed to create jobs in a nation where the unemployment rate had spiraled to 25 percent. The depression-era program gave unemployed men a chance to earn a little income by bringing them to military-style camps to plant trees, prevent soil erosion, and plan parks around the nation. When World War II became imminent in 1942, the camps closed officially on July 1.

In 1944, the country was still in conflict. Election time came again, and Roosevelt was elected for the fourth term. Everyone had high hopes of economic and financial improvement. Our family's nerves were on edge with worry. We could read and hear the news but didn't know what to believe. Nevertheless, family life kept my feet on the ground and my mind away from the horrors of war.

1935 – 1945
World War II

World War II was not as kind to our family as World War I. Both of my brothers were called into service. Lewis first served in the conflict in Europe; Arlton was called to the Orient to fight against Japan.

I am sure you will recall from your history books the details of this horrible war. I will try to give you a bird's eye view of some of the events that the boys related; although, they were both reluctant to talk about their personal experiences.

After World War I, the foreign powers that upheld the law failed. This gave the dictators an opening to carry on their secret plans to promote the idea of dividing the world into spheres, and each sphere would be under a master nation.

In August, 1934, Von Hendenburg of Germany died. This paved the way for Adolph Hitler to take total control over Germany. In 1937, there was much unrest, not over property but concerning the war. Germany invaded Poland, and, one by one, the little countries were overthrown.

In June of 1940, we heard the voice of Franklin D. Roosevelt saying, "The hand that held the dagger has struck again into his neighbor's back." Roosevelt tried to calm our nation and declared, "The boys of American mothers will not fight overseas. America is neutral." Yet, it was just a matter of time until these mothers had sleepless nights because the call had come.

Our country had a very low morale while in the throes of hunger pangs and empty pockets. President Roosevelt again promised "peace and prosperity." In his fireside chats, he said, "The only thing we have to fear is fear itself." Our President tried to remain neutral, but eventually declared war. America dropped the first atomic bomb on Hiroshima in 1945. Hitler committed suicide April 29, 1945. The war ended in 1945. Both of my brothers came home with many battle scars.

What Price Freedom?

During my lifetime, I have been touched by many tragedies, and our beloved country has been involved with warfare since the pioneer days. We have overcome each and every attack upon our nation. I heard stories about the early days from my grandparents, and in later years my brothers actually became a part of war. Our family suffered through so many perilous times, but I am listing here the suffering and strife endured in the major wars and recessions during my lifetime:

1. Terrible days of recession and depression
2. War with Germany, World War
3. War with Japan
4. War with Vietnam
5. Cold war with Russia
6. Terrorism worldwide

From all the stories I have heard and events I have witnessed, I am recommending that our history book lessons record a few atrocities inflicted upon our own boys. The following happened to my brother and your uncle. In 1941, shortly after Pearl Harbor, the Japanese captured the Island of Corregidor. The U.S. fighters were taken prisoners by the Japanese. Some of our loved ones were packed into unmarked ships and set adrift as targets. The prisoners were hot, thirsty, and starving. They were covered with their own urine and excrement. Many died, a few became slave laborers, for conditions were so horrible they cannot be described. These are inhumanities of man to man. What is the price of liberty?

Matthew 24:6 and Mark 13:7 tell us, "There shall be wars and rumors of wars," and you and yours are facing perilous times.

Historic Events That Happened During My Lifetime

1941 - We bought our first car, a "Big" Buick, License Registered 3-D1959. State and Clerks fee $10.35 each year.

1942 - Due to war shortages, many things were not on the store shelves. For instance: Sugar was rationed starting on May 5, 1942. The minimum draft age was lowered from 21 to 18 years of age.

1943 - Our general economy is holding very steady because of the manufacture of war materials.

The "Big Three" leaders of the world, Roosevelt of the United States of America, Stalin of Russia, Churchill of Europe were trying to devise ways and means to control the world conflict.

1944 - The Country is still in conflict. It is election time again. Roosevelt wins election for the fourth term. Maybe things will improve soon for the economy and everybody financially. Our nerves are all at "wits end" with worry. We hear news but what do families believe?

As for the "Tooth Fairy," he visits often and left this record of Wynn's teething progress.

>Dec. 21, 1945, upper front tooth
>Feb. 5, 1946, right lower
>Feb. 18, 1946, upper front right
>March 12, 1946, left lower.

1945 - Roosevelt dies at Warm Springs, Georgia, at the age of 63. The Nation lost its "Hero." Who will be next? Our fate is dangling. Gasoline Rationing Coupons were issued. They were renewed every three months.

CERTIFICATE OF AUTOMOBILE REGISTRATION
STATE OF TENNESSEE

1941

3	D	3D-1959
Co. No.	Class	License No.

State Fee $ 10.00
Clerk's Fee .35

(Buick) (4428007!)
Make of Car / Motor No.

Total $ 10.35

( ) (41) (Sed) ( ) (✓)
Weight / Year Model / Type Body / Old / New

EVIDENCE OF TITLE

1940 Certificate of Registration _____ 1940 License No. _____

Bill of Sale _____ Check with _____

Owner's Name: Leland C. Biggs

Street: Robin Road

City: Fountain City   County: Knox

Leland C. Biggs
Signature of Owner

This is to certify that the vehicle above described is duly registered with the Department of Finance and Taxation, State of Tennessee, subject to the provisions of Chapter 55, Public Acts of 1935, as amended.

George F. McCanna
(Commissioner)

Date 4/17, 1941

Countersigned W. H. Hall
County Court Clerk

County **KNOX**

This certificate is owner's evidence of title and must be kept with the vehicle.

CERTIFICATE OF AUTOMOBILE REGISTRATION
STATE OF TENNESSEE

1941

Make of Car: Buick

Motor Number: 4428007!

License Number: 3D-1959

Correct Motor Number is very important.
Do not issue license without Motor Number.

Becky, A Blessed Event

On March 9, 1946, a pretty, petite girl was born to our family. Just what I wanted! Of course, we were back at Fort Sanders, with Dr. McElwayne in charge. Everything went fine, and all were pleased that we now had a little girl. She was so little that the boys called her a "bag of bones," but I think, "a hair in the biscuit" would have been more appropriate for now and later.

We received many cards of congratulations, from those who were very happy over a little girl. My Mama came up to Knoxville from Sheffield to help me with everything. Three little ones in the household is a handful. This left Papa Joe at home alone, and this is what I found written by him to Mama, also a card to Leland telling him when she would arrive. Notice the cards and notes on the following pages. A pretty card was received from Grandpa and Miss Emma (Big Ma). Notice that she suggested the baby be named "Joe Ann," but we decided on Rebecca Lynn. She was a pleasure to our addition, and only the boys would dare pick on her or seem jealous.

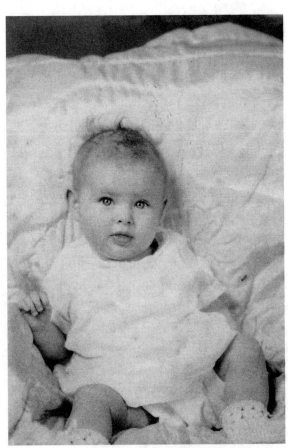

Rebecca Lynn Biggs

A brand new BABY
in your house?
No wonder you're
so proud —
For this is one time
sure enough,
When THREE is
NOT a CROWD!

Grandpa and "Bigma"
name it — Joan

For Dear New BABY

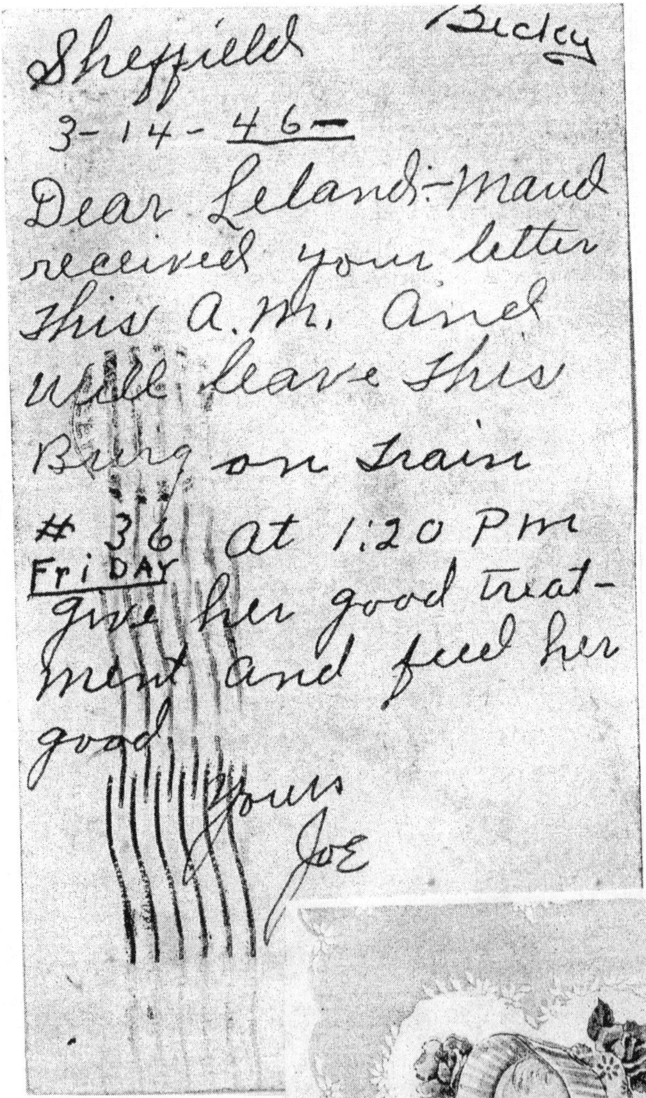

Sheffield Becky
3-14-46-
Dear Leland & Maud
received your letter
this A.M. And
will leave this
Being on Train
#36 at 1:20 PM
Friday
give her good treat-
ment and feed her
good
Yours
Joe

TO WELCOME THE New Baby

"Sunday"

2702 S. Adams St
Apt #2, ANNA VALLEY
Arlington, Virginia
Mch 19 1946

Dear Mama, Alma, Leland, Billy, Wynn, and "Rebecca":

Pearl and I were happy to hear about the wish come true and hope you are all doing fine. —

The boxes came this morning about 9 which is fast service it seems to me. Everything came in good shape and the doll was not harmed at all. I didn't mean for you to box up the golf clubs as I thought it OK to mail express as they are since there was a cover over the top —

We expect our apt to be just about complete by tomorrow but of course there are still a few things missing that we need. We haven't been able to find a radio nor lamps that we want for the money but these can wait til production starts —

This letter written to all of us— Specially "Congratulations" on arrival of Becky.

2 I have been going to a dentist since Friday for wisdom teeth trouble and he can't pull them til the swelling goes down — all four of em bucked up at the same time and I really had a big jaw for a couple of days.

   Monday A.M.

Dear Family,

  Lewis has gone to the dentist his jaw was much better an the swelling was gone, so I feel as tho' the dentist will pull a tooth to-day. I thought of going with him but didn't feel any too good myself an too, we are expecting our living room suit to-day, we hope, it was to be delivered last Monday an Sears mixed things up, so I have sure been teased about it, Joe Nelson told Shorty just to think had he not known some one from Sears no telling when it would have been delivered, an that he felt sure he'd get it by September. New Ha. It will surely come to-day they have special days for delivery.

We are just as happy as two bugs in a rug we've had 'oodles of fun fixing our place up - we have finally got all our things we need just now I guess, My nicest breakable things are still packed & at Jemison but they are not necessary just now

My Sister writes Mother & Dad made the trip from Jemison on to Robertsdale to visit them, so Mother has improved or either felt she needed the change so bad she grined & made it.

Alma Sure hope you're doing fine by now let us hear, what color is her eyes, her hair, how much did she weigh, hurry & let us hear.

Mama Dukes, don't worry about Lewis I'm sure he'll be O.K. soon, one side was hurting worse than the other - so if he pulls that tooth to-day he'll be back to work soon. I tried to get him to use warm, salt water but No, so he went to the Dr. & he sent him home to use it, until the swelling went down. Joe said had I charged him for my advice he would have taken it Ha.

We were over to Ray & Dot's Sat. nite their apt. is much larger than ours but we like ours best, Shorty doesn't leave until after the bus stops across the st. It is very convient to the buses both to Alexandria & Washington

How is the boys these days bet they were glad to see Mama Duke, how they like the girl?

Leland bet you having fun passing out cigars.'

     Write us
     Love to all
     Pearl & Shorty

P.S. our living room suit just came an Lewis is back, going to pull his teeth Wednesday.

HOTEL CARDIFF

IN THE HEART OF MUSCLE SHOALS

UNDER THE DIRECTION OF U. O. REDD, JR.

TUSCUMBIA, ALABAMA

I've not seen any of the Kin since Sunday but guess they are all OK. Talk about cold they say its been as low as 38 here its just my luck for it to do this just at a time when I've no bedfellow to keep me warm.

Hope you are having a good time and you needn't worry about me as I'm doing as I please for once in life so I'm going to close for this time and try it again soon when I'm not so sleepy.

With much love I remain yours Joe

We received many calls and cards and letters of ~~a~~ happiness ~~s~~. I am sending a special ~~card~~ letter from Aunt Ruby. ~~xxx~~

Sat. A.M.

Dear Alma,

I've heard the good news, and I'm very happy for you! I know you're glad to be your good, flat self again. I'm glad the baby is O.K. Sex really don't matter. So many other things are more important.

I haven't been able to git to Maryville to see Bill or Wynn. ~~Wynn didn't~~ call me until last Saturday. Esa & Lewis & children were out all Sunday afternoon,

Edmonds new sister came in Tuesday, and I haven't had the car. He is taking them to the Mts. today. I packed a lunch this A.M. Charles and I are sitting in the dis. office. I have a boil on my rear and Dr. may cut it open. I hope. I'll try to get over to see them tomorrow. I want to send you something. I thought of flowers, and candy, and I also thought if your pants now look like mine did, that that would do you more good than

flowers or candy. So that's what I'm going to do. Soon as I leave here. I hope you do need some. I'll do something for the baby later, and I know you are going to be careful, take it easy, and if you keep these pants on you won't get out of shape again — Don't forget I

Love you,

Ruby

Mama Was A Great Help!

Mama was a great help! Leland took her home, and the day after their return to Alabama, Leland called me. I still have trouble believing what he said. But this is the sum and substance of the conversation. Apparently, he had been secretly thinking of a move from Fountain City. Until this day I do not know the reason why; however, some say TVA's rules and regulations had something to do with Leland's desire to choose other employment. Anyway, he said, "How would you like to move back to Alabama?" This floored me, because I was still fixing up our house and never dreamed we would leave this very first home! "Well," I said, "Let me catch my breath. You will have to make me better informed as to the wheres and whys!!" So when he came home, I said, "Are you crazy? Going into business takes oodles of money! We don't have any cash on hand, let alone oodles."

"We will think about the best thing to do. I have met a banker in Tuscumbia, and after several meetings he assured me The First National Bank in Tuscumbia would finance my venture," explained Leland. "Mr. Marshall Dugger is one of the nicest bankers I have ever met. He did not hesitate to listen to my future plans. And when he finished listening, he turned to me and said, 'If you are serious about making a change in your life, now is the right time to take the step and I am in a position to help you.'"

The big venture was purchasing an on-going concern, a concrete company. Fred Bevis, a native of this area, owned the business. "Right now?" I asked. "Let's consider this leap of faith and not be too hasty in our decision."

Becky was about three months old when he said, "Sell the house, pack up the kids, cats, and dogs and sing 'I'm Going To Alabama With My Banjo On My Knee.'" Only instead, it was three Biggs babies and their pets. Mama came and stayed with us about a month, and I wondered what I would do when she went home. Of course, I was more than happy to move back where my family was still struggling to make ends meet. The promise was to be kept; the financial call was still loud and clear. Leland soon left us in Tennessee and went to Sheffield as the new owner of the Tri-Cities Ready Mix Company and Sheffield Concrete Block Company. I began to make plans to return to Alabama, first by putting our house on the market. It sold quickly, for it was new and built of the best materials. Then our new life became a reality.

In July 1946, the biggest moving van available drove up to be transportation for the whole kit and kabootle of the Biggs' earthly belongings. Our car was filled to the fullest with three children, a dog, and I think a cat. Tears filled my eyes as I looked back at our house and headed for a future unknown. I did leave, however, and never looked back again.

We had decided on buying an old house located on Colbert Heights Mountain, about three miles from Tuscumbia. This is a rural area; for I had said, "I do not want my children to be exposed to city streets and ways."

In the meantime, we had over-purchased on the big revolving concrete trucks. Very few were used, and the company yard was filled with idle trucks. Leland was a plunger. He was looking for a break and would say, "Things will work out," Well! Sure enough, a construction company located in Chattanooga, Tennessee, had been awarded a big concrete contract with Dupont. T. T. Wilson & Company had the job, but their equipment was not adequate. They had the work, and we had the trucks. So Leland packed up his almost new trucks and, with a contract from T. T. Wilson, joined hands to construct this project. Leland began working in Chattanooga, spending only weekends at home.

Leland's father, Papaw Biggs, was asked to come to Alabama to help operate the newly acquired business. He was retired and was only picking up odd jobs around Fountain City, Tennessee. He came and tried to adapt himself to all the changes in his life. Becky was his pride and joy. He would cuddle her up, and in Winter pull the chair closer to the kitchen stove. I tried, but I knew my cooking was a far cry from Mamaw Bigg's East Tennessee meals. Papaw Biggs was a good sport and somehow managed to survive.

As time went on, I think Papaw enjoyed his job, and he did at least keep things going. Bill and Wynn were in school, and Becky and I took over the housework. Leland delegated what was left in Colbert Heights to Papaw and me. We had our hands full with three children, orders and collections, and all the duties that make life go on. Papaw was very temperamental by nature, but he was a great help to me in all I was trying to do. He always enjoyed a garden and decided a flat place near the foot of the mountain would be rich soil. So he would make his way half way down the mountain with his rake and hoe in hopes of beautiful vegetables.

Late one evening from the back porch, we could hear a cry that sounded almost like a child crying. Then the top of a curly, black head was seen, and Papaw came huffing and puffing up the hill. He said, "Did you hear that cry? It was a panther! It can have the garden, I'm through!" We still talk about Papaw's hair standing straight up. He added, "There are snakes down there! Look at that snake print on the floor of the porch! I'm through!" That was the end of our dream of all those fresh vegetables.

There was a small family of black people at the bottom of the mountains. John and Ida Thomas, their children, and grandchildren used the back path that wound up the mountain as their way to the grocery stores at Colbert Heights. They came through our backyard often, and one day I asked Ida, "Would you like a baby-sitting and helper's job?" She accepted and became almost as one of the family. Ida was a big, jovial, energetic person and just filled the bill for what I needed. You will hear more about Ida as times goes on.

We soon learned that we had purchased a beautiful view, snakes, panthers, and unusual neighbors. Before we had even unloaded the van, a neighbor came over and said, "You have made a big mistake. No one can live peaceably by Mr. Berry." Sure enough, we soon learned that he was claiming about half of what we thought was our driveway. He secured his claims by paying overdue taxes. It seemed like every morning he would be closer and closer to our door with his surveying equipment. Inch by inch, we were being pushed off the mountain. This went on and on. Mr. Berry made our lives miserable. However, we still enjoyed the beautiful view from our back porch.

The children, Bill and Wynn were in school, and Becky and Ida took over the housework. I was chief cook and bottle washer, and did all the office work from our dining room table. After all the chores were ended each day, it would be supper time. Our kitchen was downstairs from the entrance. Bill and Wynn had been cooped up in school all day, and they were ready for a scuffle. I tried and tried to settle things down and with a broomstick would chase them to the stairway. They would take their seats and call down, "Mrs. Biggs is a mean old woman." I would give up, and somehow Papaw held his tongue. I said, "Enough is enough."

In 1948, the Wilson job was nearing completion, and things at home were gradually becoming worse and worse. The boys needed supervision, and I needed a breather. "Changes must be made," I said. "You come home, or I come to Chattanooga." We considered both ideas. It seemed best to stay and put some more life and effort in our weakening economy. Leland came home and believe it or not handed me $80,000 in cash. I almost fainted, but I managed to say, "Now we will be able to pay for the children's education." But money was needed everywhere else. How we saw the times through, we will never know. I guess we were just determined.

Advice To Parents

I have long been a great admirer of Erma Bombeck, and I saved this bit of advice to share with all of you. She said the following:

"Do you have MEAN Parents?"

Being a parent is not an easy assignment! Especially when it comes to saying "No!" to your children. Kids often interpret their parent's negative response to their requests as mean, narrow, or even hateful. Parents and teens, read the following article from Erma Bombeck and listen to what she is saying.

Someday I'll Tell My Children

"You Don't Love Me!" How many times have your kids said that one to you? And how many times have you, as a parent, raised the urge to tell them how much?

Someday, when my children are old enough to understand the logic that motivates a mother, I'll tell them:

I loved you enough to bug you about where you were going, with whom, and what time you would get home.

I loved you enough to be silent and let you discover your handpicked friend was a creep.

I loved you enough to make you return a Milky Way with a bite out of it to a drugstore and confess, "I stole it."

I loved you enough to stand over you for two hours while you cleaned your bedroom, a job that would have taken me 15 minutes.

I loved you enough not to make excuses for your lack of respect and your bad manners.

I loved you enough to ignore "what every other mother did."

I loved you enough to figure you would lie about the party being chaperoned but forgave you for it after discovering I was right.

I loved you enough to let you stumble, fall, and fail so that you could learn to stand alone.

I loved you enough to accept you for what you are, not what I wanted you to be.

But most of all, I loved you enough to say no when you hated me for it. That was the hardest part of all.

Making Ends Meet

A Move Back To Alabama

In 1947, Becky was about four months old, we moved to Colbert Heights, Alabama. We soon realized we were missing some very important aspects of our lives: This community did not have a Church of Christ. We decided to drive up and down the mountain several times a week to the 4th Street congregation in Tuscumbia.

The William Carroll family lived at the foot of the mountain, and Mattye and I attended Ladies Bible Class at 4th Street weekly. One Wednesday on the way back home, a thought became a loud and clear reality. I said, "Mattye, why can't we begin a new beginning right here at home and call it Colbert Heights Church of Christ?" "Do you think we can do that?" she asked.

We did not go to our homes, but pulled into the local school parking lot and timidly approached the principal's office. He was very receptive of our request to allow us to begin meeting in one of the classrooms on the Lord's Day. When the next Wednesday rolled around the ladies gathered under a big oak tree for our Bible Study Class.

The Beginning of Colbert Heights Church of Christ

Brother Harold Posey came to our group and offered a vacant lot next door to his home. This lot became the cornerstone of our dreams. At this time Leland and I owned the Tri-Cities Ready Mix Concrete Company, and he used the big revolving concrete trucks to haul concrete up the mountain from Sheffield. Please note that your grandfather was not a member of the church at this time, and I was graciously surprised that he allowed his concrete to be poured out at Colbert Heights for the foundation of our building. Now at least we had a basement, but it seemed to rain downpours every Saturday, and the basement would be ankle deep in water. This called for volunteers with brooms, mops, and buckets to work fast so we could meet on Sunday morning. The Biggs family, all of us, including Leland, took part in this mopping operation. Mama and Papa Delano lived right across the road, and they generously kept the workers supplied with the most delicious country food imaginable. Mama Delano sort of adopted Leland, and much to my surprise he soon became a part of the good work. Time moved on, and many happy memories still linger, which include so many Christian people and this country church building.

A Country Church

I think God seeks this house, serenely white,
    Upon this hushed, elm-bordered street, as one
With many mansions seeks, in calm delight,
    A boyhood cottage intimate with sun.

I think God feels Himself the Owner here,
    Not just rich Host to some self-seeking throng,
But Friend of village folk who want Him near
    And offer Him simplicity and song.

No stained-glass windows hide the world from view,
    And it is well. The world is lovely there,
Beyond clear panes,
    where branch-scrolled skies look through,
And fields and hills, in morning hours of prayer.

Violet Alleyn Storey

Our First Preacher

*Remembrance Of Work With The
Colbert Heights Church of Christ
September 1949 to May 1951
By Richard and Mable Taylor*

In the fall of 1948, Brother Ervin Lee, then president of Mars Hill Bible School, had come to Harding College where my wife and I were in our senior year. Brother Lee's assigned topic was "How to Start Bible Schools." After hearing him, Mable, my bride, and I approached him, and in complimenting him on his excellent lesson we asked how a person could get a job at Mars Hill Bible School.

He took out his pen and asked, "What's your name?" When I told him, he said, "You have a job as soon as you graduate."

After graduating in the summer of 1949, Mable and I hitched a ride with Don Healy, a Harding teacher, who was traveling to Alabama with his trailer to take a Russellville piano back to Harding. Brother Healy brought all our earthly possessions in that small two-wheeled trailer. We arrived in August just in time to settle into Brother Virgil Larimore's apartment next door to Mars Hill. When school opened, I became the teacher of the eighth grade class, swapped rooms with Brother Rayford Henry, and taught Math and Geography to his seventh graders. Mable was a homemaker, and she later became the full time librarian at Mars Hill.

That Fall, Brother Lee held a tent meeting at Colbert Heights. There were five or six families who lived in the Colbert Heights community who wanted to start a new congregation for the Lord. They were attending services with about three neighboring Church of Christ congregations: 4th St. in Tuscumbia, Littleville, and probably Leighton.

We attended the tent meeting held in Colbert Heights and met the people there. With Brother Lee's encouragement, they asked us to move there that I might become their preacher. Brother Lee must have appointed three elders, because I do not remember appointing them myself. They were Elbert Henry Sr., Burl Vandiver, and Harold Posey. It seems that we lived in Brother Larimore's apartment for only four or five weeks; then we moved to Colbert Heights into Brother Posey's house which his brother, Johnny Posey, and Damaris had just vacated. We met in the elementary school building of Colbert Heights regularly, until we were able to build a basement in which to meet.

Harold Posey had donated a lot next door to his rock house on the highway, where the present building that belongs to the Church still stands.

Mars Hill Bible School guaranteed its teachers a $200 per month salary to teach full time with them. If we got any pay from churches, it was to be deducted from the $200. So because the Colbert Heights Church of Christ paid me $50 per month, I received only $150 from Mars Hill Bible School. We had no car, so Brother Charlie Morris sold us our first and newest car ever, a 1948 Hudson with only 17,000 miles on it. Needless to say, we were strapped with payments for quite some time.

I was glad to be the regular preacher for the Lord's Church at Colbert Heights. We were young, just married, and inexperienced, but we were thankful to the Lord that we had been blessed by attending Harding College, a Christian College. We wanted to give our lives in serving the Lord through helping others in Christian education. Mable and I have never regretted our decision, and we are very thankful for the wonderful influences that have come into our lives and the lives of our three sons, through the school and church work. We have made many, many lifetime friends and have tried always to be a blessing to those we serve.

Some of the members at Colbert Heights who I remember are the elders I have mentioned, and their wives and children: William and Mattie Carroll, Bill, Paul and Evalynn; Mrs. Leland (Alma) Biggs, Billy, Winston, Becky and David; brother and sister Olen Henry, Oconee, Bonnie Lee, Claude and Geraldine; Elmer Counce family; Barry Clark family; Mrs. Marvin Saint and daughter Juanita; Edward Taylor family; Vernon Taylor family; Clarence Mitchell family; Looney Huggins family; Kelley Ellidge family; O'Neal Greenhill family; Dave McDonald family; Covey Brown family; James Delano family; Clyde Delano family; Clyde L. Jones family; Harold Posey family; Burl Vandiver family; Elbert Henry family and her sister Lula Taylor; and a son, Elbert Henry Jr. and Hope, with whom we were closely associated at Mars Hill. Occasionally, Mathis and Dot would come to visit with us from Chicago. Also, in our first year at Colbert Heights, we rode the school bus driven by Elbert Henry, Jr. It seems that I became the driver before the first year was finished, and then I drove the bus from Colbert Heights down the mountain on toward Leighton, but turned south to Spring Valley, returned and continued north, crossed the Tennessee River and picked up students all along the way.

During our second year, a basement was built mostly by members while we met in the local schoolhouse. The church was really good to us. We came from Mars Hill Bible School one day and found our table filled with groceries and a lovely bouquet in a big mixing bowl. A note said, "For our orphan kids."

We drove back home to Canada our first Christmas vacation, and the church gave us a ceramic well filled with money to help pay for the trip. We still have the well, but not the money.

The second year, we moved into Harold Posey's house, across the field from the church building and near the edge of the mountain. Mary Lou Greenhill is still living there. Our oldest son, Richard Neale Jr., was born January 22, 1951. It snowed the week the baby was born, and I couldn't get off the mountain, so I spent the week helping to take care of Mable and the baby. The churches in Tuscumbia and Colbert Heights gave us baby showers.

All in all, the time we spent at Colbert Heights working with the local church was very pleasant and enjoyable. Many brethren we knew there have gone on to heaven. We hope to see them all again someday at that greatest of all reunions. May the good Lord always be glorified in all that we do.

***

Since Richard and Mable left in May of 1951, I will continue the story with some very happy things that happened later that year. Some time in the year 1951, a gospel meeting was held at Colbert Heights by Brother Howard Allen. When the invitation was extended and we were standing singing, I realized Leland was taking the most important step of his life. He made the good confession, and many of the members went with us to 4th street in Tuscumbia where he was baptized. As I became more and more unsteady on my feet and as I sat down, I thought, "Yes, miracles do happen!" Now our children can attend Mars Hill Bible School, and we can join hands as a family in this, the greatest work of a lifetime. Even now, I want you children to know that this was a wonderful decision made on a remarkable night in the presence of the members of Colbert Heights Church. "Thank you, Lord."

After moving back to Sheffield, Lady Luck handed us Jackie Phyfer, who became my co-worker and good friend. "Thank you, Jackie."

The Children Try Their Wings

Time passed so swiftly. The children were all leaving home in the dark and returning home in the dark. Mars Hill Bible School, where they attended, was across the Tennessee River Bridge through Florence and on the outskirts of the main perimeter of the city.

I had the usual picture panels made of the boys, being sure we were at the photographers at the right age and time, so when it was time to make Becky's picture, I decided that since we had only one little girl, I would forego the panel and save my money toward a portrait. A talented Mrs. Alexander had agreed to do Becky's sitting when Becky became about four years old. So we kept that date, and I have always been so pleased with her work. This is a copy of Becky's portrait that graces our living room wall. A little 29-cents-a-yard dress and flowers from our front yard tucked into Mamaw's basket: What could be sweeter?

The Mother Eagle watched one by one as they tried their wings. Finally, when it was Becky's time to take flight from the nest, she, like Bill and Wynn, headed north toward Nashville, Tennessee, to attend David Lipscomb College (now University). I will try to describe how all mothers must feel as children separately leave the nest. We made memories as we climbed endless dormitory stairs, struggling with what Becky thought were her necessities of life. This included stereo, cooking vessels, even a refrigerator and endless decorations. Here was our little girl (the third Biggs) heading off for new friends and experiences. The nest was almost empty, just David bringing up the rear in the 1960s. We enjoyed every phase of our family life and looked to the richness of maturity that we never could imagine in all of them. From Lipscomb Becky went to Auburn, and then she married and graduated from Florence State University.

We Are Pleased to Announce That

Rebecca Biggs Hamm

has been placed on the Dean's List because of high scholastic achievement during the past semester.

Turner W. Allen _____ Dean

Florence State College
Florence, Alabama

David Is Born

1950 brought another "Bigg's" surprise. I did not feel well, and what do you think? Dr. Trapp of Tuscumbia said, "No, it can't be!" It was: I was expecting for the fourth time.

Dr. Trapp refused to believe that I was pregnant at the age of 41 plus. I asked, "How many children have you really had?" He laughed and said, "None." "Well, then I have had three, and if everything goes well, I will have another one around the middle of August."

My good neighbors, Elizabeth and George Babcock, lived just across the road from our dividing line. Elizabeth was a registered nurse on duty at Colbert County Hospital (now Helen Keller Hospital). She had graciously promised to see me through the ordeal,

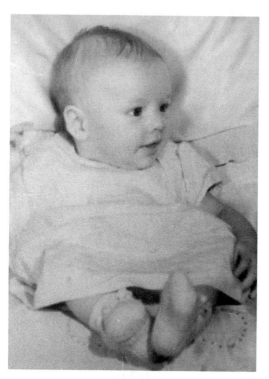

day or night: she was on call. Mother Nature did make her call in the middle of the night, and Elizabeth picked me up bag and baggage, and drove me off the mountain to the busy Colbert County Hospital. She was my "Guardian Angel" (though the Bible plainly says angels are masculine. Look this up!). After what seemed ages, I remembered hearing a little squeaky noise and a nurse coming up to my bed with a precious bundle. This little fellow had a head full of curly locks. While counting toes and fingers, I noticed his head sat almost flat on his chubby shoulders; he was so cute. He was almost a carbon copy of Winston.

Since Mamaw and Papaw Biggs were now living in Sheffield, the Knoxville relatives visited often. At this time, Barbara Biggs,

Everett's daughter was visiting. She and Mamaw came out to the hospital. We were still trying to find a proper name for the baby. Barbara said, "I like David," and since Warren is a family name on my side, his name immediately became David Warren Biggs. Barbara was a sweet girl and gave Mamaw much pleasure.

David stayed pretty much in Ida's care. Only on Saturday would I show up in Tuscumbia, and my friends would say, "Oh! Alma, your little grandson is precious!" Then I would explain, "Miracles do happen."

Leland was trying to keep things in order with the business, so he wasn't at home much. We were lucky to have Ida to help with all the chores, and almost with open arms she accepted another charge. Soon David was her "pride and joy." As he grew, Ida would straddle him around her neck in the afternoons, and off they would go. He loved the attention, and I really appreciated the help, especially when I thought, "Here comes another terrible two," maybe not so terrible, just frustrating. The only word in his vocabulary seemed to be, "No," no cereal, no bath, no bedtime. Any silence for a minute would spell trouble, but what would I give to relive those sticky, bubbly days. Even the time a little later, when young David let the brake loose on our new car and he and the car both landed in the top of a sapling on the side of the mountain, I remember with thankfulness that he wasn't hurt.

Becky was baby-sitting one day. She perched David on the see-saw made of a board nailed to the top of an old cedar post with an iron spike. She jumped off. He was left on, and his side of the see-saw came down hard. He still has a permanent scar from this incident.

Bill and Wynn also had their times of terror. Bill's job was to keep the furnace full of coal. On a trip with a bucket full of coal, Wynn caused him to fall and knock out one of his front teeth.

We moved to Sheffield in the Spring of 1955. David attended Sally Dunning Kindergarten there. He started to Mars Hill Bible School the following year. Some of his teachers were Mrs. Underwood, Mrs. Gilbert, Mrs. Kendrick, Mrs. Wilhelm, Mr. Beavers, Mr. Gooch, and Rayford Henry who was also the bus driver.

SCHOOL DAYS 1953-54
MARS HILL

SCHOOL DAYS 1956-57
MARS HILL

SCHOOL DAYS 1958-59

All of my children were college graduates and were exposed to piano lessons, but the interest was not there to become good musicians. The world of music was not taken seriously, even though Mrs. Berry and Mrs. Alexander were very able teachers.

David moved to Sheffield High School for his 11th grade, then graduated from Sheffield High in 1968. He was in the Navy from 1969 until 1973. He attended Old Dominion College in Norfolk, Virginia in 1976. He married Amy Jackson in 1994.

Mrs. Joe Henry Hancock, junior

announces the marriage of her daughter

Amy Jackson

to

Mr. David Warren Biggs

on Sunday, April twenty-fourth

Nineteen hundred and ninety-four

Nashville, Tennessee

The Bigg's Pets

Pets seem a vital part of all young families and my story tells you a little about the Biggs bunch's pets from the first to the last. Some of you remember being very responsible for these additions, and if you do not remember them all, maybe this will jog your memory.

Bill's imaginary playmate was a dog. This dog was so real to him that it almost became our pet, too. The pet was called Dog. I have mentioned him previously.

Our second pet was a beautiful German Shepherd. He became our pet in the early days while we were living in Knoxville. He was named Danny.

Next we had a cat. We named this pretty, fluffy cat, Nicko. Your Uncle Arlton picked the name from his stint in Japan during the war.

Pet number four was a dog named Jingo. He was a beautiful Dalmatian, and he would have graced any fire truck around.

Then we had a parakeet. Winston won Pretty Boy at the Memphis fair. He and his friend, Paul Carrol, won Pretty Boy and several other birds. We allowed him to bring home only one. While cleaning Pretty Boy's cage, a peephole caught his eye, and out and over he went. We watched him until he became a dot and then we began weeping and wailing to no avail. He was gone into the wild blue yonder.

Becky's black Poodle Pecot was bought from a home kennel near St. Florian. Becky's heart was broken when he first vanished. We formed searching crews, but he was never found. Maybe he was just another kidnapped pet.

Woody was number seven. We named him Woody because we found him in the woods. He was David's companion, just a plain chunky devoted dog. He was a carrier of ticks, and he kept us busy, especially in winter. The ticks loved the heat vents, and we despised finding them there.

Also, there was Blindy, Leland's dog. One morning he greeted us at the back door, an appealing and attractive mixed breed of maybe dog and wolf. We soon realized his caring mother sensed his disability and must have brought him to us. So what should we do? He was totally blind, with a keen sense of hearing and smelling. We asked ourselves, "Do we take him to an animal shelter to be disposed of?" An emphatic "No" came from Leland. So our yard was fenced in, and Blindy lived, a well-cared-for, long life, and he was a part of our every day care. His caution is still a part of our yard gate, "Beware of Dog."

We also had numerous chicks, ducks, bunnies, and whatever came with Easter. One of the baby ducks happened to run under Winston's feet and became a one-sided duck. He only had half of his face. We didn't hear many quacks out of him.

All of our pets were special and lived a normal life span for a dog, bird, cat, or chick, and I believe each was a blessing to us all, maybe creating more patience and tender love. If there is an Animal Heaven, I hope they will all declare in one big bark, meow, quack, or cheep, "I am of the Biggs Bunch."

Back To The Main Story
There Must Be A Better Way

Now back to the main stream of my story. It seemed all our business ventures so far showed "red" ledgers, and this one was about to be another trial run. I thought, "There must be a better way."

Our neighbor was Carl Salter, an engineer with Tennessee Valley Authority and a regular early riser for coffee at the Victory Café in Sheffield, Alabama. One day he asked Leland, "Do you own any heavy equipment suitable for transportation of chemicals from the TVA Plant in Muscle Shoals to their fertilizer plant across the city of Sheffield? TVA has a desperate need for this service."

Over coffee, plans were instigated to create a company for transportation of chemicals from the TVA government plant to the chemical companies at home and finally across the nation. As you children must have decided, your father and grandfather was a "plunger." So here he goes! Our past financial expenses had been as follows:

1. Tri-Cities Ready Mix Concrete, 1946
    (A) The T.T. Wilson Dupont Job, Chattanooga, Tennessee
2. Bevis Lumber, 1952-55, Sheffield, Alabama
3. Chem-Haulers, 1955. Sold in 1980 (hauled acids to Monsanto Chemical Company, Luling, Louisiana from TVA, 1956)

It was necessary for our new company to make big purchases of equipment to service a venture of this magnitude. In planning our new uncharted highway, tank-truck venture, we made the unbelievable deal with Fruehouf Trailer Company, Birmingham, Alabama, to build three huge, stainless steel trailers and trucks to operate for our future financial security. Our debt called for payments of $1,666.66 per month on each of four 316 trailers. Chem-Haulers became a national tank truck operation with home offices on Country Boy Lane, off Hatch Boulevard and Jackson Highway, Sheffield. Terminal facilities were later located in Birmingham, Tuscaloosa, Decatur, and Guntersville, Alabama, and in Memphis, Tennessee.

I am not sure that we were aware of any highway rules and regulations of the U.S. Interstate Commerce Commission. We soon learned that traveling over our free highways required special authority granted by the Interstate Commerce Commission.

Getting Chem-Haulers up and going took untold determination on our part day and night. Soon it was clear that operation costs far exceeded our income. The Chemical Companies seemed less and less in need of the service over our limited road rights. We finally decided to use a little politics, and Leland persuaded a local lawyer, (Jim Smith) and an advisor, (Jimmy Thompkins) to make a trip to Washington, D.C. They appeared before a meeting of the Interstate Commerce Commission and made their desperate survival plea. We were surely blessed; they headed back to Alabama with something generally called, The Grandfather Rights. Soon we realized we held in our hands a piece of paper granting Chem-Haulers the right-of-way, almost without restriction, across most of the U.S.A.

The sun was shining again. The company expanded, and we were the proud owners of a highly respected hometown company. Many people were employed for highway travel, and the office personnel file was bursting at the seams.

In 1956, Papaw Biggs died of a heart attack at his home. This was a blow to us all. My Papa Joe's death had come in 1956. Leland kept his promise to me when we were married that he would support me in a financial way in order to take care of my parents.

One day Leland said, "There is a little house on 9th Street in Sheffield for sale for a reasonable amount; it's where 'Aunt Maud' and 'Uncle Joe' live. Since they are on a rental basis, month to month insecurity, let's buy this for them! At least they will have one less money stress!" So the little house became their permanent earthly home, thanks to a generous and loving son-in-law.

The Sheffield Grammar School was just across the street and much of their time was spent enjoying the activity of the children, their ball games, and other events.

In 1956, emphysema took its toll on Papa, just one more cough, one more struggle for clean fresh air, and then quiet and peace. Papa Joe died in his own bed in the front room of the little house. This left Mama alone, not lonely, but very much on her own. Again the tug of the singletree—Granny's Daze was waiting with open arms.

1955
829 River Bluff Terrace

The Muscle Shoals Area already had one or two concrete industries, and our business seemed to need an additional boost. We decided to add a lumber company to our faltering business venture. The windfall was short lived. The lumber company gobbled up our fortune, and our trucks were idle again.

Bill Hamilton, a former TVA purchasing agent, was hired by Leland to operate the lumber business. He had learned his trade by spending the government's money with no thought of cost. A privately owned business couldn't survive with this mode of spending. The lumber company was short-lived and, along with the Ready Mix Company, it was soon liquidated. All of our bills were paid, but very little cash was left on hand.

In the meantime, Bill Hamilton had built a nice home for his family. Somehow he managed to take advantage of his job and used the best material available. Finally, when bad came to worse, we had to assume the balance of debt on the house. It seemed to me that we would never get this loan taken care of, but finally we did clear the debt, and it became a good investment. The house was located on 829 River Bluff Terrace which remains my address today.

Our Neighbors On River Bluff Terrace

When he moved from this area, we assumed financial responsibility for the house Bill Hamilton built on River Bluff Terrace in Sheffield, Alabama. The Tennessee Valley Bank directors said, "Someone will have to assume this debt!" That someone happened to be the Biggs.

Living in Colbert Heights was a travel burden. I had become a taxi driver for the whole family. So Leland said, "Let's move to the Hamilton house in Sheffield. It belongs to us anyway." I did not readily jump on his bandwagon, but I finally came around and agreed to make the move. This house was the first built on River Bluff Terrace. No Neighbors!

Soon Bill and Deanne Sanford chose a lot next to us. Then Walter and Marsha Gullet built across the street. Some say, "There are neighbors," and some say, "There are good neighbors." I say, "These are the best."

The Martin family lived around the circle. Wynn and Donnie Martin were buddies. They were into and out of everything. Their lives have been filled with ups and downs.

After school days, Bill Biggs and Bill Martin became friends, and they burned the midnight oil keeping the world's economy in line.

David and Ian Sanford, with their trusted two BB guns, prowled the river bank. Stray BBs left their marks, one on the dining room window and one on the kitchen window. Ian said, "David did it," and David said, "Ian did it." Who did it? Oh, well, boys will be boys.

Jim and Fran Smith became our latest neighbors, and they are tried and true. All my neighbors are good neighbors. I am here, and they are there with outstretched hands ready to help when needed.

1956
Another Family Christmas

After we were a family of four children and living at 829 River Bluff Terrace, Christmas was always a happy season for us as it rolled around each year. I particularly remember 1956: David was six years old and had decided his Santa was Mom and Dad.

Christmas was always a special time for sharing, giving, eating, and particularly decorating our house. Our house seemed to say, "Here am I; please decorate me!" A trip was always made to the neighbor's cedar tree groves. After we had placed the tree in the perfect spot, the fragrance traveled through the whole house.

This Christmas was especially remembered as Santa struggled down the chimney carrying, (would you believe) an Electric Lionel Train. The card said, "It's for all of you." Someday maybe you will draw a numbered card with your name. You will be the lucky one, for you can hand it down for generations to come.

Now these many years later we have become Grand Pa and Grand Ma. We begin to wonder how time passed so quickly. With precious grandchildren, we have little time to remember; instead Christmas is alive with laughter and wonder that can only be seen through shining eyes of the first generation, portraying kindness and love.

All Christmases signal that a New Year is just around the corner. I hope that your memories reach backward

Christmas Greeter, 1956

and forward, and your memories are as wonderful as mine are. Remember that as long as we can love we are not alone. Keep this in mind for all past and future holiday seasons.

I wish for you and yours, A MERRY CHRISTMAS.

The Electric Lionel Train

Christmas decorations in the garden room at River Bluff Terrace

1956
Chem-Haulers & The Lake Home

From 1953-55, Chem-Haulers struggled. We were all very much involved in making "hauling" go. The children—Bill, Wynn, and Becky—were in school at Mars Hill, and it seemed tuition knew no bounds. However, Leland would stretch every penny, and hide all red letter statements marked overdue. His children were his pride and joy and must not be deprived. During the year 1956, he heard of a lake residence available for sale. As the doting parent, he made another financial addition to our over burdened budget, a house on Wilson Lake Shores. The children were ecstatic!

In the meantime, Bill and Wynn enrolled at David Lipscomb College in Nashville. They each made many friends, both at home and in school. Our lake home soon became "a come one come all" haven for teen-agers from far and near, especially the Lipscomb group. They considered our house a hang out, with the welcome sign that stated, "come as you are." Leland and I would find ourselves stripping the grocery store shelves on the way to the lake every night. We would never know how many would tuck their feet under our table. It seemed to me that we added more potatoes and more of most every edible thing as every mealtime approached.

I think I am right: Lipscomb College did not have a fraternity, but our intellectuals decided to fix that. The Delta Kappa Chapter of Alpha Kappa Psi was soon in the making. Dr. Axel W. Swang, head of the Business Administration Department at David Lipscomb University, seemed to be the right person to lead this new endeavor. He was loved and appreciated by all the loyal boys. Dr. Swang was a loving family man. He loved the Lord, the Church, and David Lipscomb College. On May 21, 1960, Leland was presented honorary membership in this fraternity. Harold N. Roney was chapter president at this time. His family faithfully supported Lipscomb, and all the members loved him.

At our lake home, we had some great times skiing, arguing, and pyramiding. Sometimes, four boys would stack on shoulders. That was a real acrobatic achievement, four high. During this time, we held our breath, expecting an accident at any moment. As far as I remember, the only really frightening tragedy happened to David.

He was put into service by the older ones to take his turn at caring for the boat and other menial chores. The other boys were in the process of docking at our back pier, and David was submerged in the water when Winston realized what was happening. He knew David was in the path of the twirling propeller. He jumped in just in time to shove David in the opposite direction. The next time the propeller made its circuit, David was just near enough to be caught by the tip of the blade. His shoulder and arm were cut in several places.

After the excitement and examination of the injured, it was decided that David with a little time would survive. His new scars would take their place under the one resulting from the "Flying Jenny" accident of long ago. I'm sure Becky remembers! Winston was declared a hero, and we know his motivation was activated by "Brotherly Love."

The lake home, though it added hard work and spending of pennies from who knows where, proved to be a time of sheer joy and well worth our sacrifices. Bill graduated from Lipscomb College in 1960 and, with all the vim and vigor he could muster, joined the Chem-Haulers force. Then when Wynn graduated in 1963, he became a part in the survival of our beloved Chem-Haulers.

Both boys had married. Bill and Shelva lived on 19th Street in Sheffield, and Wynn and Linda lived on Hiwassee Avenue on the West Side of Sheffield. We, of course, were at our home located at 829 River Bluff Terrace in Sheffield, Alabama. We all lived near enough to the Chem-Haulers plant to check on SOS calls when we were needed.

The trucking business is not easy from any point of view. There were many hazards, including the possibility of overturned trucks spilling caustic acids into the environment. Hazard after hazard happened, and we received call after call for assistance. It seemed the night time buttons must have been set on SOS at all times.

I remember one Spring night, rain was pouring down, and the phone sounded louder than usual. The Sheffield police were calling for immediate help. Our tanks loaded with ammonia were parked on the lot, and someone passing reported that the dolly on one of the trucks was leaning; in fact, it was sinking in the mud. I punched

Leland and said, "Get up, we are in trouble. One of the tanks is about to roll. Hurry!" He grunted and said, "Let 'er roll." Then turned over and burrowed under the covers as he mumbled, "Enough is enough."

I was furious! I grabbed a raincoat and umbrella and headed for Country Boy Lane. As I topped the hill, I could see many people. I realized what a dangerous situation we were in, and I stopped to be of help. If this ammonia spilled out it would be a great disaster. When I pulled up, some of our employees had been called, and one said, "Mrs. Biggs, what are you doing over here?" All I could answer was, "I want you to know which side I am on, like the old woman during the Civil War with her broom."

Then bright, car lights showed up on a speeding car. It was bleary-eyed Bill. The company of men, together with Smitty and his wrecker, worked to prop the tank up, and then they stabilized it, thanks to the Good Lord, neighbors, employees, and friends.

There was excitement of some kind every hour of the day and night.

Later, while I was ironing and listening to the radio, news blared out, "A Chemical Company in Sheffield, Alabama is being sued for one million dollars due to a truck-pedestrian wreck. The victim claimed he lost a big diamond ring when his arm was severed. The ring was on his finger, he said."

I guess this could have been a compliment—a million dollars? I just kept on ironing; for there is no blood in a turnip. We survived by the hardest.

We worked beside many loyal people who also became our dear friends, and they helped us throughout the Chem-Haulers years. Here is a list of some of them: Lonnie Flippo, Lou Smallwood, Elizabeth Richards, Juanita Gresham, Annie Darrah, Mary Agnes Black, Greg Napps, Doug Logue, and Lawton Gillis.

Left: Cliff Henton on crutches after an accident.

*Drivers:
Cliff Henton,
Paul Willexson,
Ronnie Balentine,
and
D. C. Haddock.*

Our World Turns Upside Down

In Loving Memory

We lost two members of our family in 1963. Mamaw Biggs had moved back to Knoxville after Papaw's death. She lived with Ruby, her only daughter. She enjoyed life even though things were never easy for her. She was the kindest, sweetest mother-in-love that was possible for me to have. I loved her dearly.

Sarah Biggs, Mother of Leland C. Biggs

Grand Pa, S. A. Milstead died later in 1963. He was 96 years on this earth. He will long be remembered for his good work. We strive to be more like him, a Christian leader for his whole clan.

Grand Pa, S. A. Milstead

1965-1967
Any Day Is Beautiful

We were kept busy up to 1965, working with church activities, school affairs, ball games, chicken stews, fundraisers, such as "Punkin Day," dinners at the Larimore Home, and working with Associated Women's Organization (AWO). We tried to make sure our family was together, and we kept the home fires burning. At this time, Leland was sort of on the puny list. Dr. Lester Hibbett, our friend and family doctor, told him, "Leland, you must lose weight, your gall bladder is acting up, and I don't want to be called in to cut through all that fat." He did lose some weight, and it seemed to help.

We were proud of our business, Chem-Haulers. I remember a few of the girls who kept the wheels turning. Lounette Smallwood was more or less in charge of the office. Annie Darrah, Juanita Gresham, and Elizabeth Murphy operated the complicated machines that were a problem for all of us. Mary Agnes Black was a "Johnny come lately." She was in the wings waiting her time. She and Leland were buddies. She kept our artificial rubber plants watered and said, "They are putting out new shoots!" Although the ups and downs continued, the trucking business seemed to keep us all busy, and actually began to do very well. Many people contributed to this work force, pushing and pulling to make things go.

Our lives could have been called normal. Leland and I encouraged the boys to become "Truckers," and their families were beginning to be a real joy to us. We had become Grand Pa and Grand Ma, and at our age we could get away with anything. There was a folk song that said, "When we pass on, our library has gone with us." We need to share with our grandchildren our faith, sorrows, experiences of joy, and even the failures we have suffered. Tell them the "tall tales," and describe to them your world long gone. Relate to them your past childhood and courtships. They will love it! All this can be Pandora's box to the young. Make yesterday come alive! Most importantly, we must pass along the basis of our faith to our youngsters. Just talk to them about everything.

One morning, Mary Agnes greeted Leland as he came into the office of Chem-Haulers, "Good morning, Leland. It's a beautiful day!"

"Any day is beautiful when I can get out of bed and pretend to be on the up and up," he said. "Each day is made for rejoicing and gladness," Leland continued. Although he struggled to be in his place, we knew he was not on the greatly improved list. Then finally, Dr. Hibbett came into our picture again. It was a long two years of ins and outs at Coffee Hospital. After much consultation, Dr. Hibbett advised surgery. In August of 1966, Dr. Charley Pritchett performed a "heart breaking" operation at Coffee Hospital: the diagnosis was cancer of the spleen.

After Dr. Hibbett told us, he and Dr. Pritchett agreed that they needed additional professional advice. Our search for the best ended with a futile trip to Oshner's Clinic in New Orleans, Louisiana.

Now there was only time, a very short time, to spend in tender loving care and concern for his last few days of comfort. Coffee Hospital became our foster home. We spent our time with hope and prayer. Our vigil ended June 4, 1967.

Leland Calvin Biggs died and was buried at Oakwood Cemetery in Sheffield, Alabama.

Leland's Grave Site

In 1967, I was left with David in High School in Sheffield, a home to sustain, and concern for a sluggish company. Bill and Wynn were doing a good job. At that time, they had many competent, loyal employees both in the offices and as drivers. Becky and Johnny were in the air-conditioning business in Florence, Alabama.

I was tired, tired of the financial burdens, family ups and downs, and especially the business world. "You can have it," I told the boys, "Do what is best, and I promise I will never look over your shoulder to suggest or criticize." This is what happened. They struggled, and little by little they prevailed. Chem-Haulers arrived and survived. I kept my promise.

The company was founded in 1953, and sold in 1980 to Saunders and Company of Birmingham. Saunders in turn sold some rights to Ryder Trucking. These rights have made heavy traffic down the road for many years and even today.

After the sale of the company in 1980, the Biggs Bunch went their separate ways. Bill resides in both Florence, Alabama, and Carillon, Florida. Wynn headed to Nashville, Tennessee, and Becky is in Lakeland, Florida. David later located in Nashville, Tennessee. Alma, "Mom B" is still in Sheffield, Alabama, same town, and same house but now "Retired."

All the grandchildren are within "Hollering" distance.

Elected vice president

William D. Biggs, president of Chem-Haulers, Inc., of Florence, a wholly owned subsidiary of Saunders Leasing System, Inc., was recently elected as first and southern region vice president of National TankTruck Carriers, Inc. (NTTC).

He is also this year's recipient of the Alabama Trucking Association's most prestigious award, the H. Chester Webb trophy, for outstanding achievement in 1979-80.

A Bitter Sweet Sale

B'ham Firm To Purchase Chem-Haulers

Agreement in principle on the sale of Chem-Haulers, a Shoals-based trucking firm, to a Birmingham truck leasing company has been reached, officers of both firms said today.

Saunders Leasing Systems Inc. will acquire Chem-Haulers and two related corporations, Harry Saunders Jr., chairman of the firm, announced.

No purchase price was announced.

Sources said the transaction was subject to approval of three governmental agencies.

Chem-Haulers, incorporated in 1956, is a specialized, irregular route truckload common carrier of bulk chemicals, aluminum, steel and specialized ore products, operating mainly in the Southeast and Midwest. The firm began its operations in 1952 as a partnership of the late Leland C. Biggs and his wife, Alma.

In recent years the firm has been headed by a son of the founder, William D. Biggs.

Saunders said the acquisitions will broaden Saunders Systems' ability to serve its customers and enable it to offer a wider range of transportation services.

Saunders, a pioneer in the vehicle renting and leasing industry, has over 120 fully staffed and equipped truck leasing service centers in 23 states and Canada. Saunders has been in operation since 1916.

Services offered include leasing and rental of over-the-road trucks, retail sale-related parts and services, fuel tax reporting and general transportation consulting services.

Sources said the acquisition of Chem-Haulers would not mean any management changes at the office located in Florence.

The company's terminal is in Sheffield.

A decision by the Securities and Exchange Commission and the Interstate Commerce Commission, two of the agencies which must approve the sale, could come within one month.

FINALIZE MERGER — Harris Saunders Jr., chairman of the board and chief executive officer of Saunders Leasing System, Inc., Birmingham, recently announced completion of the acquisition of Chem-Haulers, Inc. The merger makes Chem-Haulers a wholly owned subsidiary of Saunders but will retain its company name. Saunders, left, is shown with William D. Biggs, president of Chem-Haulers.

Something Good Comes From Everything

When 15 years of age, while attending Sheffield, High School, David Biggs wrote this tribute to his Dad.

People experience things everyday, some good and some bad. When bad things happen, we do not stop to consider the good things that may develop from them. Just recently my Father passed away. I felt as though the whole world was against me, and I had a sorry disposition. Now that I have adjusted my life to my sorrow, I can see how I have profited from it.

The first thing I can think of is, I have gained much responsibility. I have been left to take care of my mother and see that things run smoothly. I have two older brothers and an older sister, but I am the only one unmarried and at home. It seems when something of this nature happens, the child at home has more responsibility placed upon him. I am not angry about this, but rather I am glad to have it. When I leave to face the world, I will be more prepared than other people who have never gone through anything like this. Besides gaining responsibility, I have found I must solve my own problems. Whenever I had a problem as all boys do, I would go to my father. He was to me a most brilliant man. I guess almost everyone feels like this toward their father, and if they do not they should. There are people who help me, and I appreciate them. But I now see that life is not a rose garden, and a man will someday be on his own. Being able to solve one's own problems makes a person prepared for life and able to survive it. Having to make his own decisions is hard, but it makes a person mature and ready to accept challenge.

I have also found a desire to protect my family name. One does not realize how important his family name is until he is confronted with preserving it. When one dies, there is nothing left except his name. I have heard nothing but honor for my father's name, and I realize I have to protect it from slander. I have to be careful of what I do and say, so people will realize I am half the man my father was. I could never bring reproach upon my family name for the simple fact that I loved and had great respect for my father. This, in itself, is probably the hardest task I shall ever undertake. I will try to the best of my ability to preserve the name that God has blessed me to have. So I see now that something good comes from everything. I now have three major challenges before me: they are responsibility, making my own decisions, and honoring my family name. These are things one does not really see until later in life, but I am experiencing them at an early age. There is a reason for everything. These are three I have found, but I know there are many more.

David Warren Biggs
8-15-67

This paper was submitted at Sheffield High. Mildred Kimbrough, the teacher made this notation. "Here is the real David. When you find yourself losing the path, take out this paper and re-read it. I, too, have known the emptiness that losing a loved one and respected father brings. Time softens the hurt, the emptiness. If we do nothing to soil the memory of that loved name, we become whole again and stronger for the experience."

Mildred Kimbrough
Sheffield High School,
8-15-67

Granny's Daze Antiques

Our family now numbers more than a score, and when you grandchildren and great-grandchildren visit on special days, you are cautioned over and over to "Be careful; for this is an antique." Then your interest comes out loud and clear. "What and where did this and that originate? Tell us the story about the old things." I am pleased to take the time from a busy day to encourage you all to appreciate the charm and value embedded in each and every special "don't touch" item that is tucked away for another generation.

When our business, Chem-Haulers, expanded their space for larger offices, a special room was added for Granny's Daze Antique Shop. This new home offered more items for sale, which were enjoyed by buyers and lookers. My Mother Maud, a caring shopkeeper, operated the quaint shop. She became a part of this shop and loved every minute of it as she puttered around each day of the week. Everyone expressed love and appreciation for her charm.

It seems that most people desire to touch base with ancestry. At this time of remembering so many of our interesting days, I unearthed an item written in our daily paper, the Tri-Cities, as it was called at that time. Barbara Lemay wrote an article titled "Going Antique Hunting." Since the article on the following page was written about me, and you and you, I am passing it along for you and yours. I hope you will enjoy what Barbara had to say about our "GRANNY'S DAZE," in this bit of information written on August 6, 1969.

Antiques Are Fun

... Mrs. Leland Biggs, of Sheffield, an antique collector for more than 30 years, is full of helpful suggestions for fledgling antique collectors. Mrs. Biggs is shown with a cherished grandfather clock, complete with whatnot shelves and a secret compartment.

Going Antique Hunting? Let An Expert Tell You Techniques

BY BARBARA LeMAY

Are you thinking of going antiquing? Then you're right in step with hundreds of young brides who move from "something old" on their wedding day to a love of the traditionally old in home furnishings.

This week, Mrs. Leland C. Biggs, who began collecting antiques when she was a newlywed more than 30 years ago, offers some suggestions for successful antiquing.

A past owner of her own antique shop, Granny Daze's Antiques in Sheffield, Mrs. Biggs' love for time-mellowed pieces has passed to her daughter, Mrs. John Hamm, Jr. and to her daughter-in-law, Mrs. Bill Biggs and Mrs. Winston Biggs. Even her son David at the University of Alabama is quite proud of his sofa, recently recovered in corduroy, with which his parents began housekeeping.

Family Pieces

It is through such inherited family pieces that most couples begin to collect antiques, Mrs. Biggs states. Although the proper definition of an antique is any object which is over 100 years old, a desk which belonged to your grandmother or a piece of your great grandmother's china should be loved and cherished. Mrs. Biggs' two story home on River Bluff Terrace contains such family pieces as the handsome old bed in which her husband was born, the Biggs' family mantle clock, and wooden churn and a time-worn bread tray from her side of the family.

Begin your antiquing search in family attics or old barns, as these acquired pieces will be much less expensive and have more meaning to you than pieces you add later," she tells would-be collectors.

Mrs. Biggs cautions beginners against highly-organized auctions as your sometimes get the piece on which you have bid only to discover it is not what you thought it was at all. "Do attend auctions if your are seriously interested in antiques," she says, "to see what others are buying and what price they are willing to pay for such pieces as old trunks or milk cans."

Visit Shops

The young wife interested in furnishings for her home would be safest in visiting the many good antique shops in our area, Mrs. Biggs continues. Study a chosen piece carefully, making sure furniture which will be used is of good sturdy construction. "Don't hesitate to buy a good antique even if you don't have the perfect place for it now," she says as her own den was built around a massive mantle which she had stored for years.

Do browse the pure junk shops as some of the prettiest objects Mrs. Biggs owns were discovered there, such as a tall porcelain-lined silver pitcher which she bought for 25 cents in just such a place.

Mrs. Biggs proves her statement that there is nothing wrong with mixing periods and different styles of furniture in the same room, as she points out Empire, Victorian, Early American and French pieces in her most attractive den. "Anyone with money can go to the store and buy a complete set of Victorian furniture and still have a stuffy room, but a home should show your personality through livable and loved furnishings of whatever style and period."

Many Uses

With imagination, old items can be put to many uses other than what they were intended. In her home, an old spool chest lined in tarnish-preventive material and mounted on legs is a perfect silver chest. An old wardrobe with the mirror from the door relocated in the back shows off her collection of cut and art glass. A cut down dining table makes a perfect coffee table.

"Learn about antiques in your own home by reading books on the subject," Mrs. Biggs suggests. The more expensive ones are written for galleries and dealers. Paperbound books on "Guides to Antiques" plus articles in women's magazines will be written in language you can understand and will offer information you can use.

While preparing for an antique show in Murfreesboro, Tennessee, Wynn helped me load a pickup truck with Granny's Daze treasures, and we drove up to Murfreesboro to display them for sale. Linda Jones, a friend and a classmate of my son "Wynn," came to help in the booth where we planned to display our wares. She drove a 1959 Chevolet station wagon, full of stuff from Murfreesboro. On the way home from the antique show, Wynn said, "Mother, I think I would like to make Linda a member of our family." It was then that we decided that Linda would be another "daughter-in-love."

1970
Mama's Death

In the late afternoon of April 27, 1970, Mama's friend Mrs. Vann, was sitting with her in her little house on 9th Street in Sheffield. I had used my washing machine and the beautiful sunshine to do her weekly laundry. This chore had only taken a few minutes. But when I turned the corner coming back, Mrs. Vann was standing on the front porch. I knew something had happened, and I hurriedly entered the front living room. It seemed I had graciously been spared the last few heartbeats taken by my mother. We had lost a loving, caring parent and a wonderful person and friend to all who knew her. She set an example of Christian living for her children and grandchildren. The tender loving care provided for her was no burden to me. When I think of the stitches of love that went into my Christmas Quilt, tears freely fall.

The little house on 9th street faced the Sheffield Grammar School right across the street. Mother had an open window to all the ball games and first fights between the children. This was her source of entertainment. The contrast of youth and age was only separated by the call, "Safe or Out." Her home was her haven.

Alma's Mother's Will

THE STATE OF ALABAMA
COLBERT COUNTY

JUSTICE COURT

Feb. 20 1957

CAUSE OF ACTION

To: Alma, Arlton & Lewis Dukes

When I pass from this world if I have any money left divide it between each of you three. The things in the house take what you want and no fussing over them they are not worth it. Things you don't want sell for what you can get and divide money and please put a foot stone to my grave.

Signed: "Mom."

This was printed in the church bulletin when Alma's mother died.

SYMPATHY: Our sincere sympathy to the family of sister Maud Dukes. She passed away Monday afternoon at her home on Ninth Street. She had been ill for many months. She was always faithful and devoted to the Lord and never missed worship when she was able. She will be greatly missed. Funeral services will be at the church building Wednesday afternoon at 1:00. Our sympathy to Sister Biggs, Sister Brewer, and other members of the family.

Alma and her Mother, Maud

My Mother would say to me, "If you act as good as you look, you will be alright."

And I say to you, "I have learned many lessons during my life span of almost a century. Life's highway is not easy, but I would not have missed it for anything!

"MAMMA'S THINGS"

The curtain slowly opens and there she stands
No silks, satins, frills or lovely golden bands
Our Mamma, brow furrowed and with toil worn hands
Gladly sharing her blessings with God and man

With the coming of frail health and dimming sight
Her happiness becomes our duty and great delight
The children are numbered three - two brothers and me
This plea we heed, "please, with my things leave me be"

The day came and she bravely answered her call, and
'Mid this and that we found a dim note addressed to all
Her last wish made clear, "divide my things bit by bit
Do not fuss, she said, they are not worth it"

A locket, a ring, a dish brought tears, but we were sure
That the love between her children would forever endure
We cherished items, both treasures and things very odd
But our greatest gift --- our heritage, the
word of God.

--- Alma D. Biggs
829 River Bluff Terrace
Sheffield, AL 35660

Someone left this Prayer of the Aging on the shelf just for a time like this. Thanks.

Prayer Of The Aging

Lord, Thou knowest I am growing older.
Keep me from becoming talkative and possessed with the idea that I must express myself on every subject.
Release me from the craving to straighten out everyone's affairs.
Keep me from reciting endless detail. Give me wings to get to the point.
Seal my lips when I am inclined to tell of my aches and pains. They are increasing with the years and my love to speak of them grows sweeter as time goes by.
Teach me the glorious lesson that occasionally I may be wrong. Make me thoughtful but not nosy, helpful but not bossy. With my vast store of wisdom and experience, it does seem a pity not to use it all. But Thou knowest, Lord, that I want a few friends at the end.

– Author not known to the editor

Solo Flights

1967
First Trip Solo, Bermuda

It would be impossible to relate to you every talk that I have made before Christian women. I can count (right or wrong) more than you can imagine, and I look back and mumble, "Did I write that, or did I say those beautiful words?" Memory is a great tool. However, some choice tidbits are lost along the way. Some of the locations are easy to recall, but our memories are among our most precious gifts. We must hold fast to these special moments spent with our own children, our grandchildren, and our great grandchildren, 'lest we and they forget' our blessings.

I have been a widow since 1967. This fact took its time sinking in. When a dinner or any honor was announced at the church for widows, I would wonder what I could do to help them. But then I had to realize that I was one of them!

Providence works in mysterious ways. One morning I was padding around in my yard—we were in the process of improving the front side—and a call came over my walkie talkie. Someone was calling from Florence, Alabama, wanting me to be a part of a missionary campaign planned for early fall. "Of course," I said, "Where to?" Then the answer came, "The Bermuda Islands." I stuttered without thinking, "No, thank you. I can't do that." The voice said, "Think about it. Maybe you will reconsider."

As I slowly walked into the house, I thought, "Why not, why can't I go?" I reached back into my book of memories and thought of the teenage desires to go to Freed Hardeman College and do some kind of Church work. If this was the call, it had been a long time in the calling. The thought had been planted, and I began to think that since I no longer felt the financial tug on the Singletree from Tennessee and there was no longer a great strain from the silent heart strings, I had found that my life had taken another great leap into spiritual wonderlands. This spiritual tug still continues to call loud and clear. So here I go uncharted, except by Golden Rules.

I reconsidered, and I went. The trip to Kennedy Airport in New York seemed so many miles away from Sheffield, Alabama, and then only a short jump to the Island. The people in Bermuda are not blond and blue-eyed, but they are God's children, too. Our group consisted of several young preachers and others interested in the work in the Island. My whole spiritual life was changed in those few days. I was adopted by our fellow travelers, and I gradually took advantage of them by making them my carpetbaggers. They brought treasures home for me in their laps.

Alma and Fellow Travelers in Bermuda

*Alma and
Fellow Travelers
in Bermuda*

Summer of 1975
Campaign to Jamaica

Chisholm Hills Church of Christ in Florence, Alabama, sponsored a campaign to Jamaica in the summer of 1975. The preacher, Marvin Crowson and his wife Judy, were leaders of this campaign. They graciously invited me to be a part of this group. Several members of the Church in Florence made the trip. My son "Bill," and his son "Billy, Jr." made it more interesting for me, and I said, "Yes, I will go!" While in Jamaica, we resided in Kingston. The whole experience was great from beginning to end. Billy, Jr. especially enjoyed diving and swimming in Jamaica's Black Holes.

One day we took off down the beachside; the houses were either castles or palaces. Bill, Sr. asked Marvin, "Is one soul more important than another?" "No," Marvin answered. Bill then answered, " I will just try to save as many as I can right here." Jamaica is a beautiful island. Vegetation is lush, and tropical fruit abounds. The campaign was well received by the natives, and we hope some seed fell on good ground.

On the way home, of course, we had to spend some time in the Atlanta Airport. This seems to be a must no matter whether you are going or coming. Judy, her little son, and I ate a light lunch at the airport terminal. All at once Judy looked at me and asked me a question. "Have you ever met the missionary, Otis Gatewood?"

My answer was, "No, and I think I am about the only eligible widow in the Church that has been deprived of this pleasure."

"Well, she said, "He is our good friend and really the person responsible for Marvin becoming a preacher. He plans to visit us in Florence in the near future. Would you come over and have supper with us and meet Otis?"

"No, you know, Judy, I just don't go around hoping to meet Mr. Eligible."

She suggested, "Why don't I invite our mutual friends, Basil and Margie Overton, to come along. I know Basil is acquainted with Brother Gatewood?"

I replied, "Let me think about it, and thanks for the invitation."

I went. Judy's table was groaning with good things like southern fried chicken and old fashioned egg custard. There was no sign of the stranger I was to meet. Judy said, "Oh! He will be back in a few minutes. He has just gone for a walk."

He soon came in the door. Judy introduced us, "Otis, I want you to meet our friend, *Alma Gatewood.*" That broke the ice, and the evening passed almost too fast. This blunder was made in names because, I think, the Crowsons were a little jittery, and Otis' wife of many years was also named Alma. The evening was very much enjoyed. I had been properly introduced to Mr. Otis Gatewood. Thank you, Marvin and Judy, for this invitation that opened the door to many travel experiences that I never dreamed of.

Otis Gatewood was a dreamer. When I met him, he was almost totally absorbed in the idea of a Christian College being established in Europe. Since much of his adult life had been spent working with European nations, he had a strong desire to lay a foundation for a Christian College or University there.

On a visit back home in 1975, he was in the Tri-Cities for several days. He had become a fatherly-like friend to a young man we knew, Ellis Coats. One day Ellis and I were invited to have lunch with Otis. We met at Barber's Cafeteria on Court Street in Florence. The subject that Otis wanted to talk about was no secret, a future college in Austria. It was so much on his mind that he could not broach another topic. Right there, while sitting around a well worn table, as we enjoyed southern fare, this venture took shape in the minds of all of us, especially Otis. Some of the framework for such a venture was discussed. Otis would be the very first President of the Christian College, and I would be asked to help with the paper work necessary in such an undertaking. The following letterhead was used in the very beginning of the European Christian College, located in

EUROPEAN CHRISTIAN COLLEGE
1020 Vienna, Austria

Office of
Secretary of Board
892 River Bluff Terrace
Tel. (205) 383-6448
Sheffield, Al. 35660

Lilienbrunngasse 13
Tel. 24-72-00
Mailing address:
Postfach 15
A-1235 Vienna, Austria

This letterhead shows my home address as a mailing address for all correspondence.

Lilienbrunngasse in Vienna, Austria. Ellis agreed to help as much as he possibly could in selling the idea to our own people. In fact, I believe he agreed that a much-needed van would be first on the list. This van was secured, and finally made its way via ship to Vienna. The European Christian College was actually established by Otis Gatewood in 1978, beginning in Vienna as European Christian College. It grew slowly; however, following the fall of the Berlin Wall, enrollment has multiplied many times over.

1961
The Berlin Wall

The Germans built the Berlin wall in 1961. Approximately 25 years later President Reagan made the historical demand that "This wall come down." And it came tumbling down. This thin piece of concrete, only a few inches thick divided the city of Berlin. History tells us perhaps 1,000 people died trying to cross this barrier. To keep the blockaded citizens of Berlin from starvation, the United States and our allies flew in 2.3 million tons of supplies in 277,569 flights. 1,383 planes landed in a 24 hour period during the peak of the airlift.

I am leaving this bit of information for you so you will understand the horrors of military action. This wall was real. Armed guards were almost shoulder to shoulder, as I stood next to it and had the privilege of actually touching the entrance on a visit to Germany.

Reagan Pres 1981-89

ANDY SHARP / Staff

Cobb County employees (from left) **Thomas Roberts** and **Donald Ice** help uncrate a 10-foot-tall, 2.6-ton section of the Berlin Wall, presented to Marietta officials Thursday evening.

Marietta's slab of Berlin Wall could build solid trade ties

1961
1981
1961
1989

By MICHAEL KOLBER
mkolber@ajc.com

When Chuck Clay went to Germany last summer, he expected to come back to Marietta with a chunk of the Berlin Wall.

But he never imagined he would be bringing home a 10-foot-tall, 2.6-ton section.

Thursday night, Clay presented the slab to Marietta city leaders in honor of his grandfather, Marietta native Gen. Lucius DuBignon Clay, who commanded American forces in Europe after World War II and organized the Berlin airlift.

Gen. Clay was the American military governor of postwar Germany; Chuck Clay spoke in Berlin last August on the 40th anniversary of the building of the wall.

The wall will be permanently displayed in Glover Park or another public space. Chuck Clay said the wall section will remain in storage for the next few weeks as he negotiates with city leaders about where it will be displayed and whether he should lend the section, or simply give it, to the city.

For all its historical significance, the wall is only a few inches thick.

"What's surprising about it is that a thin piece of concrete divided a city for 30 years," Clay said. "That almost 1,000 people died trying to cross this thin piece of concrete points out the absurdity of dividing a people by a piece of concrete."

Clay, a lawyer and former state senator who is seeking to return to the Legislature, said he hopes the fragment will forge economic ties between Berlin and metro Atlanta. A dozen German business and political leaders joined Gov. Roy Barnes at the ceremony Thursday at the Marietta Convention Center.

"I think a lot of people are unaware that Gen. Clay is from Marietta," said Betty Hunter, a Marietta City Council member. "I see it as very significant in building ties and telling part of our history and the history of one of our distinguished citizens."

Lucius Clay was President Kennedy's ambassador to Berlin in 1961, when the Soviets built the Berlin wall.

But history remembers Clay best for organizing the Berlin airlift for 15 months in 1948 and 1949. In June 1948, responding to the unification of the American, British and French zones into a single West German territory, the Communists in East Germany blockaded West Berlin.

To keep the city from starving, the American, British and French military flew in 2.3 million tons of supplies in 277,569 flights.

At the airlift's peak 1,383 planes landed in Berlin in a single 24-hour period.

At this time, I think everyone should be aware of just what Vienna, Austria, has meant to the world. Austria's carefree capitol is known for Mozart, not machine gun fire. Let's look at a bit of history from that part of the world. For 600 years, the Hapsburg dynasty ruled Austria.

After the First World War, Czechoslovakia and Yugoslavia were formed from the ruins of the Austrian-Hungarian Empire. During World War II the Allied Nations declared Austria to be independent, so now it is free. Throughout the years, Austrians have been hated as rulers; yet, people not governed by them seem to be able to get along with them. As a people, they have charming manners and have endured their misfortunes as becomes a people who once played a big part in history. The beautiful city of Vienna, Austria's capitol, puts sadness in the hearts of those who remember it in its prime. It was famous for centuries as the musical capital of the world, and it was the home of many of the greatest composers: Mozart, Beethoven, Schubert, Brahms, and the two Strausses. Vienna has also been the center of Austrian art, a city of magnificent buildings and of natural attractions, such as Vienna woods and the beautiful Blue Danube.

Now let us consider Hungary. Saint Stephen was Hungary's first king. Hungary was recognized as an independent nation after the World War I. It was mostly Catholic at that time; however, in 1956 they revolted against the USSR, and a very large number of people were killed. In 1968, Hungary (Yugoslavia) was forced to help the Soviet Union invade Czechoslovakia.

Since Yugoslavia's break with the communists, their name has changed to Serbia, and the United States has aided them. In visiting Zagreb, it was easy to see that Serbia (Yugoslavia) (Hungary) was the most prosperous of all Communist-ruled nations in Eastern Europe. This nation also shows the most Western influence.

The Beginnings of European Christian College

After the meeting at Barbers Cafeteria, the European Christian College began to take shape, and many people became interested in this work. 1975 is the date that marked the beginning of my interest in Christianity in Europe. The next several summers were spent in flights from Alabama to Vienna, Austria. I cannot detail the great number of lectureships and other events that took place in that part of the world.

Dr. W.B. West and his wife Velma, a teacher of Greek from Harding, and I became Jet Setters for many vacation-work summers. Many teachers from our Christian Colleges enjoyed time spent in a foreign country. I remember joining Jack and Mary Alice Wilhelm in Vienna. Our time spent together was great, and this was one of my last visits there.

In about 1977, during one of the summers while working at European Christian College, we all attended a lectureship. At this meeting Velma and I ran into one of her former students at Harding. She was really happy to spend some time with Gottfried Riechel and Hammelore, his charming wife from Munich, Germany.

When the lectureship was over, Dr. West caught the first plane to Alabama. He was scheduled to be at Alabama Christian College on their opening session. Velma and I let it be known that we would like a few more days browsing around. The Riechels graciously invited us home with them. On the way to Munich, Gottfried came near a beautiful, ancient, antique baroque church building. A trek had to be made across a barren field. I turned my ankle, and soon thereafter received the diagnosis that it was badly sprained. The Riechels took me in, and their attic became my home for the next two plus weeks. Abundant meals were carried up spiral stairs, and I counted the days.

We finally decided we could make our flight. The trip came about with a hop, skip, and a crawl. Many years in the future, Gottfried would knock on my door while on a visit to the U.S.A. Gottfried and Hammelore were a gracious pair of good Samaritans. For over 35 years, Gottfried operated the German Radio Ministry in Munich, Germany.

Please allow me to quote from a letter of Dieter Alten, longtime Evangelist and Elder of Hamburg. He wrote this letter when he learned that the broadcasts had ended.

"Dear Gottfried: Now that your longtime radio broadcasts have ended, it is a special occasion to express from the heart a word of appreciation for this ministry. This for several reasons: The salvation of souls, the spread of New Testament principles, the support of our publication, *The 20th Century Christian,* and your dedication in seeking the financial funding through your many trips to the U.S. and other contacts. No one unfamiliar with such a ministry can really imagine what a task that is. This should at least in this humble way be deemed worthy. Yours Dieter."

These words in many ways also apply to you, my faithful friends and partners. Our labors in the Lord have not been in vain. We covet your prayers.

                    Gratefully yours,
                    Gottfried & Hammelore Reichel,
                    Rasso, Siedlung 40, D-82284 Grafrath

Gottfried & Hammelore Reichel
Munich, Germany

Absender – Expéditeur:
W. B. West, Jr.
Harding Graduate School of Religion
A-
1000 Cherry Road
Postleitzahl
Code postal
Memphis, Tenn. 38
U.S.A.

Harding Graduate School of Religion
1000 Cherry Road
Memphis, Tenn. 38117 – Aug 18
1978

Mrs. Alma D. Biggs:
829 River Bluff
Sheffield, Alabama

Dear Sister Biggs:-

Velma and I have thought and have spoken of you many times since we left Memphis for Vienna. We had a good flight. Otis met us at the airport. We spent our first few days in a hotel near the location of our lectureship program. The quality of the lectures were good, but attendance was disappointing. We moved to Lillenbrunngasse where we are now. We have had two classes going at the same time for two weeks taught by Velma and me.

We leave tomorrow for seven lectures on Revelation in Nürnberg, then to Munich, Lausanne, Milano, Jugo-Slavia, Vienna, and home at 12:30 a.m. Sept. 8.

Wish very much you had been here. The Thorums from Miami, Sister Brown from Iowa, and Sis (King?) from Indiana were here. We had an unofficial Board meeting and are to have an official one in Miami Dec. 7. Otis and Bro. Thorum I am sure will notify you.

Your alms have not been forgotten. We appreciate your gift to us. We hope you are having a good August. We are looking forward to seeing you the last of September at Florence. We love and appreciate you.

Sincerely,
W. B. and Velma West

P.S. You are welcome at our house whenever you can come. We shall be pleased to have you.

San Juan, Puerto Rico
June 28, 1977

I was escorted by Guy Caskey, Bill Stewart, and Mike Wright. They explained the Rain Forest to me. I felt quite popular.

Does this make you homesick for Lilienbrunngasse?

Summer 1980 spent here

This picture shows my apartment area in the turret at Lilienbrunngasse.

1980-81

Otis and I had become best of friends and co-workers, and there was, I suppose, a touch of romance here and there.

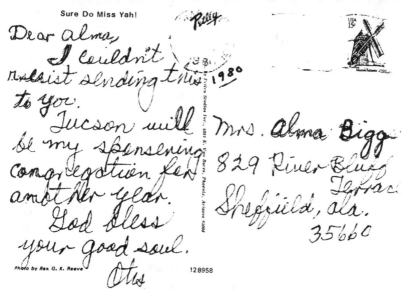

Dear Alma,
 I couldn't resist sending this to you.
 Tucson will be my sponsoring congregation for another year. God bless your good soul.
 Otis

Mrs. Alma Bigg
829 River Bluff Terrace
Sheffield, Ala.
35660

A Solo Trip From Alabama To Where?
To Vienna!

I finally reached Vienna, Austria. A Christian Summer lectureship had been scheduled for Madrid, Spain. Christians would be attending from all over Europe, America, and wherever they happened to come from.

I had been invited to spend the summer in Vienna to work with the students at the International College. There was a time conflict surrounding the time I was to travel to Austria and the lectureship in Spain. But I decided to join the group from Alabama to meet the people attending from Vienna.

Sue Warmack and I were cabin mates from Alabama to Spain. It was fun just to be with her. However, my time in Spain was cut short due to the cancellation of the Lectureship.

Dr. W.B. and Velma West were already in Vienna, and they planned to come over to Spain with Otis' group from the College. However, for some reason the Lectureship in Spain was cancelled. After landing in Madrid, plans were made for our people to tour Portugal and other points before returning home. There would be no meeting of my friends from Austria, so the telephone was kept busy trying to reach somebody, anybody to tell me what to do. Finally, I reached Otis, and he advised me to catch a flight to Vienna. By doing this, I could join them in their planned camping session in Communist Territory. This sounded simple, but with no foreign money, a grammar problem, and so many more scary details, with fear and trembling I asked the hotel manager to call a cab to take me to the airport. Upon reaching the airport, the person at the window told me, "That flight has been cancelled."

So, now what do I do? I asked, "Can you help reroute me to Vienna?" He said, "It is impossible; for who knows how long . . . ." This left me totally stranded in a foreign land with strange speaking people. Again, I had no friend, no seatmate, and no money. I could not speak a word of French, Latin, or Spanish, and it seemed my English was so bad that no one could understand a word I said. But after another phone call, I was told in no uncertain terms, "You can do it. We are waiting for your arrival to have our big banquet. What else could I do but take off.

After many delays: air strikes, labor strikes, and just plain laziness (they must have taken time for their siestas), I finally landed at the airport, which was miles out of Vienna. At one point while flying over Italy, the snow-covered Alps peeped through a frothy white cloud. I let out a cry of joy; I knew that finally these mysterious mountains would be offering their great peaks and pinnacles as an open window to reveal to my soul secrets which I thought had been firmly closed.

A kind foreign passenger (German, I think) realized what a plight I was in, and he reached into his pocket and handed me enough of their currency for a bus ride into the city. The bus driver was told to let me out at the Delta Hotel. Incidentally, this was the end of his run.

After much doubt that I was going in the right direction, all at once I saw a big sign: The Delta. Sure enough, I saw a friendly face. It was Otis, rushing me through this door and that exit, and off we went to Lillienbrungasse as specially invited guests to the college banquet.

As I looked toward the big open door, I could not believe I was face to face with my friends. There was Velma looking gorgeous in blue chiffon, and her niece was all dressed out in pink. They were beautiful sights. I tried to tell them of the obstacles I had hurdled just trying to get there. "This is not really me," I said, "I have been traveling a full week, I think." They had to listen to all the problems between Alabama and Vienna. I had crisscrossed France, Switzerland, and Italy, then had come within touching distance of the Rock of Gibraltar. Morocco and the point of Casablanca had been pointed out. All this travel had taken its toll, and I was a sight to behold as I entered the dining area. Yet, everyone was gracious and made me feel more than welcome, dirt and grime accepted.

Secrets Of The Dolomites

Dr. West, Velma, her niece from California, and I were closing the scene on another summer in and around the European Christian College in Vienna. Otis, as usual, was his charming self in his capacity as a good friend and a competent tour guide. He suggested that, since we had visited the Switzerland side of the Alps, we see the beauty awaiting us on the other side of the mountains. We all approved this short Italian jaunt and with a rented van took off in that general direction. "Have you seen The Dolomites?" Otis asked. We all unanimously answered, "No!" "This is unusual. It is a must," he told us. We eagerly continued on our way.

At about dusk, we located a quaint, rustic cabin, our overnighter. As we were unloading, Otis said, "Alma, they are such late getter-uppers, and we are early risers, why don't we take advantage of the early sunrise with all the majesty and colors emerging?" As I looked out the East window of this quaint little chalet, there seemed to be a voice calling, "Come and be a part of God's beauty." I accepted, and this we did.

All kinds of pleasant aromas greeted us at the chalet's doorstep. The enticing smell of freshly perked coffee, little breads, bacon, mountain-grown berries peeping out of jelly glasses, and even eggs in tiny white cups. It proved to be a hardy breakfast, fit for a king. The view from the window was indescribable. It was The Dolomites.

The Dolomites were named for the French geologist D'eodat Dolomieu, who discovered the magnesium-calcium rock in the Alps. Because of the minerals in them, some of the mountainsides are streaked with blue-black and yellow splotches, and others are a brilliant red, milky white or pink. The sun shining on these rocks was a magnificent sight. All of this was handed to us before a big roaring fire, with snowflakes falling on the windowsill outside. It reminded us that "it is cold outside, but oh so cozy inside."

About mid-morning, we packed up and started our real probe into the mysteries contained in these mountain peaks called The Dolomites of Italy. Since W.B. West was not friendly with heights, he, Velma, and their niece explored the popular lookout points at lower levels.

Otis and I decided that it would be just the time for us to stop at a little roadside market and pick up some picnic supplies. We found many items to our liking, little packages of Italian this and that. We also found a spectacular lookout point overlooking valleys, waterfalls, and ski slopes of the Alps. We enjoyed our lunch on paper napkins. We looked at photos and sang. Otis enjoyed singing, anytime and anywhere. "How Great Thou Art" was one of his favorites.

We were silently quiet for a long while, and then Otis seemed to come to life, leaning forward and covering my hand with his. I placed my other hand on top of his. He topped the pile with his broad hand, and we begin to laugh, talking about things we remembered that had happened to us. We wished the moment would never end. Our time together was more than enjoyable. Despite my look of supposed dignity and the aura of memories long passed, we were thankful for "our day." And yet there seemed to be a coldness about me that was unshakable and could not be moved.

Otis said, "We are two people who flew across the sky at each other and finally crashed like falling stars. Today we meet again and are in a hailstorm of wants and wishes. As the stars fall and vanish from the heavens, they seem to cry out, 'Hold to the moment, and try not to seize an entire life.'" After a long silent moment, the words began again. He said, "I admire you so much; it's funny how things have not worked out as planned. I have been weakening since the first time I met you in North Alabama. I have been fighting this, knowing all the time it was happening. Some things just happen, and they are not planned."

At this moment, his greatest desire was to protect and care for me, and maybe never leave these beautiful mountain peaks. As we made our way back to meet Velma and W.B., Otis said, "My life has been controlled by wants and needs of others; this may be my sacrifice, maybe our sacrifice." I asked myself, "Have you forgotten that you are still the hub of the SINGLETREE that pulls the load?"

From that time on, board Meetings were attended, and great Christian soldiers made up my best of friends at home and abroad.

London Trip With Tuscumbia Congregation

A group of members of the Tuscumbia Church of Christ went to London in August, 1981, to visit individuals they supported in that part of the world. They also attended the European Lectures in London. As a member of the Annapolis Avenue Congregation, I went with the group to attend the Lectures and to speak to the ladies attending the Lectureship.

Pictured in the Lectureship program include the following saints from Tuscumbia: Roland (Mac) McMackin and his wife "Mary Frances" (Honey), Ralph and Lisabeth Foster, Grace (Toots) Ward, and me (from Sheffield). Also pictured are Yann Opsitch, Nelly Andrejewski, and Christina Silva, daughter of Adelino Silva who is supported in Portugal by the Tuscumbia Church. Others supported by the church at that time were Vurel Vick and Glenn Langston.

One thing I remember especially: When I got up to speak to the ladies at the Lectureship, a call came through that my friend, Velma West, had died on August 5, 1981. This was a sad time for me.

EUROPEAN LECTURES
LONDON
AUGUST 4 – 8 1981

My fellow travelers, Mary Frances "Honey" and Roland "Mac" McMackin are two of my best friends. Honey's father, L. L. Brigance, was a member of the faculty of Freed-Hardeman College.

COME TO LECTURESHIP

PROGRAM DIRECTORS

TUESDAY- STEVE WATSON, DOUG. VARNADO
WEDNESDAY- GARY KELSEY,MALCOLM ARMSTRONG
THURSDAY- LLOYD MANSFIELD, MEL BROOKS
FRIDAY - GEORGE HARRIS, VUREL VICK

SONG DIRECTORS
DON HALL
JOE CASEY, WAYNE HINDS

TUESDAY

11:00-1:40- ARRIVALS, REGISTRATION & ROOM ASSIGNMENT

1:45- SINGING: **JOE CASEY**

2:00- STEVE WATSON: WELCOME! LONDON: PAST, PRESENT, & FUTURE

2:40- WORLD FACTS & FIGURES WHAT WE HAVE... AND HAVE NOT DONE

3:20- BREAK

3:40- **DURWARD BOGGS**: PREACH THE WORD

4:20- **HOWARD BYBEE**: SURVEY OF WORK IN EUROPE

7:00- **JOE CASEY**: SINGING & SONG LEADERS' QUARTET

7:30- FRANK MORGAN: THE CAUSE IN GREAT BRITON

8:00- CLIFF GANUS: TO EVERY NATION!

WEDNESDAY

9:00- JIM WALDRUN: THE WORK IN CHINA

9:45- BILL MCDONOUGH: THE WORK IN GERMANY

10:30-BREAK

10:45-OTIS GATEWOOD: BEHIND THE IRON CURTAIN

11:30-YANN OPSITCH: THE WORK IN FRANCE

12:00- LUNCH

1:40- SINGING WITH DON HALL

2:00- WILL C. GOODHEER: EUROPE MUST HEAR

2:45-DON YELTON:SERVICE MEN'S PROGRAMS

3:20- BREAK

3:45- JOE NISBET: THE BRITISH BIBLE SCHOOL

4:20- NORMAN HOGAN: THE DIGNITY OF DISCIPLESHIP

7:00- Wayne Hinds & The LCC CHORUS

7:30- GLENN LANGSTON: LOVE IS THE GREATEST

8:15- JUAN MONROY: NO MAN COMETH BUT BY ME!

7:30- TEX WILLIAMS: TRAINING OTHERS TO GO

8:15- REUEL LEMMONS: LET MY PEOPLE GO!

THURSDAY

7:00-8:00- BREAKFAST

8:30- DEVOTIONAL -ALSO: SPECIAL FOR LADIES WITH GAIL MANSFIELD

FRIDAY

7:00-8:00- BREAKFAST

8:30- DEVOTIONAL {SPECIAL FOR LADIES WITH ALMA BIGGS

9:00- DOYLE KEE: THE WORK IN SWITZERLAND

9:45- JOE WATSON: SOUTH AFRICA WORK

10:30- BREAK

10:45-MALCOLM ARMSTRONG: REACHING THE IMMIGRANTS

Welcome to the European Lectureship for 1981! We have some great speaker bringing messages of great importance. We hope you will hear them all. Cassette tapes will be available from Emmite Channell. There will be some good singing as we are lead by some fine singers and song directors as well as the LCC Chorus and some special groups.
We want all that can to stay on the campus as it will make it sq.handy to attend all of the lectures. The price of the room, including a full breakfast, is£9-00 (Pounds) or $19.00 per person.
There will be sandwiches available in the PUB (no alcohol) for 40 pence for lunch and the evening meal will be catered in the breakfast area for £2-00 (Pounds) including a drink. Drinks will be available in the PUB at lunch-time from the establishment.

B E   S U R E   A N D   R E G I S T E R

Tributes To Alma Biggs

Written by
Otis Gatewood

March 16, 1981
September 18, 1981

Otis and Alma

Dedicated To Alma Biggs

The mountains break forth with singing
and the hills resound with musick.

The trees of the field clap their hands
and the streams leap and roar

Because the soul of the righteous
Is filled with fatness

Oh ye that thirst come to
the living waters

Taste of the mercy of the Lord
for it is good

His forgiveness is abundant
and he freely forgives

The rain waters the earth and
the snow blankets the hills

And declare that our God
and Saviour is good.

Oh how great is his mercy.

We who serve Him lift
our heads with joy

And rejoice in the glory of
His salvation.

We lay hold on treasures
without money

And drink of living waters without
that quinch thirst in the redeemed soul.

by Otis Gatewood
3/16/81

A Tribute To Alma Biggs

The beautiful and lovely Alma,
Her face is so gentle and fair.
She walks with an air of dignity,
And stands as a queen by her chair.

She is kind, tender, and humble;
A teacher of ladies who call.
World traveler, poet, and author;
A missionary who is loved by all.

She reaches her hand to the needy
and lifts those who fall in despair.
She serves wherever she is needed
at home, overseas, with loving care.

Her home reaches out and welcomes all,
In neatness and splendor supreme.
The Sarimore house stands great and tall
Because Alma touched it with a dream.

Written by: Otis Gatewood
Sept. 18, 1981

13th ANNUAL
MISSION FORUM
November 13, 14, and 15, 1987

THEME: *"From Jerusalem unto the Uttermost"*

SPEAKER: OTIS GATEWOOD

★ 37 years in European and Russian mission work
★ President, European Christian College, Vienna, Austria

Elders, Mission Committees, Interested Parties are Invited... Come, catch the Mission Spirit — in particular learn about the work in Europe and Russia. Come Saturday evening and hear an informal talk and then ask questions about works in an European country of your interest.

Otis Gatewood

FRIDAY
November 13
7:30 p.m.
"From Jerusalem"

SATURDAY
November 14
7:30 p.m.
"Europe Is Listening"

SUNDAY
November 15
9:00 a.m.—Combined Teen and Adult Bible Classes
"Remember... in the Days of Thy Youth"
10:00 a.m.—Sermon
"Rulers Are Not a Terror to Good Works"

Church of Christ, Wichita, Kan.
8-11 Southern California School of Evangelism Lectureship, Buena Park, Calif.
8-12 Denton Lectures, Pearl Street Church of Christ, Denton, Texas.
13-14 Stark County, Ohio, Lectureship, Stark County Christian Academy, Canton, Ohio.
13-15 Mission Forum, 13th annual, Broken Arrow, Okla., Church of Christ.
22-26 Southwestern Christian College Lectureship, 50th annual, Terrell,

Church of Christ

662 East Thirteenth South
Salt Lake City, Utah 84105
Telephone 467-0974

1-801-

November 20, 1980

Mr. Al D. Biggs
029 River Bluff Terrace
Sheffield, Alabama

Dear Bro. Biggs,

Brother Otis Gatewood has informed me that the <u>Board of Directors of European Christian College</u> is planning to have its Board of Directors meeting in Salt Lake City in February just after his campaign with the church here in Salt Lake City.

Accordingly, we'd like to invite you to be with us during the campaign, if it is at all possible for you. If you cannot be here the entire week, perhaps you could plan to be with us for a few days of the campaign. Not knowing your situation nor capabilities, we're sending you complete information on the campaign, which we're sending to all our prospective campaigners. It will be information to you in any event, and if you can join us, you'll know what's going on. If you cannot come for the campaign, perhaps you know of someone who could work with us. If so, you could pass this information along to them.

May the Lord bless you richly in his service.

Sincerely,

Robert L. Wagoner

The International University
Higher Education with a Christian Dimension
Vienna · Kiev · Alicante
Mondscheingasse 16 • A-1070 Vienna, Austria
Telephone (+431) 718 50 68 11 • Telefax (+431) 718 50 68 9 • Web: www.iuvienna.edu

Office of the President   E-Mail: pres@iuvienna.edu

March 24, 2002

Dear Christian friend,

It is a great pleasure for me to inform you that our school year 2001-2002 is going very well with record enrollments.

In Vienna we have the privilege of serving students from 56 different countries. (In our more than 20 years of ministry, IU students have come from over 100 different nations). Our students represent a variety of religions and many cultural backgrounds. Also they represent a broad spectrum of socio-economic situations, ranging from refugees to children of diplomats; from people just scraping by financially through odd jobs to those with excellent positions in multi-national firms. Many of our students are here in Austria alone with their families miles away. Others are privileged to have family with them.

Our visiting faculty regularly make comments like this: "Every student seems to come with a story of a life that is hard for Americans to imagine: poverty, war, or just taking the initiative to leave their homeland where there is little opportunity for a place they hope will give them a new chance. Many have had to learn a lot of 'Street-Smarts' which, thanks to God's blessings, many Americans have never needed to learn."

Yet, in many ways our students are the same as young people everywhere: they face the same temptations, are in many ways skeptical and afraid to put their hopes in a peaceful future, have goals for the careers they desire to achieve, and experience the fears and worries typical of our modern society.

What you and I are privileged to do together is to try to show them the difference that Christ can make! Not everyone responds, but at IU everyone has the opportunity to hear about Christ through academic Bible classes, interaction with faculty, Conversational English Using the Bible, and by attending our daily Chapel.

Also, we are privileged to provide a family atmosphere and built-in support system for our students. This exhibits itself in many ways:
- Cheerful smiles and hellos on the street or in the halls – while outside of the university family people on the streets try not to acknowledge another person's presence
- Offering medicines, a phone call, or a prayer together with someone who is sick
- Frequently being a sounding board for advice in personal problems
- Noticing if someone seems sad and offering a listening ear

It is apparent that these daily things are among the most important that fill our busy schedules day after day. In thinking about Christ's ministry, it is evident that He spent a lot of time meeting needs and healing hurting people; when he could have devoted more time to the direct teaching of God's message.

Our enrollment in Vienna has continued a steady increase. The number of Austrian and EU students who have enrolled has risen, which is a good sign about the positive effects of accreditation. In Kiev we are thankful that the Ministry of Education granted an extension of our annual Fall quota for incoming freshmen from 100 to 150.

At IU-Vienna we were honored to host **Dr. John A. Quintus**, Counselor for Public Affairs from the U.S. Embassy, who works directly with the Ambassador, for an Open Dialogue with IU students. Dr. Quintus did an excellent job of explaining the U.S. position on the War Against Terrorism with clarity and cultural sensitivity, and then opened the forum for discussion. The Auditorium was packed full and students were eager to ask questions. Also in the audience were people from each of the three countries cited by President Bush as part of an "axis of evil" – Iran, Iraq, and North Korea. Dr. Quintus undergirded his presentation with references to Christian principles and also the verses on peace selected for the daily reading by **Hans Dederscheck**, Minister and Bible teacher.

This was the first presentation of a high U.S. Embassy official on campus. We have invited the U.S. Ambassador to welcome our guests during our Eighteenth Graduation in June.

Lilienbrunngasse

As of February 28, the building at Lilienbrunngasse, which earlier housed the entire university operation and three congregations (German, English, Chinese), and then later was completely used for visiting faculty, staff and student housing when the academic center was moved, will no longer serve as a bulwark for Christian education and the churches of Christ. Hundreds of IU's friends from the States have visited, taught, stayed, or worshipped in this building. Thousands of students and refugees have been taught and served here. The building was in a poor state of repair and was sold by the City of Vienna to a real estate firm which plans to renovate it – which necessitated that IU leave the building. Over the past year IU has relocated students and faculty in stages and then, in the last week of February, completely rid the building of old furniture and appliances, etc.. We are thankful that this building fulfilled such a vital role in His service, and also that God has provided the Mondscheingasse facility and Austrian dormitory space to meet the needs of the academic operation and student housing.

Needs

I know you are aware that, with the priority we place on serving needy students, your generous financial support and prayers are greatly needed. Annually IU writes-off over $400,000.00 in financial-need scholarships in Vienna. In Kiev our fees are greatly subsidized to be in line with the local economy. This means we operate on a limited, tight budget and make the best possible use of the funds God provides. It also means that you can feel assured when you give to IU, **you are giving to needy students and changing lives. This is certainly a worthwhile cause – one with which our Lord is pleased!** His goal was that His people would take the Gospel to the whole world! At IU, we have the opportunity to minister to people from around the world!

Because of the generous scholarships we provide for worthy students, we often have to wait for other needed items. One current need is a large sign for the front of our building. Several have indicated that it is time – we've been at the Mondscheingasse building over a year now. You might also be able to help in daily operational costs or in providing scholarships for worthy students.

Please prayerfully consider helping. We know that God is able, through His people like you.

Sincerely in Christ,

Wil C. Goodheer
President

Making dreams come true

A dream come true for Kiev students

Graduation is one of the highlights of the academic year — for the students, but also for faculty and staff, as we witness the joy of a dream attained. For many of the students of IU in Vienna and Kiev, their dream would never have become a reality without your sacrificial gifts. I hope that you feel pleased and satisfied knowing that you are changing lives of people from all over the globe.

In today's insecure times, when so many negative events impact us, hope is generated by the possibility of extending a positive influence all over the world.

Just yesterday a remedial English teacher informed me that her Polish student has a dream of perfecting her English so she can get a better job. Right now she cleans houses to make a living. She has much more potential to realize. We at IU have the chance to help make it possible. She is only in the beginner's level of English, so she has a long road ahead. But, with her determination and our caring teachers, I am sure she can realize her dream.

We all know the proverbial statement that it is better to teach someone how to fish than to only feed them fish. At IU we are involved in just such a venture — teaching skills that will help young people in their desired professions.

In this Bulletin you will learn of new, exciting programs in Kiev and Odessa, Ukraine, which provide students a means of making a living.

In addition, we have the weighty and unique (in Austria and Ukraine) responsibility of helping people have the opportunity to study the Word of God, with the hope that they might accept Christ. Thousands and thousands of seeds fall on all kinds of heart-soil, and it is our prayer that God will provide a great harvest. Please join us in prayer and in partnership in our mission-education outreach.

Sincerely in Christ,

Wil C. Goodheer,
President

In June, 2002, a record crowd attended the 18th graduation.

One day, a young man drifted into the office in Vienna. He was warmly greeted and seemed to be aware of our progress. This was Will Goodyear. He and I became what seemed more like Mother-Son buddies than just friends. After Otis' long tenure as President of European Christian College, the staff was passed on to Will Goodyear. Otis returned to Michigan, his former home, and enjoyed several happy years there. He died September 16, 1999. Otis Gatewood preached in communist countries for 37 years.

This just about ends the highlights of my time in Communist countries. This is the life of a very ordinary person who blossomed to full bloom by assuming and conquering extraordinary callings. Many home workshops have made the golden days of Fall and approaching snows of Winter beautiful. They seem to say, "Keep on keeping on." This I am trying to do, and I pray for God's continued blessings. I still feel the tug of the Spiritual Singletree and hear the sound of the plea, "Please come and help me." Then the answer comes, "Here am I, send me."

Some say, "Tomorrow never comes." Yet, when the sun peeps over the horizon and announces another day, it is tomorrow, today.

My Cup Runneth Over

Upon my return home in 1978, my cup was running over, and I am sharing this time with you. This was the Eleventh Mediterranean Lectureship, which took place in Athens, Greece on April 15-20, 1978. Democracy was born in Athens over 2500 years ago. In 1978, when I attended the Christian Mediterranean Lectureship in this city, it was a sprawling metropolis, traffic everywhere. It was very much alive with life and vigor.

Travel — THE WORLD EVANGELIST 1978

My Cup Runneth Over

1968

Alma Biggs
829 River Bluff Terrace
Sheffield, Al. 35660

widow — 1968

ALMA BIGGS

Since finding myself in the role of Christian widowhood, ten years ago, I have undertaken an annual journey into far places in the interest of improving myself by actually seeing, feeling, tasting and becoming, for a short time at least, a part of foreign cultures.

As I read the Bible stories I realize the entire picture is a panorama of far away places, people and personalities. I know that I have been greatly blessed by having been able to rub shoulders with so many so different people who have been created by the same God who made me. He loves us all and we must love one another.

My cup truly runneth over this morning as I, in a measure, re-live the experiences of one of my recent travels.

The Eleventh Mediterranean Lectureship took place in Athens, Greece, April 15-20, 1978. It was declared a great success by all standards of lectureships in all parts of the world. All who attended received a gracious plenty of spiritual food. Twelve precious souls were added to the church and seven people confessed public sins. This, to me, was wonderful for I remember so many lectureships, work-shops, and like sessions as being almost entirely inspirational and factual learning processes. This great response was spiritually uplifting to all of us and especially to those stationed and living in that part of the world. It was stated by some of the leaders of this effort that the whole body of Christ in Europe, the Middle East, and the entire world is stronger because of this meeting in Athens.

Each year these lectureships are hosted by the military congregations and the missionaries of the areas. The following congregations assisted in this 1978 effort: Oslo, Norway; Vicenza, San Cito and Catania, Italy; Athens and Crete, Greece; Kaiserslautern and Nurnburg, Germany; Adana, Karamursel and Izmir, Turkey; Dhahran, Saudia Arabia; Chickearda, England, and I feel sure the list could go on and on.

Approximately three hundred people attended the lectureship at the beautiful Chandris Hotel, near the Mediterranean Sea in Athens. The lectures and accommodations are made possible because military congregations unite and sacrifice financially that not only they and their families may attend but that missionaries from all over this part of the world may come at a very nominal expense.

The entire week in Athens was chocked full of good things and especially were we blessed with talented speakers from different corners of the world. The theme assigned this year was: "When the trumpet of the Lord shall sound." William H. (Bill) Smith, instructor at the White's Ferry Road School of Biblical Studies, in my opinion, proved to be the greatest of the great key note speakers. Other well knowns on the program included; Otis Gatewood, Missionary to the Iron Curtain Countries; Juan Monroy, Madrid, Spain; Dino Roussos, Athens, Greece; Elsie and Everett Huffard, Sr., Amman, Jordan; and many others.

Don Yelton, West Monroe, La., did a great job as AMEN over-all coordinator. George Dumas, Athens, acted as master of ceremonies and certainly made us (foreigners) all feel welcome and happy in our home away from home. The Huffards were placed in a team role. I am sure he did his usual good teaching and I can highly recommend her work with the ladies. She did considerable counciling among young marrieds and I know her good works will follow her. Since I am writing from a personal vantage point, I want to thank all who had a part in making this spiritual feast and experience possible for me. Thank you for including me in your guest list. I shall always remember all of you and I thank God for your dedication and faithfulness even though you are stationed so far away from your hearthstones — wherever that may be.

I am already hearing faint sounds of plans for an even greater Lectureship in 1979. May God bless and keep you all.

My cup really ran over when at the close of the meetings at Athens it was possible for Margaret Hardin, Arbyrd, Mo., Elsie Huffard, Amman, Jordan, and me to make a short trip to Bible Lands. This was especially exciting for Margaret since she had not been there before and Elsie was very pleased to go and visit her son, Everett Jr. and his family. He preaches for the church in Nazareth. Joe Shulam, who preaches at the Jerusalem church, and Everett, Jr. met us at the Tel Aviv Airport. Elsie was soon on her way to Nazareth and Margaret and I were in Joe's capable care. She and I traveled from Jerusalem to the Dead Sea and then followed the West Bank up to Nazareth.

We made all the customary traditional visits to Bible places and when we had finished we felt as if we had been from Dan to Beersheba! Our visit in the Huffard home was delightful and he proved to be a most able tour guide. We feel that we really benefited by his knowledge and ability to get in and out of so many off-tour limits.

Our time at Nazareth ended all too soon. Elsie made her way somehow across the Jordan and Margaret and I boarded a jumbo jet and flew across the beautiful Mediterranean to Athens.

Our lodging place for the few days there was a small hotel overlooking the Agean Sea. The beautiful blue of the sea dotted with white sail boats is beyond description.

While back in Athens we enjoyed visiting with Dan and Mary Smith and their family. They are great leaders in the Military Congregation there. We enjoyed being a part of their services near the base.

Dino and Debbie Roussos, Mike and Cathy Sinapiades, and George and Joan Dumas all work with the Greek congregation located in uptown Athens. These people all went far beyond the call of duty in their love and hospitality.

After these few days again in Athens George and Joan Dumas, Margaret and I visited Egypt. Margaret and I had wanted so much to go to Egypt but did not think we could brave this trip alone. When George expressed an interest in going with us we knew that was the answer.

Egypt is beyond my description. It is absolutely street to street people. Eight million people live in the city of Cairo. We were unable to find a single Christian in Egypt. If they are there and we missed them I would surely appreciate this information for it has really bothered me that in this ancient Biblical country no one has answered the call — surely someone has said "Here am I, send me."

There is so much of Biblical interest in and around Cairo, Memphis, the Nile, pyramids, tomb treasuries, brick making, camels, desert, and on and on that it would be impossible to describe in this short travel report the many things of interest that we were able to visit.

I again say "My cup runneth over." The blessings that have been outpoured in my direction are too numerous to mention. I can only say, "Thank you, Lord" and pray that you will keep me in the hollow of your hand that I may know that each day is the day I have made for rejoicing a gladness.

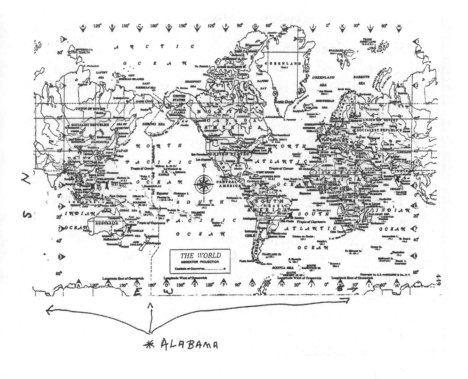

* * *

When you open your window and see crisscross lines of condensation made by planes in the sky, remember this: Alma Biggs has joined the "Jet Set" and is off again to who knows where. Her life is likened to the flight of the eagle. She knows that the wings of eagles will bear her up, and she will be carried safely on their wings to near and far away places.

Let's Go! Where?
Around The World

Since becoming an amateur traveler, I seemed to have developed itching feet. The first jump from our precious home was a missionary journey to Bermuda, and as the pages turned I took advantage of every invitation, saying, "Let's Go." At this point in August 1974, I did the unbelievable. I was invited and jumped aboard on a trip around the world. I have decided not to impose on you all the details of all the journeys that I have made. I'll just include the "biggie."

The face of the world map has changed so much, I doubt if some of the countries and cities can be identified anymore. However, change creeps into the very fabric of our lives, and tomorrow will be different, too. For your information, I have left my footprints on the soil of fifty or more nations. Several of these will be mentioned as we go on, so here goes. After sifting through many folders, I have decided that in all the miles I have traveled and of all the wonderful people I have met, maybe the best thing I can do right here and now is to include in detail my trip around the world. This is my version. When you go, you can hold onto yours.

Here are some of the highlights of my trip around the world with the Welmiths and Jack Lewis of Harding Graduate School which is located in Memphis, Tennessee. The P. D. Welmiths and I were seasoned travelers on past tours. We traveled 32 days, 30,000 miles, took 24 jets, and visited ten countries.

I left Sheffield on the morning of July 24, 1974. At the beginning of our trip, we arrived at Kennedy Airport at 1:40 PM. Our flight left the airport at 7:00 PM, Wednesday, July 24, for Paris, France, and eventually returned to Los Angeles, then Dallas, and finally home on August 26, 1974. It was all over too soon. I would not have missed it for the world. This was the Cadillac of all tours.

Traveling in these countries gave me much to think about. We live on an Island of Affluence in the Sea of Poverty. Let us be thankful.

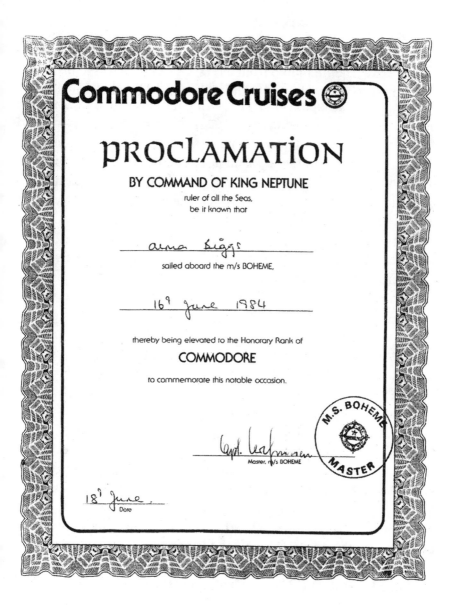

From 1982 –1995
Christian Cruises

The greatest opportunity to do a good work that could be offered to a single person (or widow) came my way in 1982. I am not sure, but I think I met Darrell Frazier, a Christian Tour manager, when I attended a workshop. I remember seeing him at several of the Annual Lectureships at the different Christian Colleges. Anyway, I want you children to know the purpose of the Christian Cruises, their beginnings, and the tremendously good works accomplished by each and everyone of us in the remote islands of our earth. So bear with me as I try to set the stage for the many stories that could be told to you and yours.

You really don't have to go to sunny beaches, walk over black coral sands, hear strange languages, observe stranger religions, and meet different people to satisfy potential disciples' desires and needs. Radio waves go everywhere! Who knows where? However, actually traveling there gives one the opportunity to answer their questions.

How did anyone dream up such an enticing way to carry the Gospel to every nation, and even to Islands? Well, just relax and believe the unbelievable as related by Darrell:

In the year 1977, Hal Frazier (Darrell's father) and Lowell Perry, both professors, were killed in a tragic plane accident on the Caribbean Island of Martinique. Their little Cessna plane crashed and became a fireball on a banana plantation at the northern tip of the island, almost over the ocean. They were on their way to Antigua, but they never made it. They were island hopping, searching for a site on which to construct a short wave radio tower to be used in broadcasting the gospel. Darrell and Lana, his wife, lived in Albuquerque, New Mexico. They received the news by telegram from the State Department. The accident, probably caused by mechanical failure, was sudden, painful, and hard for them to accept. Some things in life we never understand. We search for answers, but where are they? We know we can never stop trusting God, and He will work out what is best in our lives.

After two years, Lana and Darrell decided to move to West Monroe, Louisiana, and devote their lives to carrying the Gospel of Jesus to the nations of the world. They would be trying to follow in Darrell's father's footsteps. They were especially interested in establishing churches in the Mediterranean area and through the Christian Cruises. The name of Jesus is lifted up as the only hope of the world. It is believed that seven days together makes one "Weak, Not Stronger!" Fellowship, worshiping together, the sea, the islands: What blessings! I thank God for the privilege of spending seven days per cruise with nearly three score Christians on each of the twelve Caribbean Christian Cruises. It made me a stronger person. The "Cruisers" considered this quality time as a combination of vacation and mission work. What a wonderful way to have a perfect seven days away from home! All of the tours taken resulted in untold blessings. Each tour was more exciting than the last. Thanks to everyone.

My records show that my Christian Cruise guest speaker assignments for the Lady's Day Cruisers ran from 1982 to 1995. I missed only two cruises.

Caribbean Christian Cruise	June 1982
Caribbean Christian Cruise	June 1984
Caribbean Christian Cruise	August 1985
Alaskan Christian Cruise	August 1986
Hawaii Christian Cruise	August 1987
Alaskan Christian Cruise	August 1988
Fall Foliage C. Cruise	Sept 1989
Alaskan Christian Cruise	July 1989
Alaskan Mendenhal Glacia	August 1992
Holy Land Christian Tour	March 1993
Scandinavia and Russia (Christian Tours International)	Spring 1994
Caribbean Christian Cruise	Spring 1995

I attended a total of twelve tours. I conducted classes for ladies while traveling on the following cruise lines: The Boheme, Commodore Cruise Line, The Love Boat, The Happy Ship, The Princess, and others. At this point, I invite each of you to join with me and enjoy every hour of each day while tramping over the face of the earth.

So Here Goes

I. Continents:

    1. Asia   5. Europe
    2. South America   6. Antarctica
    3. North America   7. Australia
    4. Africa   8. England

I have touched the soil of seven of these continents, all except Antarctica.

II. States:

    1. My footprints are on all fifty States of our beloved America.

III. Countries:

1. Austria
2. Belgium
3. Bratislava
4. Canada
5. Czechoslovakia
6. Denmark
7. Dominican Republic
8. England
9. Egypt
10. Finland
11. France
12. Germany
13. Greece
14. Holland
15. Honduras
16. Hungary
17. Haiti
18. Iran
19. India
20. Ireland
21. Israel
22. Jamaica
23. Japan
24. Jordan
25. Lebanon
26. Luxembourg
27. Mexico
28. Morocco
29. Nepal
30. Newfoundland
31. New Zealand
32. Nicaragua
33. Panama
34. Poland
35. Puerto Rico
36. Portugal
37. Russia
38. Scotland
39. Spain
40. Switzerland
41. Tibet
42. Thailand
43. U.S.A.
44. Vatican City
45. Wales
46. Yugoslavia

IV. Seas and Oceans

    1. Aegean   4. Galilee   7. Red Sea
    2. Atlantic   5. Mediterranean
    3. Caribbean   6. Pacific

V. In making this travelogue, I used the following modes of travel:

    1. Walking, climbing, crawling
    2. Automobiles, all models
    3. Airplanes, jets, and a Goodyear Blimp
    4. Ships, cruises and regular passenger
    5. Donkey, camel, elephant, and rickshaw

Lectureship visitors entertained

Photographed from the stairway of their restored home, Rosetyme, 1910 North 3rd.—Mr. and Mrs. Johnny Thompson (left) greet their guests: Mr. Norval Young of Malibu, California, and Mrs. Leland C. Biggs of Sheffield, Alabama. The Thompsons were hosts Tuesday evening to a reception that honored friends of Abilene Christian College Bible Lectures. (Staff Photo by Mark Allred)

1992
Spiritual Growth Workshop
Orlando, Florida

Becoming What You Believe

This was perhaps the largest group of people I have ever spoken before. It was an honor to be invited. Many people who attended brought memories of past days at home and abroad.

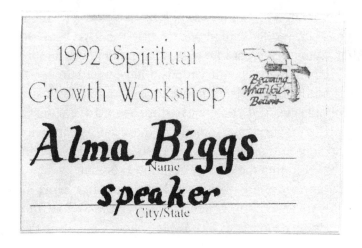

I would like to add that Mildred Higgs, Mary A. Black, and I have traveled "to and fro over the face of the earth." Just say, "GO," and we were ready. I would not have missed it for the world!

Volunteering

1868-1974
A Sentimental Journey With The Larimores

Webster defines restoration as the act of returning to the original state. Nehemiah 4: 6 says, "The people had a mind to work." Old houses seem to reflect the personality and character of the people who called them home in the long, long ago. It is possible to turn the pages back in one's mind and picture the love, harmony, and Christian living that went into making any old house a real home.

In driving along our country roads, I have many times been fascinated with the remnants of a once charming old place sitting far upon a hillside awaiting someone to offer a word of encouragement in its struggle for survival. Sometimes these calls seem so loud and clear that they are actually heard. Then after much weighing of matters and counting the cost, restoration is begun.

I have come to think of the word restoration as being synonymous with the accomplishments made at the site of the T. B. Larimore Home on the Mars Hill Bible School Campus in Florence, Alabama.

For our Christian heritage, the Larimore Home built in 1870 has a unique distinction and significance all its own. Its sturdy walls echoed to the voice of our religious faith. Its loving arms enfolded the hopes and dreams and longings of noble spirits who sought to restore New Testament Christianity.

The beautiful seasons of Spring, Summer, Autumn and Winter, each crowned with its particular charm, made successive panoramas of color as the parade of decades marched by this spacious home framed by virgin oaks, elms, beech, and hickories. No one seemed to recognize the faint sound from this knoll of nature's beauty as being a call for survival. Finally, the Associated Women's Organization of Mars Hill Bible School heard the plea as it came frantically loud and clear, and a dream coupled with determination began to take shape.

In an effort to preserve this great heritage, our vision stretched far into the future, to our children, and to their children. Now, please join me and so many dedicated Christian women in a little bit of nostalgia, and turn the pages back approximately one-hundred four years, when this stately twelve-room home was another dream, and picture it in its original state and usefulness.

Theophilus Brown Larimore was born July 10, 1843, in Jefferson County, Tennessee, a place he called "the Galilee of America." On his eightieth birthday anniversary, Larimore described that part of the country as a "land of fruits and flowers, tall men and towering mountains, fertile plains and limpid streams."

When a child, Larimore and his mother moved to the beautiful Sequatchie Valley of East Tennessee. This green valley is tucked away between two towering Appalachian Mountain ranges. The Cherokee Indians gave it the name of Sequatchie, which means "trough."

T. B. Larimore served in the Civil War. He was a soldier with the Southern Army and performed services in many hazardous situations, but he never fired a gun while he was a soldier. His sensitive temperament would have caused him to be terribly bothered over having injured or killed a fellow human. He was in the battle of Shiloh and was assigned to watch the Tennessee River for the coming of Union gunboats. He wrote the message that informed General Albert S. Johnston, who was killed at Shiloh, of the presence on the river of two Union gunboats which were escorting a fleet of troop transports. It is reported that General Johnston said, "Larimore's message is a model military document."

Soon after the war, he and his family moved to Hopkinsville, Kentucky. There he heard the gospel and obeyed it. He soon thereafter preached his first sermon. He said of that first sermon, "I repeated it over and over again in the presence of the team with which I was hauling wood to town, before I preached it to the people who patiently and politely listened to it."

T .B. Larimore married Miss Esther Gresham in 1868 near the place he later named Mars Hill, about four miles from downtown Florence, Alabama. In 1870, he had not enough money to buy a postage stamp. In fact, he lacked a few dollars yet being out of debt.

Confronted by many obstacles, he undertook to establish a "church-school" on the summit of one of the clusters of little hills, a site selected for the combination home-school building. Mrs. Larimore had inherited this small plot of ground, worth perhaps $250.00, from the estate of her mother, and this was all of their earthly possessions. They had never kept house and hence did not have enough furniture to start a home on the most economical plan. The first building, a three-story house of twelve large rooms, three halls, each ten by forty feet, and four open porches, each ten by fifty feet, was finished at a cost of $5000.00 in round numbers. To suitably furnish this building, enclose the campus, and put up the necessary outbuildings would cost approximately $5,000 more. If the time could be taken to study the resources of the field of religion on which Brother Larimore had to depend for support, the intense religious prejudice he had to combat, and the general indifference in the community, it is a wonder that he succeeded. He had to successfully manage a $10,000 debt and meet the running expenses of a well-appointed school; this would require unusual ability.

The Larimore Academy property at the beginning of 1875, only five years after the beginning of the enterprise, consisted of over 600 acres of land, more than twenty houses, and a splendid collection of school furniture; all of which cost not less than $30,000. The college was successfully managed for seventeen years with never a dollar of debt contracted that was not paid to the cent. This school was only closed when T. B. Larimore felt that he was neglecting the preaching of the gospel to lost souls. After much consideration and many prayers, he decided to close the school and hit the campaign trail to simply preach the Word of God.

A human interest statement about the construction of the home, as related in the *Letters and Sermons of T. B. Larimore,* Vol. III on page 44, illustrates one principle of his life to which much of his success is due—a steadfast determination to do whatsoever he did as nearly to perfection as possible. Here is the statement: "When the combination home-school building at Mars Hill was in the process of construction, he (T. B. Larimore) insisted that the sills should all be very heavy, of the best material, and securely fastened together so as to successfully resist time as well as tornadoes. (They have.)

One day, when all the workmen were eating their lunch and seated on the sills, which had just been put in place, Brother Srygley expressed doubt as to the securability of some part of the work. One of the men said, "Sometime in the far away future, some man swearing and sweating while trying to tear this old house down will say, 'I'd like to know who built this everlasting old house anyway; he must have thought he was building for Eternity instead of Time.'

Then some old man too old for work will say, 'I remember hearing my grandfather say that a cranky old man named Larimore had it built.' That was in the summer of 1870. The house we were then restoring is still as good as it was when it was new, and with proper care should last a thousand years and be a good house even after then."

On January 1, 1871, Mars Hill Academy, the first Christian Bible School in the South, was opened to receive students. The school term began in January every year and continued for twenty-four weeks, closing in June. Perhaps no other school in Bible School history has had such a short life yet wielded such great influence. Mars Hill was a pioneer among Bible Schools in the South. "Larimore Boys" were prominent in various fields throughout the Southern states. The name for the school was chosen from Acts 17 when Paul made his famous speech from Mars Hill in Athens, Greece. Since 1871, the name Mars Hill has been a synonym for wholesome teaching. Likewise, the memory of its illustrious founder, his noble wife, and their self-sacrifice are enshrined in the hearts of all throughout the brotherhood.

Mrs. Larimore and their six children continued to live in this home while Brother Larimore was away preaching in many parts of the nation. After the death of Mrs. Larimore in 1907 and the growing up and leaving of the children, the home was converted into rental apartments and became residences for many other families.

Approximately sixty-five years passed before another school came into being. In 1947, the new Mars Hill School opened its doors. At this time, operation began in the original Larimore Home and barn. The house was used for classrooms. The barn was constructed from materials saved from an old Civil War cannonball factory which had been adjacent to the house. Once constructed, the barn was used as the auditorium and lunchroom. Today, Mars Hill Bible School is an extension of the tradition of academic excellence dedicated toward building the whole individual. In 1956, the growing student body and the demands of expansion for educational excellence prompted a building program. The first unit of the new elementary building and a cafeteria building were erected in 1963, and the second unit completed in 1966. In 1968, the kindergarten department and elementary auditorium were constructed.

While the expansion and growth of Mars Hill Bible School was being realized, the Larimore Home was silent—no one really seemed to care about it. Women being women welcomed the challenge, and we began an effort to restore this home. Many were optimistic, many were hesitant, and a few were just plainly scared. But after much conversation and many pros and cons, the Associated Women's Organization shouldered the seemingly impossible financial and physical task of picking up the pieces and literally putting the house back together again. "We had a mind to work." This house was in such ill repair after serving the needs of so many people for so many years that we hardly knew where or how to begin, but we did begin.

It has been said that "Old houses mended cost little less than new before they are ended." We have found this statement to be so true, for we launched out on "faith" only, working frantically, not even stopping to count the cost. Please consider this to be your invitation to enjoy a "sentimental journey." Visit this historic shrine, and see the beauty and dignity of the restored home, which is reminiscent of an era when the land was still fairly new and unsettled and New Testament Christianity was being attacked from all sides. There is something about our heritage that resists being bought and sold. Everything at the Larimore Home is a little bit special. It is as special as the elusive and gracious spirit of Southern Hospitality that waits to welcome you as you make entrance to the peace and quiet of the North Veranda. The lovely wide porches offer big old-fashioned rocking chairs that extend you a gracious invitation.

Brother Virgil Larimore, the last of the Larimores, passed away December 30, 1972 at the age of 93. We are so happy that he seemed pleased with what had been done to his ancestral home, and when asked, "Brother Larimore, How do you like it?" He said, "Well, it doesn't look exactly like Mamma's house," and then after a pause he continued, "But I guess it looks like Mamma's house should have looked." He visited the restored home several times and recommended it as an ideal place to eat a good meal amidst the splendor of reminders of an illustrious past. In talking about his famous father, he said, "I don't understand how my father did so much." But we know today that Brother T. B. Larimore was truly about his Father's business.

We are sure that you are genuinely thrilled and inspired to see this beautiful old building again as it has taken on new life and looks forward toward another long and useful era. It has truly been connected with ETERNITY from its beginning. Today, the hub of activity at Mars Hill centers around the Larimore House. All proceeds from the house go toward fulfillment of Brother Larimore's DREAM, through us, for CHRISTIAN EDUCATION.

> Alma D. Biggs, President
> Associated Women's Organization
> Mars Hill Bible School
> Florence, Alabama

T. B. Larimore and Family

Home of
T. B. Larimore

Erected in 1870

Restored in 1971

~

Restored and Operated by
Associated Women's Organization
Florence, Alabama

History of the Larimore Home

The Larimore home was built in 1870 by Theophilus Brown Larimore. Following his marriage in 1868 to Miss Esther Gresham, they decided to establish a school on 27 acres of land she had inherited from her mother's estate. Using the home and approximately 20 other buildings on the same site, a school was operated from 1871 to 1887 which has significantly affected the history of the Shoals area — and much of the nation.

The Larimores built their spacious 12-room home of virgin oak, elm, beech and hickory. The following interesting note about it appears in one of Larimore's books:

. . . *When the combination home and school building at Mars Hill was in process of preparation, I insisted that the sills . . . be very heavy, of the very best material, and securely fastened together, so as to successfully resist time, as well as tornadoes, should tornadoes ever pass that way . . . (Note: they have!) . . . One day when all of us then working on the building were eating our lunch, seated on the sills that had just been put into place...I expressed doubt as to the security and durability of some part of the work. John Thrasher, a good worker, a good man and good friend to me, noted for his humor and good nature, remained sagely silent till the discussion of the imaginary defect ceased, and he soliloquized thus, "Sometime in the faraway future, some man, cursing, sweating and swearing, while trying to tear this old house down, get sills apart and remove the rubbish, will say, 'I'd like to know who built this old house, anyhow. He must of thought he was building for eternity instead of time'..."* The house we were building is still as good as it was when new, and with proper care, should last a thousand years, and be a good house even after then... (Letters and Sermons of T.B. Larimore, Vol. III, p. 44)

In 1947, the present Mars Hill Bible School began a new era of training, making use of the home for many years for elementary and high school classes. When the new high school building was erected, the status of the home was uncertain for nearly a decade.

The Associated Women's Organization of Mars Hill, visualizing the dignity and service the home could again provide in its setting, committed its membership to a seemingly impossible physical and financial task of restoring the home.

Restoration of the home was initiated exactly one century after its original construction. Continuing efforts are underway to furnish it authentically for the period and to beautify the grounds. Many of the Larimore family possessions, including personal items of T.B. Larimore and his descendants, have been given to the home.

The home is used extensively as a serviceable community and school center. The "north veranda", the lovely foyer, the large living and dining rooms, the bedrooms, the study — all of these rooms bespeak a noble vestibule into antiquity. Descending the stairs into "Virgil's Cellar", one is ushered into yesterday with all of the sights, sounds and smells of true southern hospitality!

Mars Hill Bible School

In Appreciation of Service

Associated Women's Organization
Mars Hill Bible School
Florence, Alabama

Recognizes _Alma Riggs_

for outstanding support and continued interest in Christian Education with your labor of love in A.W.O.

_1985_ _Frances E. Williams_
Date President

Tributes

Times Daily, Sunday, January 20, 1985

> "First you get a vision of something worthwhile, spread your enthusiasm and watch as people get interested and start things happening."
> — Alma Biggs

Home's restoration proves daydreams really do come true

By Lucille Prince
Staff Writer

Daydreams do come true.
Alma Biggs of Sheffield can tell you how. Her dream 14 years ago to renovate the historical Larimore Home in Florence not only came true, but has snowballed and gets bigger every year.

The plantation-type home, then 100 years old, was restored within a year. Biggs and the other energetic women whose efforts made it all possible then turned their efforts to other projects — projects that have yielded approximately $145,000 for Mars Hill Bible School, located on the home's grounds.

"First you get a vision of something worthwhile, spread your enthusiasm and watch as people get interested and start things happening," she said. "Just wishing, or dreaming, won't do any good. It takes action."

Peggy Simpson first caught the vision and is credited with organizing the Associated Women's Organization of Mars Hill Bible School.

"Mrs. Simpson, along with other women active with the Churches of Christ of the area, saw potential in the old home built by T.B. Larimore in 1870," Biggs said. "The home was in bad condition and many people thought it should be torn down. But the women, admitting the task of restoring the home sometimes seemed physically and financially impossible, tackled the job of raising money and rolling up sleeves to do a lot of cleaning."

The 12-room home was constructed of virgin oak, elm, beech and hickory. Used as a combination school-home, the Larimores named the school Mars Hill, apparently for the Biblical Mars Hill.

The AWO's efforts paid off as the home took on the appearance of a stately mansion and the grounds were beautified. Many of the Larimore family possessions, including a communion set given to Larimore in 1878 by Mrs. Alexander Campbell for use in worship services, were given to the home.

It was placed on the National Register of Historic Places in 1974.

After the restoration project was completed, the AWO turned its efforts toward using the home to help the Mars Hill School.

"One of our projects was to let people use the home for events such as weddings, receptions, dinners, luncheons and club meetings," Biggs said. "This is still going over big. Right now we're booking bridal parties for next summer."

AWO members use their tastiest recipes for luncheons and dinners, which are served in a basememt room known as Virgil's Cellar, named for the Larimore's youngest son.

The AWO's year-round money-making events include a gift shop, fashion show and luncheon, a variety show called "Musical Starburst," and a Shoals Holiday Tour of Homes. Pumpkin' Day, the association's largest event, last October netted approximately $15,000.

The school has used AWO money to help buy air conditioning, science and home economics equipment; start a first aid room and construct a bus garage.

Biggs' dream has not ended. Younger generations of women have grasped hold of it, and they, too, are continuing the work of the Associated Women's Organization.

"The dream of one lady has become the answer to dreams of many other people," said Barbara Young, current AWO president.

State of Alabama

LARIMORE HOME

The National Register of Historic Places
by the
United States Department of the Interior

Alabama Historical Commission

The above certificate, giving notice of the Larimore Home to the National Register of Historic Places by the United States Department of the Interior on November 21, 1974 is a treasured symbol of the cooperation that has long existed between the A.W.O. and local and state officials interested in historic preservation.

Proverbs 31:10
Who can find a virtuous woman? for her price is far above rubies.

Associated Women's Organization
Mars Hill Bible School

I am only one, But still I am one.
I cannot do everything, But still
I can do something.
And because I cannot do everything
I will not refuse to do the Something that I can do.
—*Edward Everett Hale*

For every right that you cherish,
you have a duty which you must fulfill.
For every hope that you entertain,
you have a task that you must perform.
For every good that you wish to preserve,
you will have to sacrifice your comfort and your ease.
There is nothing for nothing any longer.

— GEORGE WASHINGTON

1969 - 1995

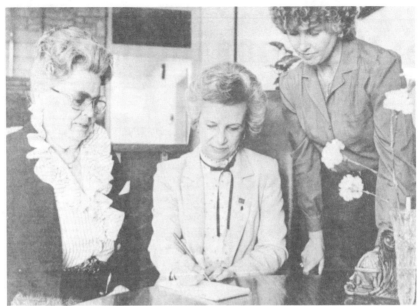

AWO Fashion Show Committee

Members of the Associated Womens Organization at Mars Hill Bible School are making plans for their annual fashion show. This year's event will be a luncheon and spring fashion show to be held April 9 in the school auditorium. Making plans for the event are, from left, Mrs. Alma Biggs, Mrs. Gertrude Hill and Mrs. Becky Hamm. All proceeds from the show will go to the school.

Spring Fashion Show, an annual Fund Raiser

Mars Hill's Associated Women's Organization and Parisian Annual Spring Fashion Show is scheduled for Saturday, April 14, at noon, at Mars Hill auditorium. Ann Harris of Parisian (second from left) shows AWO members (from left) Becky Hamm, Johnnie Lou Cochran, Alma Biggs and Edith Presley one of the dresses in the show. Tickets are $10, and will be available at Parisian in Regency Square Mall or at the school house gift shop at Mars Hill.

AWO 1969, Johnny Lou Cochran and Alma B. enjoy a fun dress up Luncheon at the Larimore Home.

Blanche Horseman and Alma B. at an AWO meeting.

MAKING PLANS — Members of the Associated Women's Organization of Mars Hill are busy finalizing plans for 'Punkin' Day' which will be held Saturday. Pictured are, from left, Alma Biggs, Edith Presley, Becky Hamm, Barbara Young.

'Punkin' Day Set For Saturday

The annual Mars Hill Bible School 'Punkin Day' will be held Saturday, beginning with breakfast at 7:30 a.m.

'Punkin Day' is major fund-raising event for Mars Hill sponsored by the Associated Women's Organization.

According to chairman Barbara Young, this year's festivities will include new events such as a moonwalk, train ride, dunking machine and chances to ride in General Lee's car.

Doug Letson will perform a magic show at noon and the rock group "Heat" will be on hand to entertain guests.

As always, a variety of arts and crafts will be available in the gym.

There is no admission charge and the parking is free.

SPRING FASHIONS — Mattie Carroll (left) and Alma Biggs will participate in "A Runway to Fashion," a spring fashion show and luncheon sponsored by Associated Women's Organization of Mars Hill Bible School. The show will be held Saturday, March 28, at noon at Mars Hill Bible School auditorium. Proceeds will benefit Christian education at Mars Hill Bible School in Florence. The public is invited to attend. Tickets are on sale at the Larimore House in Florence, Mars Hill Book Store, and from any member of the AWO. For more information call 766-9191.

AWO Sponsors Spring Fashions

*Alma as Hostess for Paul Harvey at the Larimore home.
He was featured speaker for the annual
Mars Hill Benefit Dinner.*

*Art Linkletter with Alma at the Larimore Home.
He spoke for the annual Benefit Dinner at Mars Hill.*

School House Gift Shop

Unique Collectables
Charming Ideas for
Holiday Giving

698 Cox Creek Pkwy.
Just off Mars Hill Rd.
Florence, AL

10 a.m. to 4 p.m.
Monday — Friday
Phone (205) 767-2839

GRAND OPENING — The School House Gift Shop, next to the Larimore House, Mars Hill Road, recently held its grand open house. The School House Gift Shop has nicities from the present and pretties for the present. Back row from left, Ralph Snell, Larry Hayes, Jim Odum, William McDonald, Johnnie Lon Cochran and Graham Edwards. Front row from left, Bobbie Crittenden, Ralph Foster, Mayor Bill Batson, Alma Biggs, Senator Bobby Denton, Peggy Simpson, Becky Hamm and Gertrude Hill.

September of 1982
World's Fair

After having the opportunity to visit World's Fair areas in other parts of the world, I became aware that the World's Fair was to be in Knoxville, Tennessee, in 1982. I decided I would like to be part of this fair. My early roots were there. I made application to work as a volunteer for two weeks. This time expanded to two more weeks. The Church of Christ booth was located right in the middle of the whole activity. I wondered about a place to stay. Then I was invited to live with some other Tennessee natives: Delphie Harvey and Daphene Kennedy, who were there from Freed-Hardeman University. It was a real pleasure to come home at night and share the places, times, and personalities we had experienced that day. After a month of work and play, I received a note from them: "We enjoyed living and working with you at the World's Fair in 1982 in Knoxville, Tennessee. Perhaps our paths will cross again. If you visit F.H.U. please look us up."

They were both employed at F.H.U., and they were a real joy to me during this time. I feel that this was a month well spent with representatives from so many nations of our world. If any of you have this opportunity, be sure and jump on the "Band Wagon."

Alma at World's Fair

Attending lectureships and being honored for work at Alabama Christian College in Foley, Alabama.

ACC President Ernest Clevenger, Jr. (center) is shown with Mrs. David (Susie) Boyd (left) and Mrs. Alma Biggs at the college lectureships.

Mrs. Alma Biggs, Florence and Mrs. Martha Carmichael, Selma, were presented certificates of Honorary Life Membership to the Women's Council at the recent Ladies Luncheon. Mrs. Suzie Boyd, Chattanooga, who was not present, was also awarded the same honor. Mrs. Don (Audrey) Gardner, (right) Houston, Texas, was the guest speaker for the event.

THE WHITE HOUSE

WASHINGTON

April 18, 1983

To the Class of 1983:

I extend to you, the first baccalaureate class of Alabama Christian College, my warm congratulations! Your valued degree attests to the fact that you have completed the demanding intellectual challenges set before you by a distinguished American college.

As graduates of Alabama Christian, you have proven your academic abilities and you have acquired a rich spiritual inheritance prepared by the saints and sages through the preceding ages. With that legacy comes the responsibility to do your part in making America and the world a better place. You will face obstacles and disappointments along the way, but nothing worth achieving was ever easy.

You should never forget the hopes that rest on you and the sacrifices others have made so that you can succeed. As you move in new directions, use your skills and talents creatively, share your hearts, your love of God generously, so that you can pass on an even richer bequest to new generations.

Again, congratulations on your graduation, good luck and God bless you.

Ronald Reagan

The Class of 1983
Alabama Christian College
c/o Dr. Ernest Clevenger, President
5345 Atlanta Highway
Montgomery, Alabama   36193

New Trustees Announced

Mrs. Alma D. Biggs of Sheffield, Ala., and Mrs. David (Susie) Boyd of Chattanooga, Tenn., have recently been added to the ACC Board of Trustees, according to Board Chairman J.H. Faulkner, Sr.

The widow of Leland C. Biggs, Alma Biggs has gained renown as a speaker who is in demand throughout the United States and Europe. A member of the Annapolis Avenue Church of Christ in Sheffield, she teaches three ladies' classes there every Wednesday and has been very active in the Associated Women's Association of Mars Hill Bible School in Florence, Ala., since its beginning.

She has had a part in the production of two inspirational books—*What Are We Doing Here?* and *Something Special.* Both have won acclaim as inspirational and study material.

Mrs. Biggs is a guest writer for the *World Evangelist,* a publication of the International Bible College in Florence, Ala.

In 1981 she spoke to the missionary women of Western Europe in London, England. She has spoken in Germany, Austria, Puerto Rico and was the guest speaker on the Christian Cruise to the Caribbean last June. She has been invited to spend a great part of the summer of '83 in Cambridge, England, working with ladies who are new converts.

In addition to her duties as an ACC Trustee, she is also a member of the Long Range Planning Board at David Lipscomb College in Nashville, Tenn.

Mrs. Biggs is the mother of three sons and one daughter and has six grandchildren.

"I am very impressed with the atmosphere here at Alabama Christian," states Mrs. Biggs. "The student attitude is just great!

"I feel that tremendous progress has been made here at the school during the past several months," she continues. "I hope to contribute myself to the success of ACC...I particularly would like to strengthen the Florence Center of ACC."

Changing Times

1945-1950
Dame Fashion Rules, The Demise Of Our Hats

I guess I am writing mostly to my girls. We all know fashions come and go, and fads and new fashions are adopted. Sometimes these changes receive a welcome to our bulging wardrobes, and sometimes they are a pure abomination. Anyway, I surely do miss donning my beautiful hat, whether the event calls for casual or dress-up. However, it surely came to pass that the millinery shops no longer exhibited their wares on Main Street.

The last hat I wore, I think, I wore to church. Then it was stored away for generations yet to come. This hat had a high crown, which I cut out, leaving a large hole for my figure eight bun to fit into.

After this last appearance, I thought it fitting that we honor the apparel of yesterday—the hat. Our hats were often decorated with roses, veils, and luscious ribbon and lace. Then came the fatal illness. The funeral was conducted by the Ladies Guild. Our hats had suffered many years from symptoms of yellow jaundice, which produced a dropping of the brim. Our ladies ordered the removal of yellow daisies and chrysanthemums, which had involved numerous stitches, but the beauty failed to survive. This cutting away brought to a close the most colorful part of our attire. Pallbearers were selected from the popular shops in whose employ the hat had played and paid no small part.

"Moma B" Has Had Her Hair Cut

Several years after the slow demise of the popular hat, I was talked into getting my hair cut, following years of wearing it long and twisted up on top of my head. It happened this way: One day in the late 70's, I stopped at the beauty shop. I was on my way to do some volunteer work at the Larimore Home at Mars Hill Bible School. My friend Lurene McKinny worked at the shop.

I said, "Please, shampoo my hair."

It was long, and I mean very long. Lurene proceeded to comb, brush, and put in tangles so it could be piled high on my head. I don't know why I had been so determined to be different.

Lurene said, "Alma, let's cut your hair."

I must have said or uttered what she thought was telling her to "Go Ahead." Anyway, I looked down, and there were all my tresses piled on the floor. What could I do or say? Nothing. What was done was done. Afterward, when I arrived at the home, I received so many compliments I decided I had done the right thing.

In 1927, the great Edgar Guest must have heard about a similar loss and immediately picked up his pen and put into words his version of the last holdout to have her tresses bobbed.

I had tried to convince myself and others that I had not been Biblically scriptural, and told them to read Matthew 24:17, which reads, "Let him that is on the housetop not (knot) come down to take anything out of his house." This is mentioned with a smile. It is certainly out of context but is fun to apply to the situation.

For many years, Becky and I have visited "Louise and Ronnie's" beauty shop. This is my before and after story.

Louise and Ronnie Kimbrough.
My favorite beauticians for lo these many years.

The Last Holdout Surrenders
by Edgar A. Guest

One by one the hold-outs weaken,
  One by one Dame Fashion wins!
Custom, with her flashing beacon
  First with youth, a style begins.
Then the brides of June affect it,
  Next the matrons tall and fair.
Now, from whom we'd least expect it,
  Auntie Mabel's bobbed her hair!

When they started shortening dresses
  Auntie Mabel shook her head.
Then when maidens clipped their tresses
  Many bitter things she said.
Oft she muttered: "I abhor it!
  It's a silly fad, I swear!"
Now at last she's fallen for it,
  Auntie Mabel's bobbed her hair!

Now at last one in our fortress
  Has surrendered to the foe,
Joined the camp which wears the short tress
  And we grieve to see her go.
She was all we had, still clinging
  To the wealth the poor could share,
Set the bells in dirges ringing,
  Auntie Mabel's bobbed her hair!

(Copyright, 1927, by Edgar A. Guest)

1975
Joe Wheeler Park

The photograph is of the 50th Year Reunion of our Sheffield High School Class. I am out front, of course, wearing a green jacket. The third man left to right is Jimmy Green. After 50 years, it is hard to remember names and faces. Jimmy finally decided: "Oh yeh! You are that little 'blue-eyed girl.'" I said, "And you were the captain of Sheffield's first football team. Now, I guess we do know who we are." Jimmy and I renewed our 'long time gone' friendship which continued until his death.

After he retired, he moved to Fairhope, Alabama, and many times I visited my brother at Hammock Creek, out of Foley, Alabama, and near Fairhope. Jimmy and I took advantage of these times to visit and revive some of our school day memories.

Perry's Restaurant near Pensacola was always a must for Key Lime Pie. Maybe there was a romantic touch peeping through, I don't know. Oh, well, thanks Jimmy for a nostalgic journey.

-ADB-

Achievements and Tributes

Information About Alma D. Biggs

Alma D. Biggs is the widow of Leland C. Biggs. She has been a widow since 1967, at which time she put her house in order and volunteered to go on her first campaign to the Bermuda Islands. Mrs. Biggs is a member of Annapolis Avenue Church of Christ in Sheffield, Alabama. She teaches two Ladies' classes every Wednesday. Since its beginning, she has been very active in Associated Women's Organization of Mars Hill Bible School. With Mrs. Biggs taking the leadership role, the Larimore Home at Mars Hill in Florence, Alabama, has been renovated and restored. This home stands tall in the Florence area as a beautiful landmark, reaching backward and forward in the interest of Christian education.

Two inspirational books in which she had a part are now on the bookshelves: *What Are We Doing Here?* published in 1972 and *Something Special* published in 1977. Both books have been very favorably received as inspirational and study material. All proceeds go to Mars Hill Bible School. Mrs. Biggs is a former guest writer for *THE WORLD EVANGELIST,* published and edited by Basil Overton of Heritage Christian University in Florence, Alabama. Also, she is a sought after speaker for retreats and lecture series, and this service takes her to many places both at home and abroad. Her enthusiasm for travel takes her much further. In 1981, she spoke to the missionary women of Western Europe in London, England. She has spoken in Germany, Austria, and Puerto Rico, and, she was guest speaker for the Christian Tours International in West Monroe, Louisiana, during twelve cruises. In 1991, she was invited to spend a part of the summer in Vienna, Austria, to teach conversational English at the International University. In 1992, she joined the cruise to Alaska as guest speaker.

Mrs. Biggs is the mother of three sons and one daughter, six grandchildren, and one great-grandson.

Accomplishments And Achievements
of
Alma Dukes Biggs

1. Graduated Sheffield High School, 1925
2. Attended Secretarial College, Sheffield, 1926-27
3. Secretary for A.G. Milan Transportation Company, 1926-27
4. Secretary for Congressman Edward B. Almon, 1928-33
5. Secretary T.V.A Office of Purchasing, Knoxville, TN, 1934-40
6. Co-owner family business, Chem-Haulers, Sheffield, 1955-67
7. Active in teaching role, Annapolis Avenue Church of Christ, Sheffield, Alabama
8. Helped write two inspirational books suitable for lesson material: *What Am I Doing Here?* and *Something Special*
9. Founder of Associated Women's Organization of Mars Hill Bible School, Florence, Alabama
10. Elected President of AWO for four terms, 1973-79 and 1987-88
11. Member, Development Council, David Lipscomb College, 1981
12. Member, President's Development Council, Mars Hill Bible School, 1983
13. Life Member, Women's Council, Faulkner University, Montgomery, Alabama
14. Life Member, International Bible College (now Heritage Christian University) Woman's Organization
15. Life Member, Freed-Hardiman University Woman's Organization
16. Member, President's Association, International Christian University, Vienna, Austria. Taught conversational English at this University.
17. Now serves as advisor to the A.W.O. board, which meets monthly. This association supports Mars Hill Bible School in all its needs. Assists in recruiting students who can best profit by the service of the school. We promote a clear understanding of Christian Education. We foster a spirit of friendship among

women interested in the development of spiritual values in education. We spearheaded the restoration of T. B. Larimore home, a historic landmark on the Mars Hill Bible School campus.
19. Traveled the world in the interest of Christianity and Christian Education and spoke for Ladies' groups world wide and on 12 different Christian cruise trips to different parts of the world.
20. Guest writer for the "World Evangelist" with articles on the Women's Page.

September 30, 1982

A Tribute To Alma D. Biggs
Life Membership Luncheon, Larimore House, Florence, Alabama

The Associated Women's Association welcomed Alma into its fold in about 1969 or 1970. From that first day, we knew we had a prize. Her brain is so filled with ideas to make things better that you can almost see the wheels turning and the images taking shape. Alma, you have proven many times over that you know how to get things done.

The first job to tackle was this house. It was in shambles when we finally got the word from the Board of Directors to see what we could do with it. Most of us stood back and wondered, "What could we do with it?" Alma, like Nehemiah, had a mind to work. Alma, you are a true workman. You lead the way, and the rest of us follow.

Perhaps some of you can remember—others of you joined us later—that we have said many times, the house was dirty, and the basement was filled to the ceiling with junk. The walls were literally crumbling, and the floors were not any too sturdy, or at least they didn't look in very good shape. The windows were just so dirty that we were not able to see through them. All of this made a bleak picture. We said, "Well, we asked for it, but what have we got?" Alma said, "We've got a prize. Let's get busy!"

And busy is not the word for it. There is not a one of us who would even think of working so hard at home. With Alma leading the pack, we would quit in the evening so tired and dirty that we would go home and fall into the bathtub. Those of us who had families somehow got through without having to see a Marriage Counselor, probably proving that hard work is good for what ever ails us. Alma, we thank you for showing us, helping us, and proving to us that the word "impossible" is only something in the dictionary. It does not exist in the mind of Alma Biggs.

First of all, we hauled all of the junk from the basement. It was separated into piles of good junk and bad junk. The good junk was sold (with most of us buying it), and the bad junk was hauled off to its doom. To be hauled off—take my word for it—it had to be terrible junk. Alma was right there saying, "Don't get rid of that. I think maybe we can make something useful out of it." And she would. We have seen you, many times, take horrible looking junk and work your magic, and out would come lamps, or candle holders or maybe just something that would make you wonder.

When finally, we had all of the junk hauled out, hauled off, or sold, Alma, you would be here at 8 a.m. with your cotton dress on, and ready to work. And work you did! You had some good reliable help, but you were the one who could work the magic! Coming next are a few of the "for instances."

The late Johnny Thompson and Sue, his beautiful wife, came several times to visit while the work was in progress. They had had experience in restoring and offered whatever help they could to you from the beginning of our big project. With minds working together, it was decided that we would simply capitalize on our crumbling walls in the basement. We would put spots on the parts that felt sturdy and finish crumbling off what was loose. They called this process by a beautiful sounding name, but we who see it now call it magic.

Alma, you scouted the backwoods and byways looking for mantles for the fireplaces. You would come into this house with a different man every day with another mantle in his pick-up truck. Sometimes we wouldn't be able to recognize what it was supposed to be. It would be boards nailed to other boards with twenty-seven coats of paint on it, and we would exclaim, "What is that?!" You would calmly say, "It is going to be a mantle for Miss Ettie's room if you'll just hush and get busy with the Kutzit."

Alma, you did this not only with mantles but also with missing stair spindles. Some of us would stand back and look at the staircase and say, "With the spindles missing, it looks like an old man with his teeth missing." You would say, "If I can just think where I saw it, I think I may be able to find a piece of a stair case. It was probably at Plow-Boys. I'll go there tomorrow and see if I can find it. Maybe I can talk him out of it." You could . . . you did . . . and no one would ever be the wiser as to how the stair case remained in such good condition these hundred years.

Alma, you would not want to forget, nor would we, that during all of your hard work and sweating (when you work that hard, it ceases to be perspiration) that Brother Snell was right here with us. We feel sure you would agree that his constant encouragement and knowledgeable background helped you help us to get the job done.

When we took a look at the pine floors upstairs, all any of us could see were dirty, rough-looking planks. You could see the rich, wide pine boards that were planed and finished from the timber grown right here on this property. Some of our hard working women thought that we could refinish them ourselves, but you said they needed to be done right. We had a professional to come in and redo the floors. They were so beautiful that we could almost see ourselves in them.

Alma, when there is love in the work we do, there is joy in the heart. Your heart must be filled-to-overflowing with the joy that comes from all of the work you have put into this place in the past twelve years.

In thinking of your hard work, there are those who would say, "Sure, Alma can work and do all of those impossible things. She has the talent for recognizing a prize where we see junk, and making beautiful things out of nothing." But it is a fact that any talent that we may possess is at least 90% hard work. Talent without work is useless. Alma, you have multiplied your talent a hundred-fold.

It would probably not be out of order if we mentioned that we owe a great deal to Plow-Boy. He and Alma had been friends for years and years. So much of what you see and what you don't see is due to Alma being willing to go every morning as soon as Plow-Boy opened up, and standing on her head and stepping through litter and dust and stripping away cobwebs to find ever so many little and big things that had been sitting in his place for years. Alma had been there so many times, she knew the place as well as Plow-Boy. Plow-Boy is gone now, but maybe he can look down and see what beauty his bits and pieces and guess-whats and treasure-finds have brought to this house and Gift Shop . . . all due to you, Alma.

Those of you who have been with AWO since its beginning already know all the things we are talking about today. But for the benefit of you who joined us after 1971, you cannot possibly know of the many things Alma did for the restoration of this Larimore House. Did you know that the beautiful, rich, red velvet drapes on the windows in the parlor did not get there by way of Lavish Windows and Interiors? Surprised aren't you? Those beautiful drapes came by way of Alma and the Annapolis Avenue Church in Sheffield. She knew that the interior of the church building was about to be redone. She asked if the drapes were going to be discarded. They were, and you now see them in the Larimore parlor.

How do you think the lace panels got on the windows? Someone or maybe several someones discussed what would be pretty on the windows. Only one thing would look really good: Lace panels. Alma said, "I'm leaving next week for Scotland. Don't do anything until I return. I'll see what I can find while I'm over there!" Many of the details have faded with the years, but the truth of the matter is, as soon as her feet touched Scottish soil, Alma began to ask every store keeper she could see, "Do you know if one can still find cotton lace window curtains? I want to find some while I am here." Finally she found someone who thought he knew of a warehouse where a few handmade cotton lace panels might be stored. Alma got directions, and off she went. If my memory serves me correctly, she climbed ladders herself to get down bundles off high shelves. She searched until she found handmade, cotton lace panels. You see them every time you go into any of the four rooms on the first floor of this house.

Alma, we recall the day you went into a store in Sheffield, and while making your purchase, you noticed a box of what most of us would call junk. You looked at it very closely, and then asked the store owner what he would take for that box full of parts, fittings, pipes, and things. He looked at it and said, "Well, if you see something there, you can just have it." On the day of our Grand Open House in 1971, you invited that storeowner out to see the restored Larimore House. You pointed out the beautiful light fixture in the study to him, and told him the light fixture was out of the box of junk he had given you. He was so surprised at what he saw, he wanted you to sign a paper saying that he had donated a brass light fixture worth so much money to the Larimore House. We feel that many of his friends have heard of his generous donation to the house.

Then what about the lovely red runner in the hall of the first floor—where did you get that, Alma? You salvaged it also from the Annapolis Avenue Church building as they were redecorating. You did remarkable things for this house. We can't help but wonder what it would look like if you had not been with us. You scouted the entire state looking for rugs to go on the floors. The writer of this tribute does not recall where you got each one, but we know that each one was searched from nooks and crannies at someone's house or store.

The furnishings throughout the house were sought from Larimore family members still living and from people who you knew had some connection in some way either to the Larimore family or to the house itself. They were brought in from far and near. You would be someplace and see a pedestal or a shelf or maybe a stool and say to yourself, "If I can get this cheap enough, I feel sure we can find the money somewhere to pay for it." And so many were bought, and you would be heard to say, "Well, I'll go ahead and pay for it. If I don't get it back, I don't think it will kill me." Several pieces you did bring from your own home, office, basement, or garage. We know that many pieces came from others as well, but today, Alma, we are talking about you and a few of the things you have done for us. The very lovely piece in the parlor, just to the right as you step through the door, is an example of Alma and her family's generosity.

After the house was completed and the doors opened wide for the friends throughout the whole area to come and see, you rested for a little while. Perhaps you were a wee bit tired. You took a few marvelous trips around this great world of ours and did many things that few of us ever dream of doing: traveling, teaching classes in far-away places, sailing into the Caribbean Islands on a cruise ship with about 200 other Christians and many other well deserved delightful pleasures. But you did come back home. About two years ago, you asked, "When do we start on the little house next door?" To be answered with, "What's wrong with, now?" So the story starts over again.

Alma, there is a commercial on TV that goes something like this, "We did it!" And we did! You and Plow-Boy and many of us.

The house next door was opened up, cleared out, swept down, and taken in. It did not seem to be in quite the desperate shape as was the house, or maybe it just wasn't as big. Anyway, you helped tackle that job with the same vigor as you did the big house. If it is possible, maybe with more vigor and energy, because this was your dream as well as the dream of many others to have the house readied for a gift shop.

Plow-Boy was about to go out of business. Everyone thought that nothing was left there but the junkiest of junk. You knew better. You said there was still treasure in some of the junk out back. You had it hauled over here for absolutely pennies, considering what it is worth now. The beautiful large piece that graces the back wall of the gift shop is what we are talking about. And that was just the beginning.

Next came the mirrors you remembered seeing propped against the wall at Plow-Boys (I think). You had some of the men from here go over and get pieces as you would find them. The men brought the mirrors, and as they were unloading them they remarked that they must be made out of lead, they were so heavy. Someone got busy scraping through the twelve coats of paint on the frame to discover the mirrors were framed in marble.

You would call up furniture stores and ask for their very lowest price on rugs, and while they were at it, you asked, would they throw in a few paintings to go on the walls . . . it was for a very good cause.

WE LOVE YOU, ALMA!

While you were helping to clean up Plow-Boys, you even got old plows and seeders for the yard, in and around the gift shop. We think the day we may have wondered about you, though, Alma, was when you brought in a flimsy brass-plated headboard. That caused us all a little concern, especially when you asked one of the men to hang it upside down in the entrance of the gift shop. Now really, Alma, you've got to admit, that seemed a bit strange. But we should not have given it a second thought. It is our elegant entrance piece, and a topic for many a conversation. Everyone thinks it is so clever that we would all like to be able to say, "I thought of doing that." But it was you and your creative mind.

You would hear of a store about to go out of business and here you would go, to see if they would give (or sell very cheaply) some of their display cases and shelves.

You put in long hard hours (as did many others) to get the quaint and charming gift shop next door. Choosing the right color paint, deciding what should go on the windows, what to stock to sell once we got it ready, and who to stock it, who to run it, and who to set up a book-keeping system. All this had to be decided, along with all that had to be done to meet the standards of our AWO and you, Alma. We are all very thankful to have had you and are deeply thankful that your standards are so high. Things couldn't be done halfway. They had to be done right. You didn't want anything shoddy or anything that anybody would be ashamed of . . . you just wanted it right to begin with.

We are sure that the Lord was with you and us in everything we did. Things went well, considering we were all amateurs at everything we were doing. In generations to come, as young men and women look about the Larimore House and School House Gift Shop, perhaps many will be heard to say something like this, "Where do you suppose the women got the money and the know-how to restore this old house and the little school room next door?" And some will answer, "They probably had several rich women interested enough in the project to pay for having it done." But Alma we hope and pray that there will always be someone present in AWO who will be able to say . . .

"They had Alma Biggs!"

A letter written in 1969 to Alma Dukes Biggs and read at the Ladies Bible Class of Annapolis Avenue Church of Christ in Sheffield, Alabama as a tribute to Alma from Peggy Simpson.

I Wish Everybody Knew "Miss B"

A friend and I share the joy of writing a children's bulletin for the benefit of our friends between the ages of two and twelve at the Annapolis Avenue congregation in Sheffield, Alabama. Recently, when it was my turn to write the bulletin, I went into great detail on being willing to share—not the things we do not want—but blessings and joys that we love; for only then do we know the real happiness of sharing. Several weeks after that bulletin had been mailed, we received a letter thanking us for the bulletin and that story in particular. As I read the letter and was glorying over the good things this mother and teacher had to say, it suddenly dawned on me that we were failing to share something we have at Annapolis Avenue that we love dearly.

"Miss B" as my family affectionately knows her, is Mrs. Leland C. (Alma) Biggs. She has all the qualities of a virtuous woman, plus. It is this plus in a person that makes her outstanding. There are perhaps thousands of good Christian women whom we know and love, but it is when they possess that extra plus that they become special. This is true even of the women in the Bible. Surely there were scores of truly good, devoted Christian women of whom we have no record. The Lord lets us know about only the ones who have that special quality in their lives.

About four years ago when Mrs. Biggs lost her good husband to cancer, she was grieved, as any devoted wife would be. This is when I first knew that she was a special person. I had not known her well before this time. After our children are all grown up and away from home, the majority of us, if we had to watch the person we love most dearly lose the battle with cancer, would be ready to give up ourselves. But in a few months following his death, when she was in her deepest sorrow, she heard of a campaign for Christ soon to be in the Bermuda Islands. She wrote to the proper officials and made her plans to go. She worked for two weeks there, going from door to door telling people "the wonderful news," while at the same time her heart felt as though it would break. As soon as she got back home, she immediately went to the Bible school director and asked to be put to work. She was given the task of not only teaching the Wednesday morning ladies Bible class, but the Wednesday evening class as well. At the same time, she also enrolled as a student of religion at our local University to further her education in Bible. Added to these duties, she has her invalid mother to care for, a large house, and several flower gardens on a two-acre lawn to tend.

Her remarkable abilities make it possible for her to do a most thorough job of each task. She makes the women of the Bible (our Wednesday morning study) seem so real that we find ourselves becoming close friends with little known characters such as Rizpah, Jedidah, Huldah, and Manoah's wife. Then on Wednesday evenings in our detailed study of the Law Books of Moses, it is as if we are encamped there at Mount Sinai, awaiting orders to move and be on our way to Canaan.

She is an excellent teacher and a most gracious, genuine lady. She has a deep love for antiques. Our youngest son, who is beginning to share her love of antiques, was overjoyed one day when she brought him a pair of old Roman axes. After giving her a big bear hug, he looked at me and said, "I wish everybody knew Miss B."

In February, she will be going on a tour of the Holy Land with a group of other Christians. We can be assured that we, in her classes, will benefit about as much from this trip as she, because she also has the ability to tell us her experiences in the most picturesque manner.

Someone has said that to be successful one must win the respect of intelligent people and the affection of children. This she has done with everyone who has known her. We love her so much at Annapolis, and we wanted to share her with others.

Peggy Simpson
October 24, 1969

A Tribute To Our Bible Class Teachers

I dreamed the pearly gates were opened wide
And I had entered in for I had died;
And now must give account for all my acts
I saw a Book there opened with these facts.

I thought, "My role upon this earth was small
Just teaching a Bible Class, my call."
For I saw all the saints of God up there,
And mine was, at most, a meager share.

I heard the master call for my report;
I stood afraid for mine was short;
I trembled and felt I would not pass,
Then whispered, "I just taught a Bible Class."

And from the throne I heard His voice, "Well Done,
Come and share eternal life, my son;
Although your place was humble and obscure,
You led the thirsty to the waters pure."

And then it seemed that from eternal plains,
There came the sound of voices in refrain
That rolled across the mighty sea of glass,
"These are the great — the teachers of a class."

When I awoke I thought of those I'd taught,
And in their lives, what glory God had wrought,
I prayed to God, and all that I could say,
"Make me a better teacher day by day."

And you who teach this Christian Way to live,
May feel sometimes you're asked too much to give,
But some day you will reap eternal joys
Because you led to Christ, girls and boys.

Author Unknown

Alma has been a Bible School teacher since 1965.

ABI American Biographical Institute, Inc.

Publisher of Biographical Reference Works
Member of the Publishers Association of the South

Main Office 5126 Bur Oak Circle, PO Box 31226, Raleigh, North Carolina 27622 USA • Established 1967 • ISBN Prefix 934544
FAX 919-781-8712

March 13, 1992

Alma Biggs
829 River Bluff Terrace
Sheffield AL 35660

Dear Mrs. Biggs:

Your name has recently been recommended to the Institute's Governing Board of Editors by Dr. Kenny Barfield for biographical inclusion in the Fourth Edition of INTERNATIONAL DIRECTORY OF DISTINGUISHED LEADERSHIP. Your nomination for this volume is a reflection of your personal leadership accomplishments.

The enclosed brochure provides you with information about the INTERNATIONAL DIRECTORY OF DISTINGUISHED LEADERSHIP. ABI reference publications have been acclaimed worldwide as valuable research documents for business leaders, biographers, journalists, genealogists, historians, librarians, scholars, researchers, and many others for twenty years.

Although purchase is never a prerequisite for inclusion, this title would be a source of pride for your personal or professional library, Mrs. Biggs. The enclosed brochure and questionnaire are for your exclusive use so that you may take advantage of our special pre-publication prices only available now. To assist our Editors, I do ask that you return the form by the date requested.

Congratulations on your nomination, Mrs. Biggs.

Sincerely,

J.M. Evans
J.M. Evans
Director
GOVERNING BOARD OF EDITORS

OFFICE OF THE PRESIDENT
205/767-1203

PRESIDENT'S DEVELOPMENT COUNCIL

Mrs. Alma Biggs
829 River Bluff Terrace
Sheffield, AL   35660

Dear Alma:

    Thought you might like to have this memento of our visit together. Surely enjoyed having you at our house. Come again.

Sincerely,
Milton R. Sewell

MRS/ss

MARS HILL BIBLE SCHOOL
698 COX CREEK PARKWAY   FLORENCE, ALABAMA 35630

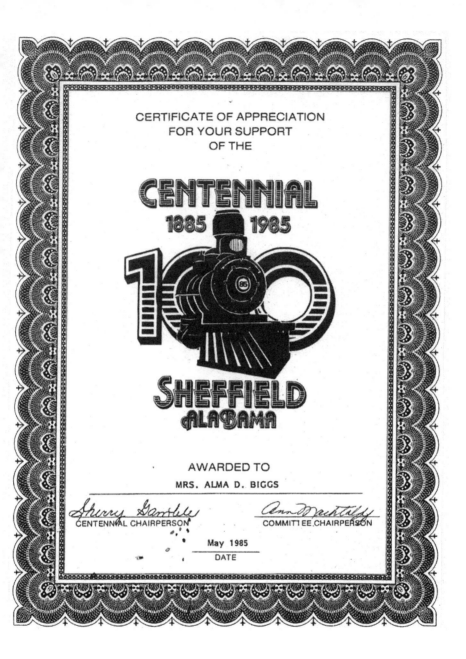

HERITAGE PRESERVATION, INC.
P. O. BOX 2836
FLORENCE, ALABAMA 35630

Certificate of Appreciation

In grateful recognition of the valuable contribution you have made to Heritage Preservation, Inc, this Certificate of Appreciation is hereby awarded to

Mrs. Alma Briggs

In witness whereof, this citation is given by the Board of Heritage Preservation, Inc.
Florence, Alabama
this the **15th** day of **March**, 1986.

Becky Mauldin
President

Billy R. Warren
Secretary/Treasurer

Office of the Chancellor • DAVID LIPSCOMB COLLEGE

• Nashville, Tennessee 37203

June 4, 1987

Mrs. Alma Biggs
829 River Bluff Drive
Sheffield, AL 35660

Dear Alma:

What a joy Ruth and I had in being with you this past weekend! We were impressed with the Annapolis Avenue congregation. I know it is home to you. We are just so very thankful that we had the privilege of being with you.

The bulletin has been read very carefully. I do not know a number of the men. However, I have talked to Tom Holland who worked in West Monroe in the radio broadcast for a time.

Here at Lipscomb, we train our young people to be missionaries. We are a training institution,
David Lipscomb College is an adjunct of the home in trying to help young people become better truer Christians. We work at Lipscomb as members of the church, but Lipscomb is not a congregation of the church.

I know David Davenport. I have been with him at one Christian College Presidents' Meeting. Howard White, in whom I have the utmost confidence, really believes in David. David was his choice to follow him as president of Pepperdine.

Ruth and I think so much of you. We do want to come down and a group of us get together. We would like to be with W. B. one day. I am going to work on this end and suggest some days to you. Would a Saturday be the best day for you? You might find this out from W. B. and then we can go on this basis. Please let me hear from you at any time.

Ruth and I are host and hostess of the "Friends of Lipscomb Tours." We take two tours each year. We are taking three this year because we had to skip one last summer because of the situation in Europe.

Mrs. Alma Biggs
June 4, 1987
Page Three

    I am enclosing the brochure about our Southwest trip and the one about our Scandinavian trip. The one to Scandinavia is going to be wonderful, and we sure would like to have you go on one or both of them. I think you would be especially interested in the bus tour to the Southwest. We will fly to Tucson and then take a bus tour with a driver and guide. A representive from Brentwood Tour and Travel will go with us to handle all the details. Ruth and I will be going along. We will just have a big time together, and we sure would like to have you go. The information as to where to send the deposit is in the folder. We guarantee to show you about the biggest time you have ever had on a trip. This is a group of Christian people, and we just have a big time and build a great deal of fellowship together in addition to seeing the beautiful sites.

    You write to me at any time. We are so glad to have Bill on the board. Ruth and I think so much of Bill and Shelva. I have just written you these things because I feel like I know you well enough that I can just talk to you frankly.

                                      Your friend,

                                      Willard Collins

WC/dcb

Enclosures

My Beloved Mother, 1984 David to Mother 12/22/84

    This Christmas I just wanted to sit down and write you in the way that writing allows me too feel. It has been too long since we used to talk.

    The times we used to sit and philosophically discuss life, relationships and those related things, well, they are the beautiful side of life.

    I could spend hours upon hours telling you tales of people I have encountered during my brief span. You have told me of some of your adventures but I honestly believe that much of my personality, if not most, comes from your adventures, of which, I do not know. How else could my thinking be so free?

    How I know you is the most personal thing in my life. How I understand you is built upon my life's experiences.

continued (2)

  I wish that, those things of life which give financial return were the same as those things of life which give because it feels better. Values cannot be justified from gainful motives.

  My above wish and synthesis is a large part of who I am. I believe that through your spiritual and literal interpretations of life, I have developed my views.

  Then there is a realistic, day to day, side of life which we rarely touched upon. Mother, you are a person of this life who has given and joyfully gained from doing so.

  I do not doubt that your Antique habits paid the price for your loved shared dream.

  I don't guess I ever got picked because I think the world is kind.

continued (3)

You have seen a lot of strange economic times. You have developed fortitude when needed which shows in the success of your style in life.

I should, at this point in my life, like to develop some of your lifestyle fortitude. I think I have and I know it's not too late to learn. I am facing an economic test of real, not academic, life. It is and will continue to forever be a mysterical stress factor upon my behavior. Whether I economically fail or succeed or manage to remain where I am, it will always be a mysterical stress factor for me.

It is mysterical because I know that I can provide what is necessary for comfortable existence but for some (mysterious) reason I cannot be a production type worker. I either have to lead the pack or work on my own. I will lead the pack as long as

Continued (4)

I can shoulder my created mystical stress, which I can't see any way out of for the rest of my life. Success has never doubted me.

I believe Thoreau said, "If a man claims to be a writer and doesn't write, he says he isn't a writer." It's too bad that it's basically a profession that's recognized post-humously. But as with any profession it's life if that's what you do.

You have instilled many noble and honest traits in your children. You have used your life experiences and Divine being in ways which have only benefited others.

I Love you,
Your Child

"Advice to Widows"

Sixteen months have passed since Jim died, and with God's love and the help of good friends, the girls and I have survived. We have grieved and agonized, but we have survived. We still miss him so much because he was such a vital part of our lives, but we can think of him now without crying. It's so hard to see clearly with tears in one's eyes.

These months have been a "real learning" experience for me. For someone who had never written a check, you know that two dollars and ninety-eight cents, I have come a long way. I have sold a house, bought a house, moved, re-enrolled in graduate school, and learned to live alone. I have learned that cars must have gas, that lawn mowers must have oil everytime they are used, that heat pumps won't last with dirty filters, that bills must be paid, and that college costs a lot of money. I have learned to close the storm windows when the temp. goes to zero, to travel on snow and ice, to change a fuse, and to drive a nail.

I have learned not to give unwanted advice or to criticize others until I have walked in their shoes, to depend more on myself and less on other people, to fully appreciate my children and my son-in-law, to smile and go on when my heart is breaking. I have learned the great truths of forgiveness, compassion, and the art of living one day at a time.

From God, I no longer seek answers because you some things, there are none, but I now seek a deeper more committed relationship with His Son. I have learned of the inequities of life and that sooner or later they come.

A Good Friend

This is a tribute to Jim Horton by his wife Patsy. It is so understanding and great advice, especially to young widows.

to everyone. I do not forget to thank God for all the years that I knew nothing but love, joy, peace, and happiness, but I do ask His forgiveness for wasting so much time on petty things and for having such misguided priorities during that time of my life.

I have no idea what the future holds for me, and I no longer try to project beyond today. Faith is not faith until it is the only thing you have left to hold to. I have stood on the bottom line where faith was the only thing left, and there has been times when it was so terribly weak. But time has passed. It is a terrible beautician, but it is a marvelous healer. I will fall again, but I know now that I will always be able to get up. Jim would expect me to and want me to. He took his illness and disappointments with great dignity and tranquility because he knew that eternal life was his ultimate goal. It is my prayer that you and I will live the remainder of our lives here in such a way that one day Jim will look around Heaven and find us there. ——— End ———

May you have a joyous holiday season and a very happy new year.

I think of you so often and still miss you, especially at this time of the year. You'll never know how much you have influenced my life for good. I love you, Patsy

Genealogy

Beginnings

The book of Genesis sets forth several beginnings, that of the world, of life, of sin, and of its consequences, and the scheme of redemption. The beginning of my story reaches back to almost a century ago.

Alma Lee Dukes Biggs
1908 – 'til?

Lest we forget, please come with me on a sentimental journey, covering a span of many years of what is called LIFE.

Maternal Grandparents

My Grand Pa Milstead (Steven Albert) was born March 26, 1867 at Pocahontas, Tennessee. He died at age 96, June 12, 1963 in Sheffield, Alabama.

He married my Grand Ma Milstead (Minnie Teresa Jane Warren). She was born in 1872 and died at 46 years of age on May 2,

1918. When Grand Ma died, my family moved to his home to help with his family while we lived in Pocahontas. His three children, contemporary with me, made a house full of Kith and Kin. His second marriage was to Frances Emaleine Stone Brooks of Selmer, Tennessee, on December 10, 1886. She died in Selmer, Tennessee.

Grand Pa and Grand Ma had six children: Maud, Myrtle, Madge and later Marie, Myron and Merritt. The last three were contemporary with me.

Pictured are all of S. A. Milstead's family except Madge, who died during the big flu epidemic after World War I. *Left to right:* Alma's mother, Maud M. Dukes; Alma's aunt, Marie Brewer; Alma's uncles, Myron Milstead, Merritt Milstead; Alma's aunt, Myrtle Shelton. *Center:* Alma's Grandfather, S.A. Milstead, who died at the age of 96. Alma's aunts and uncles.

Myron and I seemed to be on the same argumentative side. He married Louise Slay, and they had two sons, George and Bob. Louise died giving birth to Bob. He has been a very special person in our lives. Myron later married Elsie Reed, born 1915, a wonderful wife, a friend to me, and a stepmother to Bob.

Bob Milstead, born December 13, 1947 was the son of Myron Milstead (born 1908, died 1970) and Louise.

Paternal Grandparents

My Grandfather, Charles Robert Dukes, was born February 22, 1852. He died March 21, 1902 and was buried at Camp Ground Cemetery, Walnut, Mississippi. He was 50 years old.

My Grand Ma Dukes, Mary Frances Prince was born January 1, 1847 and died April 29, 1923 at 76 years of age. My Grandfather and Grand Ma Dukes were married December 18, 1823.

Since these grandparents lived on what was known as "Dukes' Farm," which was several miles from our home, I do not remember the details of the daily living out there.

My Grandfather Dukes died in 1902, and I was born in 1908, so I was deprived of the pleasure of knowing him. However, I do remember Grand Ma Dukes coming to town to visit us when I was a small child. She had totally lost her sense of hearing, and communication with her was difficult. When Grand Ma Dukes visited us, she would sleep in the bed with me, and she always kept the slop jar, a beautifully decorated ceramic pot used to relieve yourself, which I refused to use, beside the bed. On many cold frosty nights, I would sneak from our bed, wake up Mama, and we would make the seemingly endless dark trip to the outhouse.

Grandfather and Grand Ma were the parents of five children: Joe, Byrd, Vaughn, Charles, and one daughter, Lennie. They all lived in and around Walnut, Mississippi.

My Parents

My mother, Maud Milstead, was the first child born of Albert and Minnie Milstead. She was born in Pocahontas, Tennessee, on January 22, 1888, and died April 27, 1970, in Sheffield, Alabama, at 82 years of age. Maud married Joseph Fleming Dukes on February 25, 1906 at Pocahontas, Tennessee.

My father was the son of Charles Robert Dukes. He was born January 10, 1893, in Tippah County, Mississippi. He was always called Joe. He died February 16, 1956, in Sheffield, Alabama. He was 73 years of age.

My Parents, Joseph Fleming Dukes and Maud Milstead were married February 25, 1906. They made their promises on faith and young love. Their financial income hardly met their needs.

Mama and Papa had four children, all born in Pocahontas, Tennessee. The children were Vada, born January 26, 1907, died November 14, 1907; Alma Lee, born October 26, 1908; Robert Arlton, born June 11, 1914, died July 28, 1987, at 73 in Sheffield, Alabama; and Lewis Milstead, born September 23, 1916, and died May 31, 1986 at 70 years of age in Foley, Alabama.

Early in November, a little girl, Vada, was born, and happiness seemed to abound. An open, wood-burning fireplace heated their small house. This heat was also utilized for drying daily laundry. The diapers would be draped on backs of ladder-back chairs from the kitchen and placed in front of the open fire.

The toddler pulled herself around the furniture in front of the hot fire and overbalanced a chair hung with diapers. The diapers caught on fire. She died from the burns on November 14, 1907. It is hard to imagine such a tragedy, but life must go on. Pieces were picked up and scars partially mended. After this, it took a lot of living to make their small cottage a happy home.

European Christian College has received a gift in memory of

Memorial: Robert A. Dukes

from

Otis Gatewood

expressing deepest sympathy.

Otis Gatewood
President

Date June 10, 1988

* * *

Army of the United States
Honorable Discharge

This is to certify that

LEWIS M DUKES 33 098 905 Technical Sergeant
Headquarters Detachment Chanor Base Section APO 562

Army of the United States

IS HEREBY HONORABLY DISCHARGED FROM THE MILITARY SERVICE OF THE UNITED STATES OF AMERICA

THIS CERTIFICATE IS AWARDED AS A TESTIMONIAL OF HONEST AND FAITHFUL SERVICE TO THIS COUNTRY.

GIVEN AT SEPARATION CENTER
Fort McPherson Georgia
DATE 21 November 1945

CONWAY BORUFF
CONWAY BORUFF MAJOR AUS

ENLISTED RECORD AND REPORT OF SEPARATION—HONORABLE DISCHARGE

1. Last Name-First Name-Middle Initial	2. Army Serial No.	3. Grade	4. Arm or Service	5. Component
Dukes Lewis M	33 098 905	T-Sgt	DML	AUS

6. Organization	7. Date of Separation	8. Place of Separation
Hq Det Chanor Base Sec APO 562	21 Nov 45	Ft McPherson GA Separation Center

9. Permanent Address For Mailing Purposes	10. Date of Birth	11. Place of Birth
901 Annapolis Ave Sheffield Colbert Co Ala	23 Sep 16	Pocahontas Tenn

12. Address From Which Employment Will Be Sought	13. Color Eyes	14. Color Hair	15. Height	16. Weight	17. No. Depend.
Washington D C	brown	brown	5'9"	155 lbs.	0

18. Race	19. Marital Status	20. U.S. Citizen	21. Civilian Occupation and No.
White X Negro Other (specify)	Single Married X Other (specify)	Yes X No	Mail Classifier 1-18.01

MILITARY HISTORY

22. Date of Induction	23. Date of Enlistment	24. Date of Entry Into Active Service	25. Place of Entry Into Service
16 Sep 41	none	16 Sep 41	Richmond Va

26. Selective Service Data	26. Registered	27. Local S.S. Board No.	28. County and State	29. Home Address at Time of Entry Into Service
Yes X No	Yes X No	8	Washington D C	2230 Mass Ave Washington D C

30. Military Occupational Specialty and No.	31. Military Qualification and Date (i.e. infantry, aviation and marksmanship badges, etc.)
Personnel NCO 502	2nd cl gunner 30 cal MG MM Rifle

32. Battles and Campaigns

*Lewis M. Dukes
World War
Discharged 1945*

*European
Arena*

Leland's Parents

Leland's mother, Sarah Texanna Sutton, was born on May 10, 1887, in Sevier County, Tennessee. She died on March 28, 1963, in Knoxville, Tennessee. Sarah married William Henry Biggs on May 14, 1909.

Leland's father, William Henry, was born at Jefferson County, Tennessee, on September 28, 1882. He died on June 24, 1958, in Shcffield, Alabama.

The Biggs had three children: Leland Calvin Biggs who was born on February 14, 1910, and died on June 24, 1967; Everett who married Elizabeth Dooley, and Ruby who married Edmond Morarity.

Family Roll Call
Year 2003

"Be Listening For Your Name"

The beginning of this chapter may sound like a broken record going round and round, but be patient: Starting with the fourth generation, new names will catch your eye. So if you are no longer interested in earlier names, dates, places, etc., just jump down and start checking.

This roster of names of family members would not be complete without the little ones. No name is forgotten.

You all are mine—the descendents of Alma Dukes Biggs!

These dear people reach back in memory to 1867 and forward in promise to 2002.

Roll Call Of Family Generations

I am so proud of my immediate family, which grew to four in the year 1950.

As you remember, this is "your book" and "my story." Therefore, I am listing our four with only a mention of their families. I am proud of our extended families and their children. I will close this record now, and perhaps each one of you, if you have the time and patience, will add stories of your generation and others as you recall them.

As you know, our children are William Duke Biggs, Leland Winston Biggs, Rebecca Lynn Biggs, and David Warren Biggs.

Left to right: Bill, Becky, David, and Winston

William Duke Biggs
Our First Born

Bill was born August 9, 1938. He was raised by the book, "Dr. Spock." The first two school terms he attended Smithwood School at Fountain City, Tennessee. Mary E. Foster and a Mrs. Davis were his first teachers. We moved to Alabama, and he attended Atlanta Avenue Elementary School for his third and fourth grades. Mrs. Lovelace was his third grade teacher, and Mrs. Threadgill was his fourth grade teacher. He attended Atlanta Avenue School for two years, and then he registered at Mars Hill Bible and finished there.

He graduated from David Lipscomb University with a B.A. degree. He received a M.A degree from Vanderbilt University. Bill was baptized by Brother George DeHoff.

School pictures of Bill & Shelva

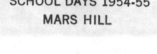

SCHOOL DAYS 1954-55
MARS HILL

Bill and Shelva Jean Chowning were married June 6, 1959. To this marriage, three children were born.

Bill and Shelva

Bill and Shelva, Desiree and Bill Jr.

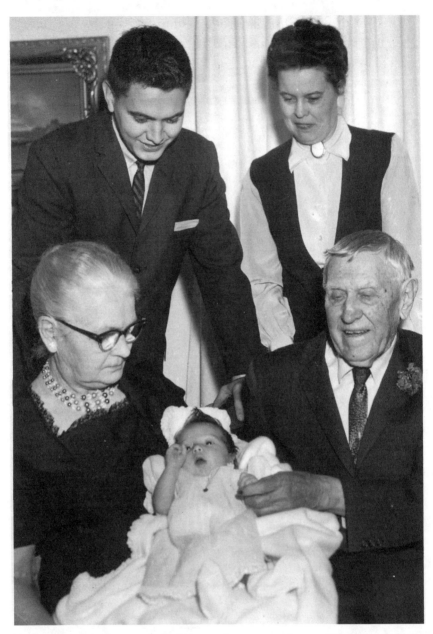

*Melissa Renee' Biggs, born December 3, 1960.
Her birth marked the arrival of a fifth generation in her family. Renee'
Biggs (Center); (Left to right) Mama Dukes, Great-Grandmother; Bill
Biggs, Father; Alma Biggs, Grandmother; S.A. Milstead, Great-Great-
Grandfather.*

I was visiting a Christian Youth Camp in Zagreb, Yugoslavia, when Bill's call finally reached me, He said simply, "Mother, Renee' has had a fatal auto accident."

My world stood still. I was at the far corner of the world. I came home as soon as possible.

Until this day, I hear her say, "Mom 'B' you are the best."

I say, "Renee', you were the best." Your Grandmother.

Melissa Renee' Biggs

Melissa Renee Biggs, lovely Christian teenage daughter of Bill and Shelva Biggs of Florence, AL was recently killed in an accident in Florence. Her paternal grandmother, Alma Biggs wrote the two following items about her.

MELISSA RENEE' BIGGS

After unbelieving shock became a reality, grief and sorrow spread like a pall and seemed to affect every person regardless of age in this area.

Now, since days and even weeks have passed Christian loved ones are accepting their loss in and through the power of faith. We say over and over "We can't understand," but "We know that some greater good is being served." "We do not sorrow as those that have no hope."

We have learned and have been reminded, that life is short and uncertain and eternity is very near to each one of us.

Our great loss (which to us still seems a high price to pay) has affected an entire congregation for good. At the Northwood Hills Church of Christ, Florence, Alabama, the following Lord's Day and the next, approximately seventy souls responded, many rededicated their lives to a closer walk with the Lord and ten young people were baptized into Christ.

The death of Renee seemed to provide needed spiritual strengthening to hundreds of those who loved her. She has accomplished in her brief sixteen years what I have failed to do in my sixty plus. What a wonderful blessing the Lord has given us, that we can bless others in life and even in death accomplish good.

Let Psalms 23 become a part of your daily life.

Thank You, God

It was such a beautiful day,
thank you is all that I could say
Her cameo features, rosebud
mouth and abundance of dark hair
Announced this wee gift from
above, our precious Melissa Renee'
Thank you for this bundle of joy
which you intrusted to our care
We watched her grow very tall,
all hands, all feet and all tears
Gathering wild flowers, for-get-me-nots,
violets and daisy chains
Reality suddenly reappears, bearing so
many frustrations and fears
Mushroom clouds are in the sky
bringing calming showers of rain
She now enters the beautiful
freshness of the spring of her life
In radiance she shines like the
morning dew, while a robin sings
Never, ever dreaming that time
will soon end all fears and strife
Life's storm strikes heavy upon us
pealing out a thundering ring
We thank you God for sharing this
life which seemed to us so brief
Nests are deserted, the robin and
the wren fly to places far away
Her bright smile and beauty
lingers on as a crumpled lifeless leaf
The wind searches for this flower
whose fragrance was only a day

"Mom B"

Alma D. Biggs,
Renee's Paternal Grandmother
829 River Bluff Terrace
Sheffield, Alabama 35660

Melissa Renee' Biggs, born December 3, 1960, was killed in a car accident August 9, 1977. This article was written by Alma and was published in the local paper.

January 30. 1978

Dear Sister Biggs:

How my heart has ached for you since I learned of your little granddaughter's death. But I know also of your great faith in God and that He knows the way even terrible tragedies can touch the hearts of many who would not listen otherwise. Having lost three of the dearest people on earth to me in the last two years, I can certainly sympathize with you. May our God comfort you and the parents of this beloved girl and may it serve to strengthen your faith in His wisdom.

I read of your summer's activities with much pleasure. I am sure much good was done as you certainly enriched my life in Puerto Rico.

The work here continues to be rewarding although not without problems. As long as Satan is at work there will be problems, and it grieves my heart to see the devious ways he has of alienating brethren in the churches. But we know that all congregations have problems and are either able to overcome them or be overcome by them.

We have a wonderful student body in the school of preaching. We are short of teachers and Jim is having to put in extra hours, but it is a joy for him to feel that these young men will be going to so many islands to teach and preach when they graduate. And most of them are very capable and talented boys. All of them seem more dedicated than one usually sees in a group that large. May God richly bless you throughout this year and give you much fruit for your labors.

                              In Christian love,

                              Joyce Massey

William Biggs and his wife, Shelva, holding granddaughter Hanna Barnes, join their daughter, Desiree Barnes, to look at the new statue in Tuscumbia. It is in memory of their daughter, Melissa Renee Biggs.

Bravery in bronze

Statue depicts teaching's challenge, encouragement

By Dia Collins
STAFF WRITER

TUSCUMBIA — The Alabama Institute for Deaf and Blind's Shoals Regional Center did not allow cloudy skies to overshadow the unveiling of the sculpture "The Young Teacher."

On Friday, the center had a reception to show off the statue for the first time and to honor its sculptor, William Binnings.

"We had a really dramatic rainy morning," said Glenda Cain, regional director of the AIDB Shoals Regional Center.

The bronze sculpture, which is posed on a granite podium, depicts a young woman holding a book.

Binnings

A quote by former President Harry S. Truman is written in Braille on the book. It says, "In your hands rests our future."

The young woman is also signing the word future.

Binnings, a resident of Meraux, La., said that the message behind the statue is duality.

"In order to be a good teacher, you must have at first been an excellent student," he said. "These people spend a lot more time in challenge, and encouragement gives way to this challenge."

Binnings said he used a sculpting process

AIDB continued on 2B

AIDB: Regional Center unveils statue

Continued from 1B
that has been in place for 3,500 years. He said the granite used as the sculpture's pedestal is from Sweden.

"I have given you my best work," said Binnings.

Cain said the sculpture is a representation of both deafness and blindness.

"The sculptor used different textures on different parts of the structure, and the visually impaired can feel that," Cain said.

The creation of the sculpture was not an overnight process.

"From the beginning to this day, it was about an 18-month process," said Rob McNeilly, chairman of the AIDB's sculpture committee.

"The sculpture should set a visual tone for the building itself," McNeilly said. "And it should reflect the purpose the building enables us to provide."

The nine-member committee met four times to narrow down the 35 proposals received from differ-

Cain

ent artists to ... one chosen.

"The co... mittee sent ... letters to a lo... artists and s... tors." Cain s...

"The commit... looked at ... ideas the art... proposed ... narrowed down from there."

The monument was given the center by William and She... Biggs in memory of their dau... ter, Melissa Reneé Biggs.

"This sculpture is not ab... donors or contributors. It's ab... serving, it's about sharing," ... Williams Biggs. "We were c... brating the gift that we were giv...

"We believe that art adds ... important dimension to the c... prehensive educational progra... we provide," said AIDB Presid... Joseph F. Busta Jr.

A proclamation was also p... sented to Busta, who will be l... ing the center at the end of Ju...

"This statue shall be a cons... reminder of our commitment t... future of those Alabamians who... deaf and those who are blin... Busta said.

Dia Collins can be reached a... 740-5744

Sculpture Committee
Rob McNeilly, Chairman, Bill Biggs, Glenda Cain,
Susan Delony, Lynne Hanner, Tommy Mathis,
Mary Lou Robbins, Jackie Smith, Di Tyree

Interpreter - Stacey Yarbrough
Key Board - Tim Sharpton and Jarrah Rutherford

The sculpture "Young Teacher" is in loving memory of
Melissa Reneé Biggs
with a quote from Harry S Truman
"..... In Your Hands Rests the Future."

Alabama Institute for Deaf and Blind
Shoals Regional Center

Sculpture and Reception
May 10, 2002 at 4:00 p.m.

I. Welcome — Ms. Glenda Cain, Regional Director

    Invocation - Rev. Gatus Cheatam, Calvary Baptist Church
    "The Lord's Prayer" - Senator Bobby Denton
    Special Guests: AIDB Trustees - Foundation Directors
    AIDB Staff - Elected Officials

II. The Sculpture, "The Young Teacher" — Dr. Joseph F. Busta, Jr., President AIDB

    1. Appreciation
    2. Sculpture, Bill Binnings
    3. Bill and Shelva Biggs and Family

III. Music Selection — "Wind Beneath My Wings", Gail Perkins, AIDB Talladega

IV. Closing — Dr. Busta

THE SHOALS REGIONAL CENTER

Since 1858, Alabama Institute for Deaf and Blind has educated individuals who are deaf and blind on campuses in Talladega. In the early 1980s, AIDB created a statewide network of regional centers to provide early intervention and preschool programs to deaf and blind children and later expanded services for adults and seniors.

Muscle Shoals was the site in 1982 of AIDB's first Kinderprep preschool class. Today, the Shoals Regional Center is the first facility designed and built exclusively as an AIDB Regional Center - a symbol of our commitment to excellence in serving individuals with hearing and vision loss and their families and communities.

DEDICATED JUNE 21, 2001
AIDB Shoals Regional Center
512 North Main Street
Tuscumbia, Alabama 35674
256/383.3503 V/TTY 256/383.3562 FAX
www.aidb.org

"I will not just live my life. I will invest my life."
Helen Keller

William Duke Biggs Jr. was born January 6, 1962. He was educated at Mars Hill Bible School in Florence, Alabama, and at the University of North Alabama. He graduated with a B.S. degree from U.N.A.

"Bill" and Kim Thomason were married in Aspen, Colorado, December 9, 2000. There are no children at this writing. They live at Carillon Beach, Florida, where he and his dad, Bill Sr. spearheaded a first-class housing development.

They have daughters,
Jessica Desiree, Sara Jeanne, and Hanna Grace

Jean Desiree Biggs was born June 21, 1964. A graduate of Coffee High School, she married Robert Kenneth Barnes of Nashville on November 14, 1987. Both are graduates of David Lipscomb University. They reside in Nashville, Tennessee.

Desiree as
Home Coming Queen
Coffee High School

Bill, Shelva, and their granddaughters, Sara, Hanna, and Jessica.

Birthdays:
Jessica – January 21, 1993
Sara – August 9, 1995
Hanna – December 15, 2000

Our second son, Leland Winston Biggs was born November 16, 1941, at Fort Sanders Hospital in Knoxville, Tennessee. We moved to Alabama when he was four years old. He attended Mrs. Morrison's Kindergarten in Tuscumbia. Then at five years of age, he entered Mars Hill Bible School, where he remained until the 10th grade. He then transferred to Sheffield High School for one year, and returned to Mars Hill where he graduated. He was a graduate of David Lipscomb University with a B.S. Degree. Brother Richard Taylor baptized Winston.

He married Linda Ruth Jones of Nashville, Tennessee, on January 1, 1961. Winston and Linda had four children. Leland Calvin Jr. was born June 6, 1962. He lived only two days and died as a newborn on June 8, 1962. Leigh Forrest was born on June 18, 1964. Mary Winston "Windy" was born January 30, 1967 and died July 29, 1967. Leland Winston Jr. was born July 8, 1970.

Winston, Linda, Leigh, and Winn Jr.

Wynn, Linda, William, Grey, Mary Winston

CONTRIBUTION — Wayne Grubb (R), head football coach of the University of North Alabama, receives a contribution from Winston Biggs representing C.K. Irby and Winston Biggs.

Leigh Forrest Biggs was born June 18, 1964. She is a graduate of Coffee High School in Florence, Alabama, and the University of Alabama. She married William Brian Reames of Richmond, Virginia, a graduate of Vanderbilt University. They have three children: William Brian Reames, born July 14, 1993; Thomas Grey Reames, born April 13, 1995; and Mary Winston Reames born August 6, 1997.

Leigh as cheerleader at Coffee High School

Left to right: William, Leigh, Mary, Grey, and Brian

Hey Mama B —

Hey, how are you? I'am doing great! Please excuse this paper, but this was all I had to write on, it's kinda cute, huh? I really miss you, I hope your taking care of yourself!

You wouldn't believe how much weight I've gained!!! I'am not fat *yet*, but I've got to start watching my weight or ya'll won't even recognize me when I come home.

The school work is *hard*, but I promise I'am studying! I feel like that's all I do! I've meet tons of new friends! You were right it's not hard at all to meet new people, It's Fun! I've told them all about you!

I'am not sure when I am coming home but I'll get in touch with you! I'll be thinking about DUMPLINGS when I come home, HINT! HINT! I can taste them now!

I love you & missya! TAKE care of yourself for me!!!

Love Ya,
Joie ('my club')
KKP

P.S. Have you traveled anywhere in the world lately?

Winn Jr. was born on July 8, 1970. He graduated from Hillsboro High School in Nashville. He attended the University of Alabama and resides in Nashville. He is not married.

He is very special to Moma B.

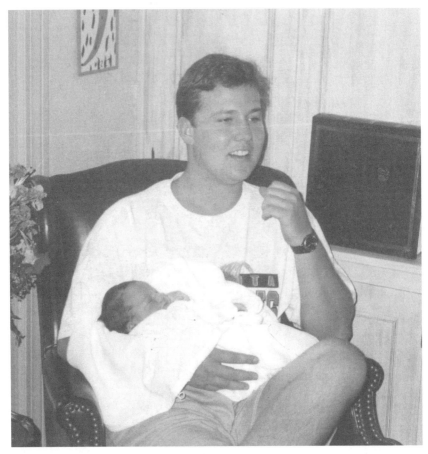

Winn Jr. and Baby William Reames

Thanksgiving 11-28-02

Grandmother of the Hills

The Path of the Just is as the Shining light that Shineth more and more unto the Perfect day. Prov.-4:18, KJV

Grandmother of the Hills

She always rose before the sun.
She watched the Birth and Death of Light
For Nintey four years of mountain dawn
and Nintey four years of mountain Night.
The mountain years are Lean and Hard,
But just and kind are all her ways.
It gentles one, she says to watch
How God begins and Ends the Days.
What all the Light revealed to her
I cannot say, but this I know:
Her Face as Latest evening Falls
Is Luminous with morning glow.

We thank thee, heavenly Father, for all people whose lives attest that at evening Time there shall be Light for those who have walked in the Light of thy presence all their days. Help us to keep times of Quiet Communion with thee at the beginning and the Ending of our Days, so that our Days and Nights may be filled with radiance, and we may understand that each ending is a New beginning.
 — Winn Jr.   In Christ's name Amen.

11-28-2002
Green Reams 74yr old —

I Love my famley very much. They of cuse to one anoter. They to they hep one anoters they bilive in god. thy tank Joe for wate they or'e thy are the bilive in the bible. I Love Grey

I my will willertil
famley

Rebecca Lynn Biggs

Rebecca Lynn Biggs, our pride and joy (a little girl), was born at Fort Sanders Hospital in Knoxville, Tennessee on March 9, 1946. We moved to Alabama when Becky was four months old. Her Grammar and High School years were spent at Mars Hill Bible School in Florence, Alabama.

Becky attended David Lipscomb University in Nashville, Tennessee, and Auburn University in Auburn, Alabama. She graduated at the University of North Alabama in Florence, Alabama. Becky was baptized by Brother Howard Allen, minister at Annapolis Avenue in Sheffield, Alabama.

John C. Hamm Jr. and Becky were married on November 7, 1964 in Phenix City, Alabama, by Brother Newborn at the Church of Christ. They have two sons: John C. III (Shawn) was born October 10, 1968, and Kevin Joseph was born May 20, 1971.

"B"

I just thought I would write this short note to you to say, I hope everything you wanted in life you have got and I hope you get what you want in the future. I Love you.

Shawn

A note from Shawn to Alma when he was young.

John (Pawpaw) and Becky with grandchildren, Blake and Hope.
Photograph made in May, 2003

John C. Hamm III (Shawn) was born October 10, 1968. He married Kristi Duncan on October 5, 2001. They have three children: Hope Joanna, Daniel Hartzog, and Kristin Duncan. Shawn has been a long time employee of the Florence Police Department. They live in Florence, Alabama.

John C. Hamm III (Shawn)   *Kristi*

Kristin

Hope Joanna

Daniel

Kevin Hamm was born in Florence, Alabama in May 1971. He married Karmen Hunt, mother of Blake Robert Hamm. They divorced. He later married Donna Matthews of Orlando, Florida. Kevin is employed by Kennedy Space Center and lives in Orlando, Florida.

Donna and Kevin

First Great-Grandchild Blake

My Great-Grandson wrote this as a class assignment: Who is your favorite older person and why? He did this all on his own.

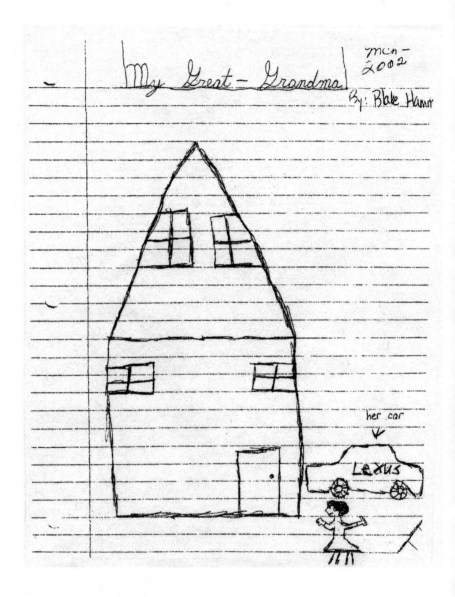

March 13, 2002

My favorite Older Person is my great grandma, Alma Biggs. She is 93 years old. She is kin to me because she is my dad's grandma, my great grandma, and my best friend in the whole world. I love my great grandma very much.

  The reason why I admire my great grandma is because she gives me old antiques that she had when she was a little girl. My great grandma also teaches me many things. The last reason why I admire her is because she is very, very good-natured.

  Now I am going to tell you why this person is my favorite. I have known my great grandma, Alma Biggs, for all of my 11 years. My great grandma is old, but whenever I go to Alabama to see her for Christmas I help her cook. I think my great grandma is very very special to me because I love her with all of my heart.

  In conclusion, my great

I told you about; how I know this person, why I admire this person, and why this person is my favorite. I can't wait till this year so I can see her and help her around her big house.

David Warren Biggs

Our fourth child, David was born at Colbert County Hospital (now Helen Keller Hospital) in Sheffield, Alabama on August 9, 1950.

He attended Mars Hill Bible School and then transferred to Sheffield High School. After graduation, he enrolled at the University of Alabama, and was then drafted into the service. He chose the Navy, serving three years and nine months. He was the only one of our family to receive this call. His time was spent at Norfolk, Virginia. After discharge, he entered Old Dominion University, where he graduated. He was baptized by Brother Howard Allen.

He married Amy Jackson Hancock of Nashville, Tennessee, on April 24, 1994. They are the proud parents of two children: Leland Calvin Biggs, III was born on December 1, 1994, and Sara Greer Biggs was born on September 22, 1999.

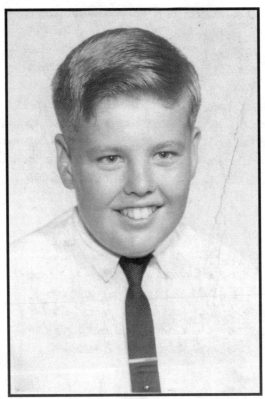

Greer, David, and Leland

Amy

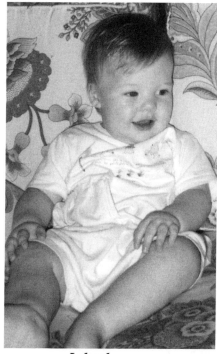

Leland

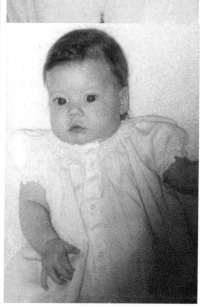

Greer

1973   9 MAY 1973

Dear Mother,

I guess this will have to be my Mothers Day card for this year. Enclosed are some pictures that we had made for you, sorry about the crease in the large photo.

We are doing fine just counting the days for my time to be up. I do think that the past 3yrs and 9 months have gone by really fast. At least I will have something to tell my grandchildren about.

I am doing really well in my law course and like I said I am looking forward to starting school full time. I plan to just go to school the first semester and then try to work part time after that.

I hope to see the family this summer if not here then at home at the end of the summer.

I think that Charles and Ayn are coming to see us at the end of this month. They are doing well, Charles said he is looking for a job and Ayn graduates this July.

Don't really have anything else to say except we love and and look forward

This was written while Dand was in Navy in Norfolk, Va — 1970

Love,
Dav.

P.S. The folder is the only thing I had to mail this in. Give it to little Bill if you want.
2°

The following is for information only, as Alexandria Rei is the last in my lineage on the Dukes side. I list my two brothers (both deceased) as follows:

Robert Arlton Dukes. He married Jean Jones and was blessed with two daughters. Pamela married Gary Chowning and became mother of two children: Brandon and Natalie Chowning. Brandon is not married. Natalie married Jeremy Humphries and they are parents of my Grand-niece-"Alexandria Rei." She was born March 12, 2002. She weighed 8 lbs and measured 20 1/2 inches.

Robert's other daughter, Teresa Dukes married David Denny, and they have two sons: Josh and Davis Denny. They live in Lanett, Alabama.

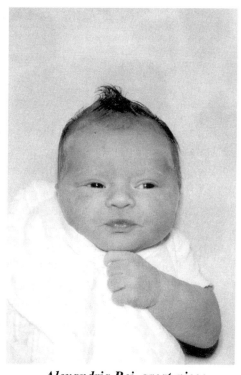

Alexandria Rei, great-niece, last born child of lineage of Alma Dukes Biggs

My other brother, Lewis Milstead Dukes, married Pearl Harrell, and they were not blessed with children.

My Prayer
by
Alma Dukes Biggs

1 Chronicles 4:10

Dear Lord:

    I am now ninety plus, and there is still so much I have not done.
    I pray I live the nineties through and finish all I need to do.
    Please Lord, let me keep on keeping on, and answer the many calls for me,
        Sometimes the way is dark, and I cannot seem to see.

    Then comes the future with many promises dear,
    Dear Lord, please show me the way without unwanted fear.

    While I am waiting in the safety of His wings,
    Please let me know the happiness this haven brings.

"Amen"

ADB

Now,
The wind in the trees whispered and said,
"The Red Sky of the evening brings tidings so glad,
        Another new birth year,
        Be of good cheer,
        My Dear."

Postscript

Since my children and especially the grandchildren have kicked, cried, begged, and pleaded for a record of my humble life to be placed on the top bookshelf of your lives, this is handed to you and future generations.

This is your book.
This is my story.

Alma D. Biggs
A Singletree from Tennessee

I want you all to know that I do not intend to paint a "Picture Perfect" family. There have been times when we might have fallen into the "dysfunctional category." Hopefully, many lessons have been learned from past experiences, and let's let "by gones be by gones" and let "sleeping dogs lie."

90TH BIRTHDAY CELEBRATION

Alma Dukes was born October 26, 1908 at Pocahontas, Tennessee. She obeyed the gospel and thus became a Christian at the age of twelve. She has been active in Christian activities since that time. She has been an active Christian for 78 years! Alma and the late Leland C. Biggs of Knoxville, Tennessee were married at the Annapolis Avenue Church of Christ in Sheffield, Alabama in 1934. Three sons and one daughter blessed this union.

Sister Biggs has long been a Bible Class teacher, and she continues in this good work. She has spoken on many ladies' programs throughout the country, and continues in this good work also.

You Are Invited!
Because you have shared in her life by your love and friendship, the children of Alma Biggs cordially invite you to join them in the celebration of her Ninetieth Birthday on Sunday, the twenty-fifth of October, nineteen hundred and ninety-eight between one and four in the afternoon at the Annapolis Avenue Church of Christ Annex, 610 Annapolis Avenue, Sheffield, Alabama 35660. No gifts please. A card basket will be provided at the reception.

The poem that follows explains why Alma has so many friends.

"I went out to find a friend,
But could not find one there.
I went out to be a friend,
And found friends everywhere!"

Alma's 90th Birthday

On October 25, 1998, everybody celebrated my birthday. I was 90 years old. My birthday is really October 26th, but my children joined hands, hearts, and pocketbooks, and decided our celebration should be on the 25th, a Sunday. To me this was another beautiful Lord's Day. To them it was a Lord's Day Plus. They made this special time a true program of celebration. I called it a "Ball." Several hundred Kith, Kin, Friends, and Neighbors elected to be a part of the Biggs Bunch. At last count, more than 100 guests had signed the register. People joined in the reminiscing, and tall tales were recalled. The children spilled the punch, and others sneaked another slice of cake. I had a good time!

The party time flew, many compliments came my way, and one even said, "You don't look 90; what kind of soap do you use?" The air was full of hugs and kisses and was crammed with Oh's and Ah's. But all good things must end. When the door finally slowly closed, they tucked me into the black Cadillac, and deposited me in my comfortable nook to recuperate and THINK!

While looking out my window, I think I heard a faint voice say, "WRITE TODAY!" I picked up my much used pen and sheet of paper, and wrote the following just for my four:

Gems Of Wisdom—My Bequest To My Children

As the world has become so materialistic in its thinking that the "things" we leave are monetary, we need to realize that everyone, will one day leave a heritage, which may or may not be money or other earthly possessions. Since I do not leave great wealth, pots of gold and silver or acres of diamonds or rubies, the lessons that you learned from the golden moments of blessings showered upon you, MUST be your "inheritance."

I hope that the "Gems of Wisdom" I have acquired in a life span of almost a century will suffice as "My Heart's Spiritual Heritage." This token of love will far outlast any works of art that I might hand you. In fact, its influence will be felt throughout eternity. I want to leave you all of the love and concern that I felt about each one of you. As David wrote in Psalms 127:3, "Children are an inheritance of God." In bundling you up and sending you to us, God knew the great happiness and blessings you would bring into our lives. I trust that you will remember me as a "kind and understanding mother," not the strict parent I must have seemed to you in trying times. My actions were always from love and concern for what I felt best.

To Bill and Shelva I say, make each day your masterpiece. You cannot change yesterday. Improve today for a better tomorrow.

To Wynn and Linda I say, "Pray for guidance, count your blessings, and give thanks for them everyday."

To Becky and Johnny I say, "I tried to live in such a way as to inspire you to call me "Mother" and "Your best friend."

To Amy and David I say, "Drink deeply from good books, but remember there is none that compares to the Bible, which purifies and refines us to glow like gold and silver."

If you, my children, desire to leave much to others in the way of spiritual blessings, you must follow the instructions given by Solomon when he said, "Walk in the way of righteousness."

Your Mother:
Alma D. Biggs

To My In-Laws

To Shelva, my first daughter in love: When Bill would be working so hard, traveling so much, and you would come to me, I remember saying, "Shelva, no matter what happens, I will always love you, and I am sure this too will pass."

To Linda, my second daughter in love. When Winston finally stammered, "Mother, I think I want to ask Linda to be a part of our family." What did I say? "Well, Winn you could look the world over and never beat her." I was right.

To Johnny, my very favorite son in love. The pattern was torn up when you were born. Thank you for graciously caring.

To Amy, my last daughter in love, David finally found you. A charming wife, a loving mother, and a happy home.

My love and best wishes for all of you in your struggle to keep on keeping on.

Love,
"Mom B"

ALMA'S FAMILY

Note: A few newcomers are missing, Sara Greer, Hope JoAnna, Kristie, Kristin, Daniel, Hanna Grace, and Donna.

Pansies At The Door

by Alma Biggs

Now that I am ninety four and almost ninety five,
I wonder what I'll do next to keep myself alive.

The kitchen window is my "door" opening to the West,
The sun finds its way to bring pink skies, which are the very best.

Morning opens with raindrops falling near the kitchen door,
Little pansy faces seem to say, "Keep faith there is more."

Their colors are like the rainbow, purple, white and yellow,
They try to tell us, " The sun is reason why we are so mellow."

How these tiny fellows can make it in rain, ice and snow,
I believe is a secret that someday we will know.

We complain of the days so dreary, dark and cold,
The pansies keep smiling, as their bold beauty continues to unfold.

2/20/03

This was Written for Our Children and YOU! Please Enjoy

To
Paul and Janet
Thanks
Alma Biggs

10/12/03